DATA JUSTICE

DATA JUSTICE

Lina Dencik, Arne Hintz,
Joanna Redden and
Emiliano Treré

$SAGE

Los Angeles | London | New Delhi
Singapore | Washington DC | Boston

SAGE

Los Angeles | London | New Delhi
Singapore | Washington DC | Melbourne

SAGE Publications Ltd
1 Oliver's Yard
55 City Road
London EC1Y 1SP

SAGE Publications Inc.
2455 Teller Road
Thousand Oaks, California 91320

SAGE Publications India Pvt Ltd
B 1/I 1 Mohan Cooperative Industrial Area
Mathura Road
New Delhi 110 044

SAGE Publications Asia-Pacific Pte Ltd
3 Church Street
#10-04 Samsung Hub
Singapore 049483

Editor: Michael Ainsley
Assistant Editor: Rhoda OlaSaid
Production Editor: Zoheb Khan
Copyeditor: Sarah Bury
Proofreader: Derek Markham
Indexer: Cathryn Pritchard
Marketing Manager: Ruslana Khatagova
Cover Design: Victoria Bridal
Typeset by KnowledgeWorks Global Ltd
Printed in the UK

Library of Congress Control Number: 2022932431

British Library Cataloguing in Publication data

A catalogue record for this book is available from the British Library

ISBN 978-1-5297-2095-2
ISBN 978-1-5297-2094-5 (pbk)

At SAGE we take sustainability seriously. Most of our products are printed in the UK using responsibly sourced papers and boards. When we print overseas we ensure sustainable papers are used as measured by the PREPS grading system. We undertake an annual audit to monitor our sustainability.

CONTENTS

PRAISE FOR THE BOOK

Here is the definitive book on the social, political, and economic dimensions of data. The authors are each experienced scholars who have produced a set of carefully integrated and clearly written chapters that cover a vast expanse of themes, from capitalism to citizenship, from social movements to social justice.

Vincent Mosco, author of The Smart City in a Digital World

Data Justice will be the foundational text for studies on the intersection of data and social justice. Drawing on their own pioneering research and an extensive engagement with the literature, the book provides a comprehensive account of data politics and power, introducing the reader to key emerging ideas and debates. Essential reading for understanding our increasingly datafied world.

Rob Kitchin, Maynooth University Social Sciences Institute

Data Justice is an essential handbook for those invested in reclaiming our digital space and reshaping data systems to align with future-oriented values of equity and sustainability. Authored by key thought leaders, this book maps a global and holistic approach to the world of data that works for radical wellbeing.

Payal Arora, author of the Next Billion Users and FemLab Co-Founder

Examining datafication – a uniquely contemporary human experience – as a site of politics, power and emancipation, Data Justice unravels the multiple and mutual entanglements of ideas of justice and idiosyncrasies of data. A contribution that is bound to animate conversations in public discourse and classrooms alike, Data Justice is an elegant addition to the body of work that helps us understand how sense-making and claims-making are connected in a world redefined by data.

Anita Gurumurthy, founding member and executive director of IT for Change

ACKNOWLEDGEMENTS

This is the first book in a new series on Data Justice for Sage Publications. We are grateful to Michael Ainsley at Sage for his enthusiasm for the series and for his patience with this book over the past turbulent couple of years. We would also like to thank the rest of the team at the Data Justice Lab, especially Jessica Brand, Harry Warne, Ina Sander, Sarah Murphy, Fieke Jansen, Philippa Metcalfe, Javier Sánchez-Monedero and Jedrjez Niklas, who have all worked on projects that have helped inform this book.

The contribution from Lina Dencik has been supported by a Starting Grant from the European Research Council under the Horizon 2020 research and innovation program (grant no. 759903). Arne Hintz's chapter 'Data and Citizenship' builds on research for the project 'Digital Citizenship and Surveillance Society', funded by the UK Economic and Social Research Council (ESRC), and the chapter 'Data and Policy' was informed by research conducted for the project 'Policy Frameworks for Digital Platforms' led by IT for Change and funded by the International Development Research Centre (IDRC). Joanna Redden's chapter 'Data and Governance' is informed by the 'Compromised Data' research workshop and book project led by Ganaele Langlois and Greg Elmer and funded by the Social Sciences and Humanities Research Council of Canada. Redden's 'Data Harms' chapter builds upon collaborations with Jessica Brand and Vanesa Terzieva and has been funded by the School of Journalism, Media and Culture (JOMEC) and Cardiff University. The chapter 'Data and De-westernization' by Emiliano Treré has been partly informed by the amazing activities and conversations carried out within the 'Big Data from the South' Initiative (with Stefania Milan), and the 'COVID-19 from the Margins' Project (with Stefania Milan and Silvia Masiero). The reflections developed in the 'Algorithmic politics and activism' section of the 'Data and Movements' chapter by Treré are partly based on the AlgoRes Project (with Tiziano Bonini), funded by JOMEC at Cardiff University. The research on which the 'Counter-data action' section of the same chapter is based has been supported by a Lakehead University SRC SSHRC Research Development Fund grant from Canada (Romeo File #1468486).

Finally, we would like to acknowledge support by the Open Society Foundations (OSF), which have funded several of our collaborative research projects, including 'Data Scores as Governance' and 'Towards Democratic Auditing', which have helped us develop our thinking on data justice and have informed several of the chapters in this book.

All four authors have contributed equally to this book and are listed in alphabetical order. However, in the interest of completion, Lina Dencik wrote Chapters 1 and 8, Arne Hintz wrote Chapters 5 and 6, Joanna Redden wrote Chapters 2 and 4, and Emiliano Treré wrote Chapters 3 and 7. The introduction was written by all authors.

INTRODUCTION

The widespread collection and use of data has been the subject of much public and scholarly interest in recent years. Data justice has emerged as a significant framework for engaging with the implications of this development, focusing particularly on key questions of power relations and social justice. The notion of 'datafication' introduced by data scientists Cukier and Mayer-Schönberger (2013) to connote the growing trend of turning human behaviour and social activities into data points that can be collected and analysed is increasingly central to debates on contemporary and future society. According to a recent review carried out by communication scholars Flensburg and Lomborg (2021), datafication research has so far focused on either technological processes or user perspectives, but often struggles to bring these approaches together and suffers from a lack in empirical grounding. Indeed, early on, sociologist Evelyn Ruppert called for research on datafication to overcome abstract analyses on technocratic or functionalist terms by advancing more contextual understandings of data (Ruppert et al. 2015). In doing so, we need to contend with both the nature of infrastructures and uses because as we come to grapple with the realities of datafication in society, we continue to struggle over what is at stake with this development. How are we to understand what the growing reliance on data-driven technologies means for society? Does it change what we are able to do and say, what we can access, how we understand ourselves and each other, and what opportunities lie ahead of us? And, who does it impact and how?

Without a grounded understanding of datafication – as infrastructure, discourse and practice – we are limited in our assessment of these crucial questions that are central to any discussion on social justice today. In this book, we highlight the issue of social justice precisely so as to recognize the significance that datafication now holds for such questions. No longer a development that can be confined to concerns with efficiency, security or economic growth, the expanding generation, the collection and use of data across areas of social and public life is increasingly seen as substantively and qualitatively transforming economic, political, social and cultural practices in such a way that entrenches and introduces power dynamics in need of scrutiny and critique. Data justice, as a framework, approach and practice, is a way to take on this challenge by privileging questions informed by social justice concerns in the examination of datafication. That is, we advance the notion of data justice as a lens through which we can interrogate, engage with, and advance and challenge the justices and injustices relating to datafication in society today.

This book has emerged out of the collaborative work of the Data Justice Lab, a research initiative that officially launched in early 2017 at Cardiff University's School of Journalism, Media and Culture in the United Kingdom. The Lab was set up in part in recognition of the need to take heed of these broader questions and to advance a more comprehensive engagement with justice concerns as they intersect with datafication. A reframing towards data justice initially offered a way to situate questions of data in relation to ongoing social justice concerns that could engage a wider political mobilization (Dencik, Hintz, & Cable 2016) and could inform debates on citizenship and governance more broadly (Hintz, Dencik, & Wahl-Jorgensen 2019; Redden 2018). Furthermore, it provided an umbrella under which to explicitly identify and illustrate the nature and diversity of harms that are caused by uses of new data systems (Redden & Brand 2017) as a way to foreground the politics of data and the significance of the contexts in which data systems are implemented. It also became an avenue through which recognition and exploration of ways of thinking and using data from the margins could be fostered, and the many Souths inhabiting our world, and as a way to promote a reparation to the cognitive injustice that fails to recognize non-mainstream ways of knowing the world through data (Milan & Treré 2019, 2021; Treré 2019).

The book provides an overview of some of the key debates that are currently central to our understanding of the societal implications of datafication. With it, we are particularly keen to shift the approach that often dominates public and scholarly debate on data-related issues that has tended to focus on individual forms of technology or abstract scenarios that position populations as equally situated in relation to data developments. Instead, in this book, we want to highlight how datafication operates, not just as a set of technologies, but as infrastructure, discourse and practice that now permeates many different societies. We do so with particular attention paid to the unevenness of this trend and the inequalities of its manifestation. We see this as a necessary contribution to understandings and discussions of the intersection of datafication and society.

Why Data Justice?

The privileging of social justice in our analysis of datafication is rooted in an understanding of technology as embedded within an amalgamation of different actors and social forces, and a particular political economy. In this sense, the way data is generated and collected, what it is used for and how, are not inevitabilities but are rather bound up with certain social structures, interests and ideas. An orientation towards justice in analysing the intersection of datafication and society asserts from the outset, therefore, that the nature of this intersection is never fixed. It is subject to continuous conflict and negotiation, advanced on the basis of competing visions. Justice concerns compel us to consider the empirical realities of infrastructures and practices in relation to normative claims on how we want society to be organized. With this book, we do not aim to set out a roadmap

for what such claims should consist of, but rather we want to pave a path that can facilitate an engagement with the continued struggle over what technology might be, and the
social and political organizations that enable it. As such, a focus on data justice advances
an orientation towards destabilizing the appearance of natural orders, sets out to reveal
contemporary power relations, and considers how they could be different.

The concept of data justice draws from a range of long-standing traditions that have
concerned themselves with the social justice implications of the nature of information
and communication systems. It has emerged prominently in the dual context of the
growing focus on so-called big data (and the more recent iterations of machine learning
and artificial intelligence), and the perceived limitations in how such developments have
been framed and approached. In particular, the revelations from the Snowden leaks, first
published in 2013, pushed the societal significance of 'big data' into more mainstream
and public view (Lyon 2015) but often in terms of a simple binary between enhanced
efficiency and (state)security on the one hand and concerns with surveillance and privacy on the other (Hintz et al. 2019). While this provided notable impetus for engaging
with the implications of emerging technologies, which included the mainstreaming of
privacy-enhancing technologies and encryption as well as the significant prominence
of digital rights and anti-surveillance campaigning in the public realm, it also privileged
particular responses that struggled to account for the implications of datafication in relation to broader social justice agendas (Dencik et al. 2016).

This has also meant that understandings of the impact of datafication have tended
to neglect different conceptions of justice, such as distributive, procedural and recognition, in favour of more narrow interpretations of individual rights and opportunities
(Gangadharan & Niklas 2019). Yet the shift to data-centric infrastructures is significant for historical and systemic transformations in relation to economic and political
interests, and the strategic alignment between state and capital that has shaped history, between and within nation-states. They are instrumental for understanding the
nature of markets and systems of governance, not just by increasing the potential for
monitoring, but as sorting mechanisms (Gandy 1993). The way these sorting mechanisms work and what their relationship is to historical contexts, social structures and
dominant agendas is not just a question of individual privacy or other human rights,
but one of justice. This focus is important because although it is clear that how we
make sense of the social world is central for how we make claims about it, systems of
communication and information infrastructures do not tend to feature in prevalent
theories of justice (Bruhn Jensen 2021). We see data justice debates as part of efforts
to address this gap.

Data justice as a concept and focus therefore speaks closely to the sorts of concerns
that inform critical data studies and related fields in that it seeks to examine data issues in
the context of historical legacies, existing power dynamics, ideology and social practices
(Kitchin & Laureault 2014; Van Dijck 2014). The premise is that developments in data
cannot be considered separately from social justice concerns and agendas, but need to
be integrated as part of them. However, what this means as an approach is varied, and

we have seen a range of different perspectives engage with data justice, often across disciplines and traditions.

Predominantly, data justice has been used and applied in recent years as a way to 'denote an analysis of data that pays particular attention to structural inequality, highlighting the unevenness of implications and experiences of data across different groups and communities in society' (Dencik, Hintz et al. 2019, p. 875). This has, in some interpretations, led to new articulations of principles to underpin data governance that can better account for such inequalities (Heeks 2017; Taylor 2017), or practices in the handling of data that make asymmetries in the representation and power of data explicit (Johnson 2018). Other approaches have foregrounded conceptions of justice in ideas about the design process and the conditions within which data infrastructures emerge. This has led to calls for more participatory design practices that emphasize the involvement of communities and that seek to build alternative bottom-up infrastructures to empower rather than oppress marginalized groups (Costanza-Chock 2018). Related to this, debates on data justice have emerged at the intersection of activism and technology, in which data is seen as an avenue to revert or challenge dominant understandings of the world, (re)creating conditions of possibility for counter-imaginaries and social justice claims to emerge (Gray 2018; Milan & van der Velden 2016).

Grassroots groups and social justice campaigns are applying a comprehensive and critical approach to datafication and, in some cases, have done so within a 'data justice' framework. The Center for Media Justice in the United States created their own Data Justice Lab as part of the annual Data for Black Lives conference. It is dedicated to thinking through ways to bridge research, data and movement work relating to issues like surveillance, carceral tools, internet rights and censorship. The Detroit Digital Justice Coalition has worked with local residents in identifying potential social harms that may emerge through the collection of citizen data by public institutions, situating these within the ongoing criminalization and surveillance of low-income communities, people of colour and other targeted groups. As a result, they have developed a set of guidelines for equitable practices in collecting, disseminating and using data. The US/Canadian Environmental Data & Governance Initiative (EDGI) has preserved vulnerable scientific data in the aftermath of the US election of Trump in 2016, and in the process developed an 'environmental data justice' framework that considers the politics, generation, ownership and uses of environmental data. Similar concerns inform an increasing emphasis on 'sovereignty' in relation to data, particularly among Indigenous communities, which is evident in the agenda set out by the growing Indigenous Data Sovereignty movement. The movement is made up of a network of alliances and groups around the world that asserts that Indigenous peoples need to be decision-makers around how data about them is collected and used. This orientation builds on long-standing struggles over the ongoing extraction and exploitation of Indigenous peoples and their knowledge systems, customs and territories (Kukutai & Taylor 2016). Themes pertaining to data justice are also prevalent in the growing 'platform cooperativism' movement, which sets out to challenge the nature of business ownership and governance emerging under platform capitalism, building on the values of cooperativism to create a fairer future of work in a digital economy. Such themes also inform a growing mobilization towards more citizen-centred data infrastructures in public governance structures, such as the visions expressed in the 'Roadmap Towards Technological Sovereignty' outlined by the local administration in Barcelona.

As we will see in this book, sometimes these different approaches stand in tension with each other, indicating that what we mean by data justice continues to be up for grabs. In this sense, we cannot understand data justice as a predefined end goal, abstract ideal with universal application, or fixed practice, but as is often the case with understandings of justice, a notion that is always subject to struggle and negotiation. We are especially guided by an ambition to expand the engagement with data justice beyond a focus on a single development or specific harm, such as prevalent discussions on algorithmic bias, digital exclusion or right to redress. Instead, we understand data justice as part of a systemic critique that levies efforts at broader transformations in society and the role of technology within them.

Our Approach

In this book, therefore, we approach data justice as a research agenda that allows us to bring together what we consider to be key areas at the intersection of datafication and social justice that stem from our work at the Data Justice Lab. The chapters in this book reflect what we regard as central tenets of data justice debates, engaging with questions of capitalism, government, colonialism, harms, citizenship, policy, activism and, ultimately, understandings of social justice. Of course this is not an exhaustive list, but rather reflective of the work we have been doing at the Data Justice Lab. They are areas that are informed by empirical research and conceptual development carried out collectively and independently over the last few years that we situate here specifically in relation to data justice.

The empirical work has investigated multiple dimensions of datafication, algorithmic governance and data uses. Several projects have addressed the use of data analytics by government and corporate actors, and the increasing automation of public services, including in welfare, policing and border control; the datafication of the workplace; state surveillance and its implications for digital citizenship; the use of data scores and 'citizen scoring' in the UK; and the failures and frequent reversals of such efforts. Other projects have explored data harms; data policy; possibilities for civic participation and intervention into the deployment of data systems; and the specific practices, visions and implications of datafication in the Global South and at the margins of the datafied society. Most of this work has been conducted as either year-long or multi-year research projects funded by both academic and non-academic funding bodies, including the European Research Council (ERC), the UK Economic and Social Research Council (ESRC), the Carnegie UK Trust, the Social Science and Humanities Research Council (Canada) and the Open Society Foundations. The empirical work has encompassed several hundred interviews with policy-makers, government officials, civil society representatives, community groups and other stakeholders; policy document analysis; media content analysis; and participant observation in relevant field-sites, forums and meetings.

In engaging with these different themes, and based on thorough insights on contemporary datafication, the aim of this book is to understand how justice concerns are implicated in an increasingly datafied society by exploring transformations that are happening across the economy, government, citizenship, policy, and civil society in conjunction with prominent concerns about the nature of harms, relations of dominance and resistance, and ideas of rights and freedoms. By bringing these together, we draw attention to the multifaceted nature of datafication and the diversity of entry-points that bring us to a collective concern with data justice. In this sense, we see data justice as a concept and practice that *continues* and *builds on* historical debates and struggles relating to oppression and emancipation, rather than as a novel normative theory based on a view of datafication as a revolutionary shift in social relations.

Holding on to this historicity is significant and evident throughout the book as it also means that we understand transformations brought about by the growing reliance on data-driven systems across areas of social and public life as bound up with ongoing transitions, shaped by a multitude of agents and social forces. Moreover, our concerns with justice implications do not necessarily seek to establish new principles or rights, but are rather oriented towards the integration of data-related developments within existing social justice agendas that encompass a wide range of principles, rights and freedoms. In other words, with this book we seek to ask what the advent of datafication means for social justice, building on concerns with questions such as equality, recognition, fairness, discrimination and human flourishing, and taking account of not just digital rights, but human rights, social and economic rights, while putting these in the context of broader systemic transformations.

As an approach, therefore, we see our engagement with data justice as an avenue through which we are compelled to ask questions about how society is organized and the role technology has within it, in order to then consider how it may be otherwise. As social scientists, our work has been informed by the desire to do research that combines breadth and depth. By this we mean that throughout our research we try to survey ideas about, and practices of, datafication so that we can gain, as much as possible, a better understanding of key shifts. We combine this with methods of qualitative investigation to ensure our research is informed by a grounded and contextually-based appreciation of the implications of changing practices. While the purpose of this book is not to provide an overview of our empirical work, the ideas presented throughout the book are informed by such research. We are situated within the field of media and communication studies, which also shapes much of our approach, but continue to extend our work through interdisciplinary collaboration. This includes an engagement with disciplines across the humanities and social sciences, as well as engineering and computer science. Our understanding of data justice is therefore informed by the ongoing efforts of a range of different scholars, practitioners and activists who push the parameters for how we are to understand what is at stake with datafication, and this book is a contribution to, and recognition of, such efforts.

Outline of Book

The book is structured according to seven thematic areas that relate to data justice in order to work towards a final chapter that advances a framework for understanding the intersection of data and social justice. While this has been a collective effort, we have each taken the lead in authoring different chapters individually among us. We start by setting the context for the datafied society, beginning in Chapter 1 with a focus on how data and capitalism intersect, looking at the growth of the digital economy, how data is valued, and what this means for social relations. As such, the chapter is concerned with examining the role of data in contemporary capitalism as a way to explore the power dynamics, values and social stratifications that condition the environment in which social justice struggles are currently carried out. It starts from the premise that datafication constitutes a 'political-economic regime' that necessitates the rooting of any notion of data justice within contemporary capitalism rather than engaging with data developments as abstract or separate from this condition. The chapter asks what the relationship between capitalism and data justice is, and whether to speak of data justice is necessarily to speak of anti-capitalism, or whether data justice is rather an avenue through which to exploit the opportunities while mitigating against the harms from the way datafication and capitalism currently intersect. It thereby sets up a key discussion that permeates throughout the book with regards to different strategic logics that inform current data justice debates, and the possibilities for radical social change.

We then move on to questions of the state and governance in Chapter 2 which considers how government uses of data-driven systems change the ways that those within government come to know about and engage with people and social issues. The chapter focuses on how a turn to datafied governance affects power dynamics as well as levels of oppression, fairness and equality in our societies. Through a survey of our collective research as well as the work of others, the chapter identifies several significant shifts in governance. The chapter traces how government uses of algorithmic systems extend longer histories of data-based ways of knowing and controlling, but also that there are new and intensified modes of datafied governance that present particular threats to our collective well-being. The chapter builds upon previous work stressing how important it is to better understand the links between information power and systemic and structural violence. By highlighting concerns about how datafied governance can lead to a distancing between those in positions of power and the people they are supposed to serve, the chapter underlines how important it is for government agencies to pursue connection as an organizing principle that prioritizes human-centred efforts, solidarity building and responsive approaches.

We end this first contextual section of the book with Chapter 3 and a focus on approaches to datafication that are often based on a problematic universalism that tends to assimilate the heterogeneity of diverse contexts, practices and visions and neglect local differences and cultural specificities. The chapter argues that this universalism can be conceived as yet another manifestation of technological determinism and reductionism. Reflecting on a problem that is of an ontological, epistemological and ethical nature, the chapter outlines problems, practices and people whose work is useful to understand data-fication and data justice beyond Western concerns and conceptualizations. More specifically, we first propose six preliminary observations that can orient our de-westernizing gaze. Then, we disentangle what de-westernization implies for data studies and data justice along four key dimensions: the academic cultures, the subject of study, the body of evidence and the analytical frameworks. In conclusion, we relate these reflections to the overall debate on the universalism of social research, the value of public sociology and the meanings of data justice.

In Chapter 4 we begin exploring some of the implications of data-driven developments outlined in the first few chapters, and argue that we can learn a lot about the transformations happening as a result of datafication by paying attention to how people are being negatively affected by these changes. In the chapter, we reflect on the lessons that can be learned from the harms documented in the Data Justice Lab's Data Harm Record. We provide a taxonomy of these harms as a means to document and identify the different and overlapping injustices occurring through the use of data-driven systems. The Record demonstrates that people are already being negatively affected by datafication, that harms are wide-ranging and pervasive and are linked to corporate and governmental practices. The Record provides an indication of how datafication is being negatively experienced by many, which provides a means to diagnose the kinds of societies we live in as well as to fuel discussions about what we can do to prevent and challenge data harms. The chapter concludes by stressing that preventing data harms will require far more than technical solutions, and that what is needed is addressing the systemic inequality and violence that leads to the implementation of systems that cause harm.

Chapter 5 expands on, particularly, the discussion on the role of data in governance by exploring the implications on citizenship and democracy. As citizens in a datafied society are increasingly profiled, categorized, scored and assessed, with data analytics determining what rights they enjoy and what restrictions they face, the datafied citizen becomes a heavily monitored and tightly managed entity. The chapter traces how the obscurity of datafication, the difficulty of interrogating and challenging it, and the focus on social management and prediction reconfigure state–citizen relations, limit the role of the citizen in governing society, and thus affect core practices and understandings of democracy. However, we also observe the increasing use of both new and established models of civic participation in the governance of datafied societies. From citizen assemblies on the use of data analytics to civil society campaigns, data literacy initiatives and data activism, a growing set of methods have emerged to enhance people's understanding of, and opportunities for intervention into, the systems that assess and categorize them, and to develop new democratic practices to ensure participation and accountability. The chapter thus discusses how both the conceptual and practical tenets of citizenship need to be reviewed – and reasserted – in the context of a data justice agenda.

In Chapter 6, we build on the question of how datafication is being negotiated by turning to the policy environment. We ask about the rules that regulate data collection and processing, their effectiveness to protect citizens from data harms, how these rules are created, based on whose interests and on what norms and ideas, and we explore necessary components of a data justice policy framework. The chapter interrogates current regulatory trends, particularly in surveillance and data protection law, that impact the control people have over the terms of their datafication. While data collection by platform businesses and government continues to expand, we observe a nascent trend towards citizen protection and control over data. However, the chapter questions the focus of predominant legal reform frameworks on individual approaches, such as personal data, user empowerment and individual rights, and points to the need for public, collective and democratic forms of governing data. Further, it unpacks the discursive struggles between different social actors and their distinct normative claims and explores the power-related institutional context in which current data policy is being shaped. It concludes that the development of a data justice policy framework requires us to reimagine concepts and institutions for organizing data and it proposes a set of starting-points.

Chapter 7 shifts the focus on policy and regulation as responses to the mutual shaping between social movements and data, foregrounding the forms of agency and social change that are being imagined and practised in the datafied society. Social movements throughout history have influenced major societal, cultural and political shifts, and their role is key in the face of rising inequality, injustice and in the context of the environmental crisis that we are confronting. Hence, we illustrate that studying movements' practices is pivotal for the understanding of the foundations, challenges and the directions of data justice. Through the evaluation of two key genres of data activism – counter-data mapping and algorithmic activism – we reflect on the dynamics, challenges and opportunities of data appropriations from below. We argue that data activism can be understood as a constitutive element of data justice, an entry-point for discussions on current injustices and ways to overcome them, by drawing on the histories of social movements, their activist repertoires and trajectory of technological experimentation. The chapter concludes by underlining that in the current struggle around data, activists are contributing not only to reorient the course of datafication to achieve their social justice goals, but also to challenge the inevitability of its application at a more structural level.

Finally, in Chapter 8 we take stock of the different thematic areas we have covered in the book and consider what these tell us about approaches to social justice in the context of datafication. In particular, the chapter argues that a concern with data justice needs to consider not only how social justice can be advanced in relation to datafication, but also how the widespread reliance on data-driven systems comes to construct and define the very terms of social justice. To speak of data justice is thus to recognize not only how data impacts on society, but the normative vision that datafication advances of how social issues should be understood and resolved. Data is therefore both a matter *in* and *of* justice. Drawing on work that has sought to explore how information, communication and media systems relate to theories and practices of justice, the chapter uses the notion of abnormal justice to move beyond the distributive paradigm of justice to consider what data justice means in terms of political and social mobilization. We see data justice as garnering meaning alongside and as part of theories and movements of social justice that attend to underlying power dynamics and conditions for social change. It is in this vein that we see debates on data justice as valuable for understanding and advancing social justice today.

1

DATA AND CAPITALISM

By Lina Dencik

The rise of the digital economy has been a defining feature of contemporary capitalism. In a relatively short period of time, companies that primarily profit from trading in digital services and technologies have come to dominate the corporate landscape and, increasingly, political and social life. In 2016, for the first time, five companies from the same industry led the world in market value: Apple, Alphabet, Microsoft, Amazon and Facebook (Mosco 2017). Predominantly operating out of the confined geographical space of Silicon Valley in the United States, the industry that has emerged around digital technologies is now a global powerhouse. The advent of information and communication technologies (ICTs) was from the outset imbued with significant transformative potentials, widely seen to overturn organizational forms central to the economy and across society (Castells 1996). Yet the turn to data – its mass generation, collection and analysis – has been instrumental to the growth of the digital economy and its role in society. Communication scholar Vincent Mosco (2017) sees it as a digital shift towards a 'post-internet' society defined by the convergence of cloud computing, big data analytics and the internet of things. In this society, the cloud stores and processes information in data centres, big data analytics provides the tools to analyse and use it, and the internet of things accelerates its generation by connecting sensor-equipped devices to electronic communication networks.

While there is widespread recognition that the advent of datafication is a significant aspect of contemporary forms of capitalism, it is less clear what the relationship between data and capitalism actually is; its history, relations and implications. For the field of data justice, exploring this relationship is important as it underpins much of how we might understand the nature of transformations happening with datafication and what might be appropriate responses to such transformations as they impact on people's rights, life-chances and well-being. As we show in this chapter (and the rest of the book), examining the role of data in contemporary capitalism is central for engaging with the power dynamics, values and social stratifications that condition the environment in which social justice struggles are currently carried out. Data, in this sense, is significant not just in terms of its role as the raw material of informational capitalism (Cohen 2020), but in the reconfiguration of social relations that happens as data is embedded in capitalist developments. The relationship therefore also poses a key challenge to ideas of data justice and how they sit in relation to capitalism. That is, whether to speak of data justice is necessarily to speak of anti-capitalism, or whether data justice is an avenue through which to exploit the opportunities while mitigating against the harms that emerge from the current constellation of data and capitalism – or indeed both.

In this chapter, we situate datafication as a 'political-economic regime' (Sadowski 2019) that attends to the role of data in advancing and shaping particular modes of capitalism. By way of background, we start by briefly outlining the growth of the digital economy in the context of big data, particularly in the wake of the 2008 financial crisis. We then go on to discuss different understandings of the value of data in contemporary capitalism and what form data-driven modes of capitalism are said to take, from cognitive capitalism to surveillance capitalism to platform capitalism. From this, we consider the implications of these dynamics for the transformation of social relations and the nature of classifications that shape the environment for contemporary struggles around data and social justice. As we go on to argue in this book, the abstraction of data from the dynamics of capitalism, understanding data in the absence of historical and social context, risks making any account of justice as it applies to the consequences of datafication void of the explanations needed to pursue it. We therefore see the relationship between data and capitalism as a suitable place to start our exploration of the different tenets of data justice.

The Rise of Big Tech

The digital economy has long been the subject of great fascination based on both fear and hype about its transformative potential for capitalism, often without clear parameters as an object of analysis (Jordan 2020). Digital technologies are now embedded in most economic activity in one way or another, and underpin financial and production trends that go far beyond any particular sector or industry. As such, it is worth pinpointing the aspect of the digital economy that we are concerned with here. To ground the further exploration of the relationship between data and capitalism, we focus here on so-called 'Big Tech' and how the development of data-intensive technologies has intertwined with the rise of global corporate monopolies. This is not to suggest that Big Tech summarizes digital technology as it exists today, but, in line with Mosco's (2017) notion of the 'post-internet' age, we understand the rise of Big Tech as indicative of a significant shift in the nature of the digital economy towards an onus on data infrastructures. This aspect of the digital economy therefore has fundamental implications for how we might consider data justice concerns and how they relate to value generation, elite interests and historical trends. As social scientist and finance anthropologist Martha Poon (2016) has argued, data systems have been spurred on by agents of corporate capitalism seeking to maximize profit through market devices reconstituted in the form of networked technology. Companies create data systems that are designed to enable and empower themselves as business operators. The speed with which such ambitions have been realized is not necessarily a matter of technological advancement but needs to be understood in relation to the longer history of capitalism and recent conjunctures in the modern world system. In his influential book *Platform Capitalism*, Nick Srnicek (2017) points to three significant moments that set the stage for the digital economy as we know it today: the response to the 1970s economic downturn; the boom and bust of the 1990s; and the outcome of the 2008 financial crisis.

In the first instance, the response to the economic downturn of the 1970s radically transformed the international political economy, driven by a neoliberal ideology that saw increased global competition, shifting supply chains and the deregulation of industries, matched with widespread attacks on labour and increased pressure to lower production costs (Harvey 2007a). Advancements in systems of communication and information flows led to 'time–space compression' that enabled global product markets to develop and less tangible relations of exchange to occur that facilitated greater capital mobility and the fragmentation of labour processes (Harvey 1992; Wood 2020). This period drastically overturned the tenets of industrial capitalism as advanced economies transitioned away from a dependency on domestic manufacturing towards service industries, global production networks and a sharp decline in trade union membership (Dencik & Wilkin 2015; Hudson 2014). As manufacturing in advanced economies declined, the promises of the launch of the internet in the 1990s and its potential for commercialization saw a frenzy of investments in new online businesses peddled by a widely chronicled myth of wealth accumulation (Curran 2012). These businesses encapsulated an ongoing power shift from consolidated firms and managers to investors and securities analysts who measured success primarily on the basis of stock price (Davis 2009). US political-economic institutions, in particular, actively nurtured new corporate models that not only centred asset-stripping and outsourcing, but that sought to build alliances between investors and consumers aimed at winner-take-all market strategies (Rahman & Thelen 2019).

This was a time of great promise for the digital economy, which also underpinned political engagement, particularly in the United States where President Bill Clinton, backed by tech-enthusiast Vice President Al Gore, sought to encourage the growth of US technology companies in the context of a largely unregulated internet. Already in 1993, Clinton and Gore unveiled a $17 billion high-tech initiative to Silicon Valley with the view to revitalize the economy, in recognition of 'the strength and potential of America's scientific and technological resources to change and improve the quality of [...] lives' (San Francisco Chronicle 1993). This kind of engagement with the technology industry set the scene for an exponential growth in new internet businesses.

The tech bubble of the late 1990s quickly burst with the stock market crash in 2001, but Srnicek (2017) traces much of the infrastructure that underpins today's digital economy to the level of investment into new technologies during this period: millions of miles of fibre-optic and submarine cables, major advances in software and network design, and large investments in databases and servers. This infrastructure is at the heart of power dynamics in the digital economy today. Moreover, the crash triggered a race for online technology companies to identify a new way to make money that also aligned with strategic security interests intensified by the terrorist attacks of 9/11: the collection and analysis of vast quantities of data (Angwin 2014). That is, we saw the emergence of a congruence of interests in state–capital relations that satisfied both commercial and geopolitical priorities in the form of mass data collection. Alongside a post-crash loosening of monetary policy that lowered interest rates and increased provision of liquidity to restart the economy, the scene was set for Big Tech to manifest its dominance out of the ashes of the 2008 financial crisis that followed.

The financial crisis of 2008 catalysed the dominant position of Big Tech in several respects. For one, following its own earlier bust, the technology sector remained relatively unscathed as the financial crisis took hold in other parts of the global economy. At the same time, corporate savings and tax havens resulted in a glut of cash in search for low interest rate investments (Berry 2019; Srnicek 2017). With finance marked by toxic assets, this saw an injection of large amounts of capital into start-ups and technology companies chasing high-risk innovation, a funding model that marks much of the inner workings and culture of the digital economy to this day (Liu 2019). The investment of venture capital into technological innovation has catapulted the growth of digital developments. According to political economy researcher Franziska Cooiman (2021), this financial structure now constitutes the backend of the digital economy and encompasses not just American investment chains but also European investment based on a deep entanglement between public and private actors dating back to the 1990s. The shift in capital was one that changed the terrain; one that saw the momentary collapse of Wall Street cement a new financial powerhouse in the form of Silicon Valley (Sadowski 2020a).

Moreover, the 2008 financial crisis accelerated an overhaul of the public sector across advanced economies that paved the way for increased privatization and a significant rise in precarious labour (Standing 2012). These conditions suited a largely unregulated digital economy that promised efficient solutions to entry barriers and production costs. They also suited a rapidly established trend of acquisitions and monopolization that has come to define the technology sector despite early proclamations of the digital economy as a great leveller that would lead to democratization and decentralization (Freedman 2016). The promise was that lowering the costs of barriers to entry and bypassing institutional hierarchies would allow for new players to enter and lead to distributed control. Instead, it quickly became clear that market dominance and scale would be central to the story of profitability that technology companies needed to seek out to make good on the massive influx of capital investment.

In just a decade or two, Big Tech has come to represent a sector organized around a handful of mega corporations that constitute the most valuable public companies in the world by market capitalization. They now shadow previous giants from fossil fuel to finance. While their businesses and focus vary, they share enough features to constitute a segment that can be seen to exercise enormous collective power, not just in economic terms but politically and socially too (Barwise & Watkins 2018). Indeed, their power lies not so much in their 'size' as a traditional measure of companies but, as we shall see, in their ability to *control* markets as 'regulatory structures' that dictate the terms of interaction (Rahman & Thelen 2019; Zysman & Kenney 2018). Big Tech in this sense encapsulates not only the big five of Apple, Alphabet (Google), Microsoft, Amazon and Facebook, but refers to technology companies at large that have come to dominate and scale across markets and sectors. As such, the rise of Big Tech is one that is intimately intertwined with the history of capitalism and capital's continued advancement in the wake of significant crises.

This dynamic has only been reinforced during the most recent global crisis surrounding the COVID-19 pandemic, which has catapulted digital technology companies – and the big five in particular – into unprecedented levels of wealth and control. It is estimated that just in the third quarter of 2020, when the pandemic had taken hold across most of the globe, Apple, Google, Facebook and Amazon brought in $38 billion in profits on nearly $240 billion in revenue, with Amazon's profits in particular rising nearly 200 per cent from a year earlier (Molla 2020). Yet Big Tech's sheer dominance and power has instigated significant debate about whether its rise has also fundamentally changed capitalism, how it operates and the social relations that are constituted through it. The generation and collection of data and how it relates to value generation is a significant part of this debate. As we go on to discuss below, data has a rather nebulous role in contemporary capitalism and has been interpreted in several different ways that solicit different kinds of responses. This is important, as how we make sense of the value of data and what it means for capitalism has implications for how we might understand the nature of conflict and struggle that has emerged around datafication, as we discuss in this book.

The Value of Data

While it is widely accepted that datafication and the ability to exploit data generation for profit is a significant aspect of the rise of Big Tech and its continued power, determining the actual value of data in contemporary capitalism is a matter of continued contention. The frequently referred to understanding of data as the raw material of the digital economy is only one part of the story. As we will see, to contend with the way datafication intersects with social and economic justice concerns, the value of data needs to be understood in relation to wider issues of infrastructural power and domination. Moreover, it needs to be understood in relation to a longer trajectory of value generation in capitalism that can help us assess the extent to which we are dealing with a fundamental shift in how capitalism operates. Scholarly debates on the transformative potentials of new technologies have often signalled changes through new labels for capitalism (X-capitalism), but a concern with data justice necessitates a certain anchoring of transformations that allow us to contend with where the target of any analysis of injustice should lie. In other words, while the notion of data justice in part emerges from the recognition of changes in how justice is understood and pursued that, among other developments, stem from transformations in the economy, it is important not to lose sight of the continuation of operational logics that have long been at the root of social conflict. Making sense of the value of data can help us some of the way.

Understandings of data in relation to capitalism emerge out of a longer-standing discussion on the knowledge economy and changes brought about by the spread of information and communication technologies (ICTs). Notions such as 'cognitive capitalism' elevated the role of ICTs and advanced an argument that they brought about a significant transformation in capitalism towards 'a mode of accumulation in which the objects of accumulation consist mainly of knowledge, which becomes the basic source of value, as well as the principal location of the process of valorization' (Moulier Boutang 2011, p. 57). That is, knowledge-based economies are the result of the subsumption of knowledge and information to the laws of capitalist accumulation, rather than the production, valorization and accumulation of knowledge for knowledge's sake (Celis Bueno 2017; Vercellone 2005). From the outset, this orientation requires a shift in delineations of productive and unproductive labour so that capital's command over life includes not only labour time but also leisure time (Marazzi 2008). The concept of the 'social factory' put forward by autonomist Marxists in the 1960s provided an early offering to consider this expansion of capitalist social relations outside the sphere of production that had defined industrial capitalism (Tronti 1962). It underpinned ideas about the need to incorporate 'immaterial' and 'free' labour that stems from the production, distribution and consumption of *information* into the valorization process in capitalism (Moulier Boutang 2011; Terranova 2000).

This perceived shift in the valorization process away from the sphere of production informed many early discussions about the relationship between data and capitalism, encapsulated by the later focus on 'digital labour' (Scholz 2013). Drawing in part on the work of media studies scholar Dallas Walker Smythe, who wrote about media audiences as a commodity in the 1970s and 1980s, the notion of digital labour suggests that data generated by users through their engagement with platforms could be considered a form of work (Fuchs 2014). The argument is that platforms such as Google and Facebook produce very little, if anything, themselves, but are able to generate revenue by tracking user activity that allows them to sell targeted advertising space. Social media theorist Christian Fuchs (2014) argues from a Marxist perspective that digital labour in this context refers to the unpaid productive surplus-value generating labour that comes from generating user data from which platforms profit. The way value is produced and exploited in what Celis Bueno (2017) labels 'the attention economy' is therefore markedly different from the traditional category of labour based on industrial modes of production. It is a shift in capitalism, he argues, in which subjectivity itself gradually becomes the territory of production and exploitation of value as well as the territory of reproduction of capitalist power relations. On this reading, data is therefore tied up with a valorization process that broadens and redefines labour as previously understood.

The cognitive capitalism thesis and debates on digital labour have been criticized for undermining the significance of wage dependency in definitions of labour and of underplaying the continued centrality of production and extraction of value from labour in supply chains (Thompson & Briken 2017). Indeed, one consequence of the focus on the 'immaterial' has been a neglect of all the intricate ways the value of data is connected to decidedly material processes and realities (Graham 2013). However, the commodification of data about users and its role in contemporary capitalism has continued to be central to analyses of the digital economy. Zuboff's (2015, 2019) prominent thesis on surveillance capitalism, for example, argues that there has been a fundamental shift in capitalism as capital moves from a concern with incorporating labour into the market, as it did under previous forms of capitalism, to a concern with incorporating private experiences into the market in the form of behavioural data. Pivoting the shift on Google's plans to generate revenue from its search engine in the wake of the crash in 2001, Zuboff outlines the workings of a new business model that seeks to capitalize on an infrastructure that can track user activity across the web, quantifying and tabulating such activity as data-points to collect and analyse for the purposes of gaining more extensive and granular profiles of users. This business model, she argues, relies not on a division of labour, but a division of learning: between those who are able to learn and make decisions based on global data flows, and those who are (often unknowingly) subject to such analyses and decisions. It is an accumulation logic driven by data that aims to predict and modify human behaviour as a means to produce revenue and market control.

In her account of informational capitalism, critical legal scholar Julie Cohen (2020) similarly refers to an alignment of capitalism as a mode of production with informationalism as a mode of development in which market actors use knowledge, culture and networked information technologies as a means of extracting and appropriating surplus-value. Although both data and algorithms have been resistant to formal propertization, the movement to an informational economy is reconstructing labour, land and money as datafied inputs to new algorithmic modes of profit extraction at the same time as data and algorithms have become the subjects of appropriation strategies. Importantly, for Cohen, this has been made possible in conjunction with platformization. As she argues, the legibility stemming from new techniques of tracking and data analysis became a service most effectively and profitably provided at the infrastructural level in the form of the platform. She states: 'Venture capital investors whose support offered a path to wider capital markets demanded a revenue model, and the demands of that model in turn began to drive platform design' (Cohen 2020, p. 41). It is a development in information infrastructures that Helmond (2015) has linked to the erosion and centralization of the open web through the penetration of platform extensions and the drive for third parties to make their data 'platform ready'.

The demands for a revenue model therefore drove data flows as an informationalized factor of production that underwrites a variety of profit-making activities. Yet the commodification of data does not sit easily alongside how we might value other commodities or goods. While it might be tempting to speak of a data market in which data is commoditized and traded, it is not at all clear that this makes sense in terms of how we otherwise think of markets, even though access to and the processing of data can generate market power (Graef 2018). According to the characteristics of data outlined by the UK's Competition & Markets Authority, data constitutes a non-rivalrous good, which means that the same piece of data may be used by more than one actor at the same time (Competition and Markets Authority (CMA) & Information Commissioner's Office (ICO) 2021). In addition, the value of data often does not lie in the collection of information itself but depends on the knowledge that can be extracted from it. Finally, the value of data is very diverse with some data having lasting value whereas other data is only valuable for a particular time or for a particular purpose (Graef 2018). These characteristics do not undermine the commodified nature of data, but they do call for an analysis of data and its (economic) value that can account for the relational features that are inherent to datafication (Ruppert et al. 2015; Viljoen 2020).

The onus on data in sustaining new accumulation logics has led some to expand on its value beyond thinking of it as merely a commodity. Political geographer Jathan Sadowski (2019), for example, regards datafication as a political-economic regime in which data is not just a commodity, but should be considered a form of capital. That is, data is both valuable and value creating. Data is essential for companies to extract more profit and it propels new ways of doing business and governance. In this context, data collection is driven by the perpetual cycle of (data) capital accumulation, which in turn drives capital to construct and rely upon a universe in which everything is made of data. Rather than seeing this as a break with capitalism *per se*, this process extends longer trends of assetization and financialization (Srnicek 2017). The aim is to turn everything into a financial asset as a way to latch onto circuits of capital and consumption for the purposes of rent extraction (Sadowski 2020b). The digital platform is central for this process in that social practices are reconfigured in such a way that enables the extraction of data (Couldry & Mejias 2018).

Under this 'rentier capitalism', datafication is part of a system of economic production and reproduction in which payment to an economic actor (the rentier) is made purely by virtue of that actor controlling something valuable. Profit can be attained from this control due to the particular circumstances of a dearth of market competition (Christophers 2020). While this logic is not new for capital, Sadowski (2020b) argues that what is new are the complex technologies that have been designed to extend and empower capital's abilities of assetization, extraction and enclosure. Market dominance is achieved through the provision of platform infrastructure to intermediate between different user groups that rely on network effects (the more users, the more useful the platform) to reduce transaction costs while the authority over important functions and the extraction of data locks users in (Srnicek 2017; Wood & Lehdonvirta 2021). That is, platformization disciplines infrastructure so as to thwart defection of transactions and networking to elsewhere (Cohen 2020). The main strategy of platforms is to turn social interactions and economic transactions into 'services' that take place on their platform. Seen through the lens of rentier capitalism, platforms are therefore intermediaries in the production, circulation or consumption process, and capture value from all the activities and operations that make up the platform ecosystem, extracting both monetary rent and data rent (Sadowski 2020b).

The value of data in this context is not necessarily as commodities but rather as capital that drives monopolization and other profit-making activities. Van Doorn and Badger (2020) argue that its value derives in part from its expected or actual practical utility (achieving functional goals and systems optimization), but also from the expectation of data-rich companies to achieve competitive advantage, and thereby attracting venture capital and higher financial valuations. Assessing the value of data therefore points us towards the cascading logics of datafication as a political-economic regime. As we become dependent on these platforms, we engage not only in the commodification of information about our behaviour, but also become locked in to a form of social ordering that restructures practices to uphold a regime of data accumulation. That is, we become part of a mode of capitalism that propels the further datafication of social life and that relies upon and drives particular social relations (Dencik 2022; Fourcade & Healy 2017).

As we will see in other parts of this book, datafication as a political-economic regime manifests itself therefore in terms of an *infrastructural dependency* on data-driven technologies that perpetuates the extraction of value through exploiting new technical capabilities for data accumulation. This is significant as it means that different social actors, including the state and civil society, are essentially positioned within a tenancy-type relationship with technology providers, in which it becomes increasingly difficult to shift this political economy over time. That is, when the public sector, for example, becomes dependent on a mode of capitalism in which revenue is predominantly extracted from rent (money or data) in exchange for services, it also facilitates a configuration of the terms upon which public institutions are able to operate. As will become evident in later chapters, this dependency relates to processes of outsourcing and privatization in part, but also threatens the *displacement* of public infrastructure with (private) computational infrastructure (Dencik 2022).

Social Relations Under Datafication

The issue of infrastructural dependency is a significant aspect of how social relations are configured under datafication in the context of capitalism. It highlights the importance of how power dynamics are manifested through this political-economic regime that shape how injustices may be experienced and the parameters within which they may be addressed. The dependency and potential displacement is bound up with fundamental questions of inequality and exploitation. Indeed, as has already been mentioned above, a significant framing of social relations under datafication draws on ecological language and consider them as *extractive*. Both in Zuboff's account of surveillance capitalism and in the analysis of rentierism in platform capitalism, data is raw material or rent that is *extracted* from a range of infrastructures; sensors to government databases to computer-mediated economic transactions alike that relate to profound and intimate aspects of social life. This framing speaks to a lack of reciprocity and consensual exchange that we might otherwise expect from a social contract in democracies (Zuboff 2019). Moreover, it links datafication to the history of capitalism bound up with neoliberalism that has sought to exploit resources through both creative as well as environmental and social destruction. As the prominent geographer and Marxist scholar David Harvey (2007b) has argued, the consolidation of class power that has been advanced under neoliberalism relies on not only the destruction of institutional frameworks and powers (e.g. the supposed prior state sovereignty over political-economic affairs) but also of divisions of labour, social relations, welfare provisions, attachments to the land, ways of thought, and so on.

In this sense, the active advancement of data-centric technologies extends long-standing concerns about the political, environmental and social conditions that enable the growth of the digital economy and their deterioration as it continues to expand (Gabrys 2011; Mosco 2014). Others have taken the emphasis on extraction further by likening social relations under datafication to a form of colonialism, in which processes of dispossession facilitate the extraction, appropriation and exploitation of data for value (Couldry & Mejias 2018). Discussed further in Chapter 3, the notion of data colonialism struggles to account for the violence of dispossession under colonialism, but used differently it points to the power dynamics embedded within datafication as a political-economic regime and that these overwhelmingly follow the historical legacies of north-south, rich-poor relations across the globe (Arora 2019b; Madianou 2019). In this respect, both the development and the implications of data-driven processes are deeply contingent upon the social relations of the existing global political economy. At the same time, the growth of the digital economy and the turn to data infrastructures across economic, political and social life reconfigures social relations and introduces new forms of social stratification.

Media theorist Lev Manovich (2012), for example, refers to the emergence of different 'data classes' in which new stratifications are being established along the lines of those who create data, those who collect data and those who analyse data. These different data classes point to inherent power asymmetries that play out as data infrastructures are embedded in society. Moreover, they suggest the need to consider how power is established through datafication that may not be adequately captured in class divisions as understood during industrial modes of capitalism that centred on ownership of the means of production. Instead, the critical media theorist Mckenzie Wark (2019) suggests, we are confronted with a new set of class relations in which power increasingly rests in the hands not of the owners of the means of production, but the owners of the vectors along which information is gathered and used, what Wark describes as the 'vectorialist class'. This class controls the patents, the brands, the trademarks, the copyrights and, most importantly, the logistics of the information vector. As such, while a capitalist class owns the means of production, the means of organizing labour, a vectorialist class owns the means of organizing the means of production. Such stratifications, Wark contends, constitute fundamentally different social relations from those that existed under previous understandings of capitalism.

The extent to which a vectorialist class should be considered as discreet from the capitalist class can be debated, but Wark's analysis highlights an important power shift that centres informational logistics as infrastructural power upon which other economic activities increasingly depend. This power shift does not make away with the exploitation of labour in value chains and productive value in contemporary capitalism, but it does indicate that this value generation is increasingly bound up with advancing infrastructural power through control over informational logistics. As Srnicek (2020) has pointed out, data-intensive technologies such as artificial intelligence (AI) systems rely not just on vast amounts of data, but on significant computational power and control over labour to drive monopolization. Divisions of labour remain fundamental in the digital economy, but their relationship to value has become more complex. Gray and Suri (2019, p. ix) refer to a growing economy based on 'ghost work': a new digital assembly line that aggregates the collective input of distributed workers, ships pieces of projects rather than products, and operates continuously across a host of economic sectors in order for data-driven systems to function. Communication scholars Jack Linchuan Qiu et al. (2014) describe a 'circuit of labour' that underpins data-driven processes, connecting the miners mining for minerals in the Democratic Republic of Congo to the factories producing hardware in Taiwan to the software engineers of Silicon Valley. As noted above, users themselves, who generate data through their engagement with digital platforms, are sometimes also included in this circuit as performing labour (Fuchs 2014). Alongside this, platforms have created multi-sided markets in which they are intermediaries for new types of work in the form of platform labour that they connect and manage

(Wood & Lehdonvirta 2021). These different dimensions point to the ongoing relevance of divisions of labour for value-generation in the digital economy.

Yet in contemplating the specific social relations that emerge from and drive datafication as a political-economic regime, we are asked to reckon with a particularly insidious form of power that is not just economic power but, as we shall see throughout this book, manifests itself as both social and political power. Culpepper and Thelen (2020) refer to 'platform power' as a way to describe the political power that they see as new to technology companies, unlike other businesses that have political influence. As alluded to in the previous section, this is a form of power that stems from the control platforms have over access to key services upon which people depend. Importantly, while market dominance is a necessary condition for platform power, it is not sufficient. Rather, they argue, 'the mechanism that translates market power into political clout ... flows from the appreciation, verging on dependence, that consumers have for the convenience these companies provide' (Culpepper & Thelen 2020, p. 290) As we illustrate in this book, this dependence increasingly stretches to citizens and governments too as technology companies have come to embed themselves as public infrastructures, while still operating on commercial logics (Morozov 2015).

The shift within engineering and computer science from shrink-wrapped software to 'software-as-a-service', as outlined by critical computer science and legal scholars Seda Gürses and Joris Van Hoboken in what they refer to as the 'agile turn' (2017), therefore indicates not a technological development *per se*, but a political-economic one that shapes social relations. The agile turn refers to the shift towards binding users into long-term transactions with software companies based on constant monitoring and amendments through user analytics. Under this model, these companies are positioned within different social and public domains, from media to transport to policing, not simply as providers of one-off tools and products, but as service providers that seek to continuously optimize such domains. Importantly, this positioning means that social issues need to be understood and approached on terms that are conducive to such service provision. That is, public domains are turned into problems that necessarily have to be optimized computationally rather than engaged with through human experience and expertise. What is more, software-as-a-service embeds these domains within an ecosystem that endlessly perpetuates this reconfiguration (Dencik 2022). Gürses, Dobbe and Poon (2020) use the term 'programmable infrastructures' to refer to this political, economic and technological vision that advocates for the introduction of computational infrastructure on our existing infrastructures. This vision, they argue, features the management of human behaviour, the standardization of values, a dependency on the economic terms of technology companies, a power asymmetry of cloud providers, and an avoidance of democratic governance.

In this context, data justice concerns need to be oriented towards the conditions that enable such power as well as the impact it yields. Engagement with how data-driven processes shape life-chances and the possibilities for human flourishing cannot be approached in isolation from these wider structural developments that facilitate the extraction of data for control. The perpetual accumulation of data is creating classification systems based around the value that data holds for platform-led markets. In this context, Poon (2016) notes, it is not technical accuracy that is the foundation of profitability, but rather the endless possibilities to manipulate financial elements tied to the managing and processing of data. These market-based evaluations are seeping through public life, invoking new struggles over classification as they shape people's position in society (Fourcade & Healy 2017). While we might be reluctant to see the advent of datafication as a fundamental disruption to capitalism that requires us to find new hermeneutic tools and frameworks to contend with its transformations, we do need to recognize what aspects of capitalist operations are being advanced and how these in turn shape social relations. Such an understanding can help inform what might be appropriate responses to injustices that people experience as they are confronted with data systems in their lives.

Conclusion: Is Data Justice Anti-Capitalist?

The financial crisis of 2008 ushered in a reckoning with the inherent fallacies of capitalism and its failure as a system to serve the needs and interests of the majority of the world's population. In its wake, we saw this reckoning find expression in the symbols and actions of large protest movements in different parts of the world, from 15M to Occupy to Syriza, that catalysed capitalism's failings and the growing desire for something else; an alternative way of organizing society to uphold values of equality and solidarity over profit. The early promises of digital technologies to aid the pursuit of such social change, however, quickly translated into a different story as the rapid growth of the digital economy, and the production model upon which it came to rely, proved to be directly at odds with such aspirations. Rather than spelling the end of capitalism, the financial crisis of 2008 instead saw the stratospheric rise of a new powerhouse that would be at the heart of capitalism's advancement.

The role of data in sustaining and furthering this advancement has been the subject of a range of interpretations that seek to assess its value in different ways – as labour, commodities, assets and rents. They unite around the pertinence of data for understanding significant power shifts that for some signal a fundamental transition in capitalism while for others they extend and entrench existing dynamics within capitalist modes of operation. Regardless of the extent of transformation brought about by datafication, it is clear that the way data is extracted, accumulated and exploited in the name of capital is increasingly central for understanding social relations. As we have seen, the proliferation of data systems has been a way to enable and enhance business operations for a range of corporate actors. Increasingly, the premise of such data-driven operations extends to other types of actors too. A concern with data justice therefore needs to confront the capitalist drivers of datafication as well as the datafied drivers of capitalism as they come to order society in new ways.

What does this mean for data justice as an approach? In Erik Olin Wright's last book before his untimely death, *How to be an Anti-Capitalist in the 21st Century* (2019), he wrote passionately about the need to continue to assert the possibility of another world that can improve the conditions of human flourishing despite the resilience of capitalism in the face of repeated crises. Similarly, the despair with which Mark Fisher (2009) outlined the prevalence of 'capitalist realism' in response to the devastating effects of the financial crisis of 2008 was a call to action to disrupt the appearance of capitalism as a natural order to which there could be no alternative. As we shall see throughout this book, much of the current efforts of data justice are precisely at the level of imagination, breaking through the stifling parameters of what is considered acceptable conflict, and pushing back against dominant logics of data accumulation. For Olin Wright (2019), anti-capitalism and creating a more just world did not have to come about by revolution, but could come about through identifying and advancing elements of a new world that are already being created in the world as it is. The stance was moral as well as practical. In what he referred to as 'strategic logics' – smashing, dismantling, taming, resisting and escaping – he argued that the erosion of capitalism would have to come about through the combination of different strategies that each constitutes a distinct way of responding to the harms of capitalism.

Data justice as an ideal and practice in many respects embodies these varieties of responses to capitalism, stretching across a spectrum of norms and activities that all seek to point to alternative ways of ordering society so as to advance human flourishing. Problematizing the extraction, accumulation and exploitation of data for capital is at the core of such efforts. A diagnosis of datafication as a political-economic regime allows us to consider how practices and concerns pertaining to data sit alongside historical developments that have been central to social justice struggles for a long time, and what responses to the harms of such developments have been effective. It is an approach that takes lessons from connected but often tangential debates, such as on environmental justice, that have similarly sought to privilege an understanding of climate change as a capitalist phenomenon. As Klein (2014, p. 20) argues, by pursuing climate justice without connecting with economic justice movements, 'large parts of the climate movements wasted precious decades attempting to make the square peg of the climate crisis fit into the round hole of deregulated capitalism, forever touting ways for the problem to be solved by the market itself'. It is a lesson we can equally draw from many racial justice and gender justice movements too. As we will go on to discuss further in later chapters, a key task for the field of data justice is therefore not only to diagnose, but also to find ways to identify and elevate strategic logics at the intersection of datafication and capitalism that can respond to the injustices that emerge from this intersection. Such a task is no doubt daunting, but also rescues the concept of data justice from serving as a mere fig-leaf in the momentous challenge that datafication poses for the future of a just society.

2

DATA AND GOVERNANCE

By Joanna Redden

This chapter focuses on government uses of data systems and it does so by considering how the datafication of government services and decision-making influences *governance*. Specifically, the chapter asks: How does government use of data-driven technologies such as artificial intelligence (AI) and automatic decision-making (ADS) systems shift the way governments come to know about and engage with people and social issues (Berry 2011; boyd & Crawford 2012)? What do these shifts suggest about the way governance is changing? The chapter argues that while government uses of algorithmic systems extend longer histories of data-based ways of knowing and controlling, the use of these systems also introduce new modes of governing that we must contend with from a data justice perspective.

The algorithmic systems discussed as objects of concern in this chapter are generally defined as technical systems to help or replace human decision-making across areas of public service administration. They rely on large, linked datasets and are introduced with the aim of improving services and productivity and often involve the collection and sharing of data in real time; for example, some make use of data analytics to predict the likelihood that individuals will commit crime, abuse their children or defraud benefit systems (Gillingham 2019). Globally, government agencies are using AI and ADS systems in the areas of security, fraud detection, benefit administration, policing, education, taxation and immigration. Governments are often said to be using these systems in attempts to improve planning and services, to be more efficient and to target resources better. The adoption of these systems is being done as government agencies struggle to meet public need in contexts of resource constraint and cuts to services.

Challenging the Faith in Data

The hype surrounding the use of big data, AI and ADS systems that dominated discussions of government uses of these systems over the last decade may have waned in light of much research pointing to harms, but the continued 'faith in data' is still evident in media, corporate and government discourses. Research shows that the way people think and talk about artificial intelligence and uses of digital technologies and data more generally can be influenced by the dominance of voices including government, technology companies, AI investors and management consultancies (Bourne 2019). As argued by David Beer (2019), we can see the 'faith in data' all around us, which includes visions about how data analytics will help us address social problems more effectively and efficiently. That is, corporate and government materials often promote data-driven systems as a means to increase efficiency and to enhance organizational decision-making by enabling greater insights – a phenomenon referred to by Evegny Morozov as technological solutionism (Morozov 2014). The authority of this discourse has been criticized for not attending to the limits of data-driven systems, particularly to where and how these systems fail or work in ways not intended (Beer 2014; Mosco 2014). There is too little information available about how data systems, particularly AI and automated decision-making support systems, work in practice. The questions about shifts in governance raised in this chapter are informed by our research at the Data Justice Lab to better understand where and how AI and ADS systems are being used by governments and efforts to investigate the social justice implications of changing government systems.

The data justice questions posed throughout are also informed by the strong body of evidence demonstrating that AI and ADS systems more generally can exacerbate bias and inequality, shift government operations and knowledge systems in ways that limit access to services and lead to harm as people are wrongly scored or denied benefits (Benjamin 2019; Eubanks 2018; Molnar & Gill 2018; Robertson, Khoo, & Song 2020). For example, research details how AI and ADS systems are being used to socially sort in ways that disproportionately and negatively affect Black, Indigenous and people of colour as well as discriminate on the basis of age, gender, sexuality and income (Gandy 2005; Gangardharan, Eubanks, & Barocas 2014; Lewis 2020; Lum & Isaac 2016; Lyon 2002).

Analyses of predictive policing systems as well as those in the area of child welfare have detailed how some of the most highly weighted variables in the systems analysed, such as postal code or whether or not a person accesses benefits, are proxies for ethnicity or poverty which mean that the poor and marginalized are disproportionately targeted through the use of such systems (Eubanks 2018; Gillingham 2016; Keddell 2015; O'Neil 2016b). Another common problem that spans a range of AI and ADS applications is a lack of transparency and access to the means to interrogate how the systems work (Pasquale 2015). There is a growing body of work discussing how government uses of ADS and AI systems may violate people's rights, including: social rights, rights to a fair trial and due process, to protection of personal data as well as human rights (Niklas & Dencik 2021; Yeung 2019).

While social justice debates about government uses of AI and ADS systems has raised concerns about transparency, accountability, bias, fairness and privacy, recent research raises questions about the effectiveness and usefulness of AI and ADS systems for public service provision. One of the first organizations to test the ability of predictive analytics to predict life outcomes, and to make the results publicly available, was the UK's What Works for Children's Social Care Centre. They partnered with local authorities to develop and test the use of ADS systems in the area of child welfare. They conclude, in contrast to corporate promoters of ADS systems, that the systems do not work and that the use of these systems would put children and young people at risk (Clayton et al. 2020). In response to the findings, the chief executive of the Centre, Michael Sanders, argued that organizations need to exercise caution before implementing ADS systems and that those wanting to use these systems should be more transparent about them and to be required to prove they work (Sanders 2020). This study is remarkable because of its findings, but also because it provides one of the few publicly accessible accounts of government ADS piloting.

Other research raises questions about the ability of data systems to predict life outcomes at all. A global group of researchers recently came together to predict six life outcomes using machine learning methods (Salganik et al. 2020). In this case, 160 teams built predictive models to forecast six life outcomes based on data from the Fragile Families and Child Wellbeing Study, a rich dataset. The teams found that even the best predictions were not very accurate and that, overall, there are limits to our ability to use such methods to predict life outcomes.

Data Governance and the Importance of Attending to History

This chapter contributes to the body of work detailed above which outlines the harms caused by government uses of AI and ADS systems as well as the limits of these systems. It does so by turning attention to governance and asking: How does a turn to datafied governance affect power dynamics and the levels of oppression, fairness and equality in our societies? We live in an age of striking inequalities and injustice, fuelled by oppressive structural arrangements, and we need to be alert to any changes in governance that makes this worse. Given the central role of information systems in influencing the way government agencies define and engage with people and social issues, attending to these information systems is key. As information systems become datafied, a crucial element of this discussion involves interrogating how processes of datafication may change ways of knowing.

As has been argued and will be detailed below, data provide a 'means through which people, phenomena and territory can be surveyed and regulated' (Kitchin 2014, p. 16). However, data is not neutral or objective; instead it is the product of processes of abstraction, selection, negotiation and convention. Further, data does not provide mere selective representations of the world; it leads to real-world impact as people make decisions and act on the basis of the stories being told with data (Kitchin 2014, p. 20). Informational power, argues Hoffmann (2020), is central to the exercise of other forms of power, including instrumental, structural and symbolic power. Further, once data systems are in place, and the narratives become relied upon, they can reinforce and reify particular ways of seeing, making them very difficult to dislodge. For this reason, data systems should be approached with caution and careful consideration, particularly when they are relied upon to inform decision-making that affects people's life-chances.

Johns (2021) describes governance by and within states as 'mechanisms of steerage' that are regular, normalized and systematized. AI and ADS systems are similar to older methods governments have used to represent data, such as the census, map and museum, in that AI and ADS systems are also 'performative technologies' that go beyond description to actively participate in 'making up' people and problems (Hacking 2007; Isin & Ruppert 2019). There is a long history of state consolidation of power and violence through data and performative technologies (Hoffmann 2020; Milner & Traub 2021) and work detailing how computing advances were used to discriminatorily socially sort in ways that affect life-chances (Gandy 1993).

Key to investigating data governance, from a data justice perspective, is attending to how data systems are part of longer histories of structural inequality and systemic violence, much of it linked to administrative classification systems that can be used in ways that provide security or lead to greater vulnerability (Spade 2011). Isin and Ruppert (2019) argue that a new regime of government is emerging through increased datafication. This new regime extends older practices of domination while also introducing new power dynamics that draw upon the ubiquity of data processing. As with older regimes of government, such as sovereign, disciplinary and regulatory, they argue that an emergent 'sensory power' is central to contemporary state consolidations of power (Isin & Ruppert 2019). Contemporary digital tracking technologies make it possible to render people and problems 'sense-able' more extensively and pervasively than was possible before the emergence of big data, and in the process new areas of life are brought into being to be governed (Isin & Ruppert 2019).

Previous work examining data governance makes use of similar terms, such as algorithmic governance or algocratic governance (Aneesh 2009; Danaher 2016; Yeung & Lodge 2019). This work discusses how the 'techniques and logics of state governance have changed and are changing', which is leading to 'new ways of seeing and being as a state' (Johns 2021). Fourcade and Gordon (2020) call this new form of governmentality the 'dataist state', a mode of governance that values data, prediction and control more than 'the will of the people'. Scott (1999) points out that state administrations use their information systems to make people and places do what is desired. Aneesh (2009) raises concerns about how algorithmic systems present new opportunities to regulate social behaviour. The concern, expanded upon by Yeung and Lodge (2019), centres on how algorithmic decision-making influences government decision-making more generally, specifically in relation to risk management and behavioural interventions. While governments have long relied on data and computing technologies to inform decision-making, concerns about contemporary algorithmic processes centre on the way they 'intensify and accelerate' power imbalances, inequality and discrimination (Milner & Traub 2021).

Hoffmann (2020) draws our attention to data violence to make links between the violence done through data systems historically to the ways violence occurs now through the use of AI and ADS systems. Contemporary and historical instances of violence are facilitated by force and coercion, but also by informational power imbalances. 'As with militarization, datafication does not only depend on a reconfiguration of material resources, labor and production; it is also a discursive process, one that routes and assigns value to human life through the logic of quantification and statistical methods' (2020, p. 5). Data systems can be used to consolidate power because of the way they can reify assumptions about people's value and tell influential stories that suggest what is at stake and what should be done to address people and problems. Categorization structurally embeds classifications of what is normal or abnormal in ways that create advantages for those treated as normal and disadvantages for those treated as abnormal (Crenshaw 1989; Spade 2011). Citing Gandy (1993), Hoffmann argues that 'the disaggregation of people in the form of data is never merely descriptive – it is always implicated in broader systems of power, norms, and normalization' (2020, p. 6).

Contemporary efforts by governments to quantify and datafy people and social issues needs to be done with recognition of how these processes have been abused and used for racist, sexist, classist and ableist violence historically if we are to prevent similar practices going forward. Data systems have been essential tools for colonialism and slavery. Drawing on Benedict Anderson's (2016) work on imagined communities, Isin and Ruppert (2019) point to the census, map and the museum as more than descriptive. They argue for the need to see objects and practices as performative given the way that they actively produce the realities they claim to merely describe. Performative technologies like the map and census have been used by colonizers to surveil and control Indigenous and First Nations peoples (Arora 2019a; Kukutai & Taylor 2016). Milner and Traub (2021) argue that Chattel slavery 'was the first use case for big data systems to control, surveil and enact violence in order to ensure global power and profit structure'. Colonizers and slave owners and traders reduced human life to quantifiable measures and also collected massive amounts of data. As noted by Milner and Traub (2021), in this case data processes were not just about generating and collecting particular kinds of data, but also about restricting and controlling information. The use of data systems to facilitate state violence spans the 20th and 21st centuries. Hoffmann (2020) provides a range of examples, including American government use of population data to force the removal and murder of Indigenous Americans, the use of census data to intern Japanese Americans in the Second World War; Nazi use of population records in Europe to murder Jewish and Romani peoples; and the use of registration systems in Rwanda to target and kill Tutsi people.

These data systems present us with blatant demonstrations of how discrimination and ideology can be embedded in the creation of data systems and how these systems can be put to violent use. For example, in Canada, maps produced by colonizers drew borders as if land had been ceded by the Indigenous communities living in those places when this was not the case. Similarly, critiques of historical census data collection point to the way a system like a census can force people into rigid categorizations that serve the interests of those wanting to manage populations (Hacking 2007). Maps and classification systems are examples of what Bourdieu has referred to as symbolic violence, given the way these tools legitimate and naturalize the ideological positions of those developing them. Classification systems, as argued by Hacking (2007), play an active role in 'making up people' and can have a 'looping effect' once in place as people classified interact with these modes of ordering, defining and sense-making. As institutions introduce and administer classificatory systems, they are 'firmed up' and normalized. The danger with classificatory systems is that they 'invite stereotypes' (Hacking 2007). Scott's work makes clear how state's force people and places into simplified categories that serve the interests of the observer. His key criticism is that administrative processes of ordering nature and society leads to tragedy and failure when accompanied by: state power, ideological interests and faith instead of rigorous scientific practice, authoritarian rule and a civil society that does not have the resources to resist (Scott 1999, pp. 4–5). His work details how different governments have used information power in ways that have led, globally, to human tragedy and failure.

Data systems threaten marginalized communities when used by those in positions of power as 'tools of proof' and 'tools of coordination' (Desrosières 2015). Measurements of poverty present an illustrative example of how numbers are used to serve political ends. In the UK, poverty has been measured since the 19th century. These measurements were used in the 19th and 20th centuries to punish people who were poor by incarcerating them in poorhouses or workhouses, where death due to detestable living conditions was common (Platt 2005). In contrast, measurements of poverty before and after the Second World War were used by social justice advocates to secure key welfare state protections such as universal family allowances, a free national health service and a unified flat-rate social insurance system for all people (Abel-Smith 1992, p. 5). With the rise of neoliberalism, living conditions reversed again. Margaret Thatcher used the doubling of poverty under her reign to justify intensifying the same neoliberal programme that had led to these high numbers (Platt 2005). Measurements of poverty present a continually contested terrain as those in positions of power argue over whether to rely on definitions of relative or absolute poverty and use poverty counts to reinforce arguments for more equitable distribution of resources and opportunity or to justify increasing punitive steps.

To quantify is to convert something into numbers and this conversion is informed by locally-specific conventions that range from language, compromises, procedures and calculations. Although often presented as an objective and neutral process, quantification in practice involves social and cognitive creativity (Desrosières 2015, p. 333). The quantified representation of the human is never a full representation; it is a representation that is partial and abstracted, which makes it amenable to being placed into the stories told by others.

> Statistics and all forms of quantification in general (probabilistic or accounting quantification) change the world through their very existence, their circulation and their rhetorical usage in science, politics or journalism. Conventions of quantification are themselves products of the history of the state and forms of government. (Desrosières 2015, p. 333)

If viewed in this way, the tools used for measurement cannot be separated or viewed as independent of the way they are used (Desrosières 2015, p. 342).

Datafied Governance Through AI and ADS

Data, the ways data are used and modes of governance are mutually constitutive; these elements influence and change each other. As argued by Kitchin (2014), people commonly think of data as something out there, aspects of life that simply exist and are waiting to be captured through processes of data collection. The research detailed above has discussed the ways that data is performative; how data makes up people and issues (Hacking 2007). As humans are constructed through data, these constructions have real-world impacts on people's lives.

> Thus, while data is seen as something that is out there – something that is about the real, they are more productively understood as both a component of the real and a producer of the real. Data are not merely an abstraction and representative, they are constitutive, and their generation, analysis and interpretation has consequences. ... If data are somehow subject to us, we are also subject to data. Data are captured from the world, but in turn do work in the world. Data are not, and can never be, benign. Instead, data need to be understood as framed and framing. (Kitchin 2014, p. 21)

To understand data and data systems as components of the real and producers of the real raises questions about what this means for governance in our age of 'big data': advanced data production, collection, storage and processing. How has the turn to 'big data' processes shifted the way governments come to know about and engage with people and social issues. Are there changes that raise specific social justice concerns? In what ways are AI and ADS systems, government practices and modes of governance making up each other?

Part of what is new about AI and ADS systems is the way that they are being used not only to learn things about people but also to try to use contemporary data-gathering capabilities to shift behaviours at both the individual and population level (Zuboff 2019). For Henman (2018), it is the anticipatory aspect of algorithmic governmentality that is unique. He argues that the new regime of truth informing contemporary data governance is one that is increasingly based on 'digitally concocted subjects' as combined with a drive to rule based on logics of prediction and anticipation. This is paired with a shift in State goals, as governments increasingly turn to trying to manage the effects of social problems rather than their causes (Fourcade & Gordon 2020). 'Governing the effects often means striving to identify which people are vulnerable to a social problem – illness, gang membership, medical bankruptcy – and triaging resources their way, even at the expense of attacking the underlying problem. It also requires subjecting the entire population to invasive surveillance, since everyone is a potential candidate for such interventions' (Fourcade & Gordon 2020, p. 87). A justification for increased predictive surveillance is that states will be able to target those in need with better and earlier support. Government agencies making this claim need to be held accountable to this promise.

Our own empirical investigations of government uses of data systems raise concerns about how anticipatory and predictive systems are being used without adequate justification and appreciation of their impacts or limits (Dencik, Hintz et al. 2018; Redden, Dencik & Warne 2020). In some cases, harm occurs because of blind spots; developers fail to recognize that all knowledge is partial and situated (Collins 1997). Richardson (2021) points to police use of geographic information systems (GIS) in the United States to illustrate this point. GIS technologies provide outputs, like crime maps, that present visual representations that are informed by processes of selection. While the map appears as merely a visual description of crime in a city, in practice the data that feeds the system and the details visualized offer a small selection of all of the possible data that could be used to better understand the city, its people and crime. Crime maps, she argues, present visualizations that focus on street crime like vandalism and burglary, instead of crimes that actually cost society as a whole a lot more, such as corporate crimes or cybercrime (Richardson 2021, p. 120).

Data Governance as Distancing

While big data presents the illusion that through having access to ever more data and computing power we can know more, the research summarized to this point challenges this idea. The research highlighted above instead raises concerns about how a reliance on data, even if we have more of it, leads to selective, partial and biased representations. Another related concern is that rather than building information systems that bring government agencies closer to the people they serve, these systems lead to a distancing between government administrative systems and people. Human efforts to shrink the world so that we might claim to understand it has only increased in an age of big data. While datafication presents the illusion of objectivity, processes of datafication involve reductions of information and a distancing from the knowledge of complicated realities (Duffield 2018). The potentials of humans are reduced to a statistical analysis of their past behaviours (Duffield 2015, p. 9). Duffield sees in this distancing a worrying change in the way those in positions of power view their fellow human.

With neoliberal governance, we witnessed a shift in the logic informing modes of governance. No longer was it the objective of post WWll government administrations to ensure everyone had access to equal opportunities and the right to a dignified life, as was the objective of Keynesianism to ensure that all lives are valued as equal. The objective of neoliberal governance is to extend the logic of the market to all spheres of life. Under this mode of governance, adopted to differing degrees by different governments, it becomes the responsibility of the individual to respond to the crises imposed by marketization without social and collective protections from the harms caused. With neoliberal governance, everyone is trained to become rational entrepreneurs of the self, with privileges limited to the wealthy who already hold their positions and those who are able to turn themselves into entrepreneurs of the self successfully while simultaneously struggling to escape structural and systemic inequality and violence.

Duffield argues that with datafied governance we again see a shift in how humans are valued. In this latest phase, he argues, humans are increasingly viewed as void of rationality and any thinking power at all. Instead, humans exist as objects to be nudged to behave in ways desired and continuously surveiled in case they don't. We would add to this, concerns about how government uses of predictive systems create narratives about people's lives that they are increasingly subjected to without their knowledge, and despite and even when these narratives are proven inaccurate.

The use of algorithmic systems to make decisions that affect life outcomes do not merely change administrative processes; through their use they also change the way those using the system relate to the people who depend on it. The relations a person has to themselves and to others is a 'political formation' (Amoore 2020). As these formations are transformed on a unit-by-unit basis across societies, such micro formations work to change the whole. 'Contemporary algorithms are changing the processes by which people and things are rendered perceptible and brought to attention' (Amoore 2020, p. 15). With datafied government systems, such as risk scoring systems, people's identities are being digitally made up often without their knowledge. Further, these digital identities are populated by data that individuals have not entered and have not had a chance to verify. As the systems used to score individuals often draw on data collected and practices designed for consumer profiling or marketing, the process is pervaded with commercial logics, including those of value and worth (Johns 2021).

The presence of a commercial logic is already identifiable in specific examples of government applications. For example, through government reliance on data about citizens produced by and purchased from credit-rating companies like Experian. Further, global technology and consultancy firms like Google, Amazon, IBM, KPMG and EY are trying to sell their ability to help governments better manage people and problems. Governments facing resource constraints and greater community need are turning to companies that promise the ability to help them better target services and increase efficiency. A turn that has increased during the COVID-19 pandemic. These companies become more involved in decision-making as they are increasingly relied on to store, manage and make sense of data collected about people and social issues. They are selling their services across public service administration. We have found governments buying services and systems off the shelf or entering into long-term public private partnerships (Dencik, Hintz et al. 2018).

Concerns have been raised about how, through datafication, government and business spheres become ever more intertwined and business interests rather than public service values influence decision-making (Garrido et al. 2018; Redden 2018a). Others raise concerns about how the more that government agencies contract private companies to help run public services, the less they develop in-house expertise and over time become locked-in to these public private partnerships. In the process, this renders some of the practices they are engaged in inscrutable to the public because of arguments that doing so will compromise company commercial interests (Kitchin 2015). As argued by Dencik (2022), with this shift governments become complicit in corporate efforts to commodify citizens through datafication, but also empower a rentier trajectory of public service provision that locks in commercial social ordering and actuarial logics. There is a danger that these computational logics of 'subtraction' reinforce the intensification of neoliberal lines of thought in ways that lead to further cuts in services and reinforce more punitive approaches in ways that increase inequality while simultaneously obscuring its causes (Redden 2015).

Government uses of automated fraud detection systems are coming under increasing scrutiny. A number of these systems have been publicly criticized, such as the Netherlands System Risk Indication (SyRI), the Australian Online Compliance Intervention system (RoboDebt), the American Michigan Integrated Data Automated System and the use of Risk Based Verification Systems in the UK. One of the elements of criticism that unites these systems is the way that people are automatically targeted for risk assessment through their engagements with public services and the absence of information that is provided to those deemed guilty, almost as if such information was proprietary.

Legal challenges were eventually successful in stopping the use of three of the four fraud detection systems listed above. These legal challenges required much time and energy, with many lives destroyed in the meantime. Of particular importance, from a governance perspective, is that the data profiles that may influence someone's ability to be prioritized for benefits or ranked according to riskiness are themselves inferences. These inferences can carry enormous weight, despite the, often, lack of effort put into investigating their veracity. For example, inferences about whether or not someone was a gang member in London could lead to their name being added to a database of suspected gang members (Amnesty International UK 2018). The database continued to be used even after significant concerns were raised about how the database reinforces racist stereotyping and accuracy: some of the factors used to estimate gang membership include music listening habits and friendships. The database was shared with job centre and housing workers, head teachers and school principals, and representatives from local hospitals. Once a person's name was added, the suspicion that they were a gang member could influence access to benefits, housing and education. Public criticism led to a public review, which found that young Black men were overrepresented in the matrix and, further, that 38 per cent of the people listed posed little or no risk (Dodd 2021). Systems like the gang matrix, which make inferences about people based on connecting selected data points, create stories about people that affect how they are treated and their life-chances.

Where and how governments are making use of AI and ADS systems is important. These systems are being used in risk assessment for policing and justice systems, in benefits administration, to detect benefits fraud and for surveillance and security. It has been argued that while governments have been innovating through the introduction of computing systems across the public service, the use of AI and ADS systems are unique in that these systems are being used in ways that are 'closer to the coercive and redistributive power of the state, particularly in the allocation of benefits (adjudication) and the direction of punishments and sanctions (enforcement). Also these new governance tools sit closer to the decision-making point, and thus entail greater displacement of human discretion than past rounds of innovation' (Engstrom & Ho 2021, p. 4).

Our own research into where and why government agencies across Australia, Canada, Europe, New Zealand, the United Kingdom and the United States are cancelling their use of ADS systems suggests that experimentation with AI and ADS systems is occurring in the areas of justice and policing, welfare and benefits administration, child protection and to a lesser extent education and immigration (Redden et al. 2020). The fact that these systems are being paused or cancelled demonstrates that government uses of AI and ADS systems are not inevitable, that there are competing struggles over whether and how these systems should be used, and that there are differences in how government agencies are making decisions about uses, with some taking the very cautious approach proposed here. However, the areas we identify across our own Data Justice Lab research as areas of public sector experimentation with AI and ADS systems raises questions about who is most affected and *stands to be most negatively affected* when things go wrong. The kinds of automated decision systems being introduced, and in some cases cancelled, are social sorting systems that in many cases are used to surveil and risk score (Gandy 2005; Hoffmann 2019; Lyon 2002).

Decisions about where they should be used to inform government decision-making and service delivery are political, whether explicitly discussed in these terms or not. The politics of these systems becomes more explicit when asking: In what areas of public service are they being implemented? Who stands to be directly affected by these systems and who will not be affected? Our research in the UK and in other Western democratic countries, as well as the research done by others, demonstrates that social sorting and risk scoring systems disproportionately affect people on low incomes and people of colour through their reliance and emphasis on data including benefits access or history of, charges of street crimes, immigration status, etc. Further, there is often little effort to investigate how the use of predictive systems are affecting those who are subjected to them or the decision-makers who are asked to rely upon them (Dencik, Hintz et al. 2018; Redden et al. 2020). Too often there is little public debate about if, where and how ADS systems should be used and little effort to include the people who will be affected by these systems in decision-making about their use. This leads to significant blind-spots that could be avoided, in part, by working with affected communities and those with experience redressing social injustice from the outset.

Our research into cancelled systems reveals how long it can take, in some cases, for governments to pause or cancel a system known to be causing much harm. Further, this research on cancelled systems demonstrates how much work is needed in many cases to ensure redress and to stop harmful practices. All of these factors reveal how binaries of 'deserving' and 'undeserving' are embedded not just in the data, but in the decision-making surrounding the development, implementation and use of ADS systems.

The more we learn about how people are being negatively affected by government uses of data systems, as detailed in Chapter 4, the more it should become clear to all how important it is to take time and care to investigate the impacts of data systems before they are implemented. There is now an abundance of research demonstrating that AI and ADS systems do not always work as intended and that much harm can be caused by them. Despite this, AI and ADS systems continue to be introduced without an obligatory requirement of government agencies to make clear how they will learn from previous applications. This failure to ensure that implementers prove usefulness and that effort is made to avoid harms is connected to a phenomenon that Shunryu Garvey (2021) refers to as the amnesia of AI. Garvey points to a pattern of those using AI often refusing to account for its history. Yeung (2018) stresses that those benefiting from and implementing uses of AI and ADS systems must be held responsible for the risks and consequences that come with these systems. She stresses that: 'this includes obligations to ensure that there are effective and legitimate mechanisms that will operate to *prevent and forestall* violations to human rights which these technologies may threaten, and to attend to the health of the larger collective and shared *socio-technical environment* in which human rights and the rule of law are anchored' (Yeung 2018, p. 4, original italics). Although AI and ADS systems are often presented as scientistic and as benefiting from highly specialized expertise, one of the limitations in their development is that they are often not subjected to the kind of rigorous critique employed in other areas of the natural sciences and engineering.

Uses of AI and ADS systems are supported by Silicon Valley funding, lobbyists and promoters with connections. AI in particular has been prone to a significant level of hype for these reasons. Collins (2021) argues that given the reach and potential impact of AI-fuelled processes on all of our lives, it needs to be subjected to the same levels of rigorous examination as other sciences, such as Physics. Doing so means developing norms to enable internal and external critique to ensure integrity in knowledge and implementation. Further, such an approach would benefit from including social justice organizations with expert knowledge. Collins refers to the need for 'productive technical criticism', meaning that the criticized learn from and act on the criticism provided.

The lack of effort to investigate impact is a key data justice issue, revealing a lack of concern about how marginalized people will be affected. This lack of concern and devaluing of people on the basis of age, gender, sexuality, ethnicity, disability and income is not new. What is new is that the data systems being introduced present potential for harm while also arming those who use them with an unprecedented ability to monitor and surveil people subjected to these systems. Eubanks (2018) and Roberts (2019), drawing on American examples, raise concerns about how datafied government systems create 'new punitive and antidemocratic modes of social control' that are more efficient in punishing the poor for their poverty than previous systems (Roberts 2021). Roberts argues that AI and ADS systems are part of a broader shift towards punitive governance, a mode of governance tied to neoliberalism which brought cuts to public services, more crises, the privatization of state functions and increased efforts to behaviourally modify and criminalize the same people who have been devastated by the effects of neoliberal governance (Roberts 2019, p. 1708).

> Computerized risk assessments are based on data taken from a social context that has already been shaped by hierarchies of race, class, and gender. Predictive algorithms package this unequal social structure into a score that necessarily reflects individuals' privileged or disadvantaged positions. The aphorism 'garbage in, garbage out' captures an important aspect of data collection but doesn't capture the nature of built-in structural bias. 'Inequality in, inequality out' is more apt. (Roberts 2019, p. 1708)

Roberts, like Eubanks, draws attention to the limits of data systems in the areas of child welfare, but stresses that the fundamental problem with these systems is deeper than how they work. The problem, argues Roberts and Eubanks, is that datafied child welfare systems do not help families with their needs. Uses of data systems in child welfare expand carceral regimes of governance, a mode of governance that seeks to control people and not deal with questions of guilt, innocence or need. Roberts stresses: '[T]he way to stop big data's threat to society is not to improve big data. It is to work toward changing the unjust structures that big data supports' (2019, p. 1725).

Conclusion: Considering Potential Datafied Futures

Our research into government uses of AI and ADS systems shows that a number of government agencies are deciding to cancel their uses of these systems. In some cases this is connected to careful review, but most often decisions to cancel follow civil society mobilization, critical media coverage, legal action and politicization. These examples, as well as much of the research cited in this chapter, demonstrates that the ways technologies are developed and implemented are not inevitable. Rather, such work presents an illustration of the fact that technologies are sites of struggle (Eubanks 2011; Dyer-Witheford, Kjøsen, & Steinhoff 2020). Across our studies of government uses of AI and ADS systems we find competing values, politics and visions informing these struggles.

There are a range of ideas being presented about how to ensure our datafied future is one in which we will all want to live. Some of these ideas focus on the need for governmental institutions to change in response to our changing contexts, particularly by working with affected communities. The ideas animating a number of these proposals for institutional change place political and democratic value on inviting critique and dissent. One step that governments could take would be to ensure more rigor in decision-making around the use of ADS systems through adopting an extended peer-review process, ideally before development (Veale & Brass 2019). As outlined by Veale and Brass (2019), this involves extending the review process to ensure the inclusion of all those who have a stake in a system, particularly those who will be affected by it and those with experience of challenging injustice. Others are focusing on making the public private partnerships that are driving the government implementation of ADS systems more transparent and accountable. Bloch-Wehba (2021) argues that transparency obligations need to be imposed, and that these obligations should be controlled by the community and include principles of direct participation.

In the United States, Eubanks (2018) and AI Now (Whitaker et al. 2018) have argued that people need to decide on no-go areas, that there are some areas where the potential harms are so great that the public needs to decide if AI and ADS systems should be used in these areas at all. In addition to arguments to enhance due process protections, others are arguing for the need to ensure proof of effectiveness, ethics and legality (Layton et al. 2020). More examples of efforts that could enhance civic participation with datafied modes of governance are discussed in the next chapter.

The larger story that this chapter tells is that datafied governance presents us with both intensified and new forms of oppression and violence that we must contend with. Roberts argues that we need a radically different vision of the relationship between technology and politics, 'one that facilitates justice, equality, and democracy' and works not to replicate past injustice and instead to build a more humane future (2019, p. 1727). These ideas are discussed in more detail in Chapter 8, which focuses on social justice. From a governance perspective, Lewis (2021) and Eubanks (2018) argue that central to moving forward is to push governments to reject the logics of austerity and scarcity they have adopted. Richardson (2021, p. 138) argues that rather than developing technical fixes, governments would be better to address the social systems and structural conditions that lead to harm and injustice. She points to the need for transformative justice, because it requires examinations of harm to extend to a focus on individual and collective abilities to cause harm as well as fix it. This approach requires also attending to bystanders who are complicit, including institutions.

Such comprehensive and shrewd analysis is necessary because many algorithmic harms stem from or are related to long-standing, systemic issues (e.g. racial segregation, poverty, and police misconduct) that are not only the result of bad or misguided actors, but also bystanders that facilitate or ignore harms, as demonstrated in this Essay. Therefore, a transformative justice approach can fashion radical social changes, as well as a variety of technical and non-technical interventions that can adequately confront the intersectional and intergenerational nature of technology-mediated problems and withstand the current pace of innovation. (Richardson 2021, p. 139)

The goal with taking this more holistic approach is to work to change social systems and structural conditions leading to harm (Richardson 2021).

This chapter has discussed the data justice implications of a turn to datafied governance by focusing on information power. The chapter outlines how contemporary concerns are linked to a longer history of structural and symbolic violence. The research surveyed describes data systems as performative and constitutive as they are used in ways that make up people and places. Further, it describes how these data visions then in turn inform decisions that are made about people, places and issues in ways that lead to real-world impact. This effect continues in an age of datafied modes of governance. However, governance itself is said to shift through the ability for vastly increased and ubiquitous data collection and analysis, leading to new modes of power referred to as 'sensory power' (Isin & Ruppert 2019) and a surveillance-driven 'dataist state' that values datafied control more than the will of the people (Fourcade & Gordon 2020). Logics of prediction shift government focus to managing problems instead of trying to identify the causes of these problems and fix them.

Concerns are raised about how data enables control from a distance which further entrenches dehumanizing approaches to administration, service provision, people and problems. This distancing makes it easier for administrative predictive systems to be introduced that regulate on the basis of inferences instead of meaningful engagements with people and problems. People become subject to these anticipatory, partial and biased stories told through data. As argued by Eubanks (2018) and Roberts (2019), continuing down this path will only lead to greater punitive and anti-democratic modes of governance. However, this path is not inevitable. Government administrations are not monolith, and as our study of paused and cancelled systems demonstrates, government administrations are responding in different ways to the challenges that these data-driven systems present, with some taking more human-centred and responsive approaches. As discussed in the following chapters, these efforts are linked to civil society and social movement efforts.

3

DATA AND
DE-WESTERNIZATION

By Emiliano Treré

As we have explored throughout this book, the rapid datafication of society compels us to confront key issues in the way data intersects with capitalism, governance and citizenship. However, while most of the world's population today lives outside the West, key debates on datafication, AI, democracy and justice are still framed with reference to the social contexts, infrastructural arrangements, visions and practices of Euro-America. This chapter shows that most approaches to datafication are relying on a problematic 'data universalism' (Milan & Treré 2019) that tends to assimilate the heterogeneity of diverse contexts, practices and visions and gloss over differences and cultural specificities. It demonstrates that this data universalism can be conceived as yet another manifestation of technological determinism. This way of understanding data, we reveal, should be critically engaged with, and overcome, if we are to understand the specificities of datafication in both the Global North and, above all, in the often-neglected Global South. In thinking about data justice at the social, political and epistemic level, we need to recognize the way the diagnosis of (in) justice itself is a manifestation of power that has tended to follow historical Global North–South relations. Hence, this chapter addresses and deconstructs universalistic claims regarding the nature, the dynamics and the supposedly inevitable character of datafication and data justice. It represents an invitation to think beyond the conceptual and territorial constraints of the West, when reflecting on the social, cultural and political implications of data justice. It foregrounds the tensions, the differences and the imbalances in the processes of data appropriation across the many South(s) that inhabit our world. In the following lines, we engage an inquiry into the conceptual and epistemological tools that can be used to destabilize and unsettle traditional conceptions of data and their relation to social justice.

More specifically, we map the parameters of a de-westernization of this field of studies and discuss the key elements (assumptions, conditions, meanings and dimensions) of the de-westernization of data studies and data justice in/from the South(s). The South is conceived as a plural entity subsuming the underprivileged, the different, the alternative, the resistant and the subversive (Santos 2014). Reflecting on a problem that is of ontological, epistemological and ethical nature, this chapter foregrounds the problems, practices and people whose work is useful to understand datafication and data justice beyond data universalism. In so doing, it also critically engages with the universalism of social research (Connell 2014) in its approach to datafication.

The chapter starts by engaging with the issue of data universalism and then moves on to disentangle what de-westernization implies for data studies along four key dimensions: the academic cultures, the subject of study, the body of evidence and the analytical frameworks. We conclude by relating these reflections to the overall debate on the universalism of social research, the value of public sociology and the meanings of data justice.

The Problem with Data Universalism

The Internet has reshaped how humanity communicates. Big data is different: it marks a transformation in how society processes information. In time, big data might change our way of thinking about the world. (Cukier & Mayer-Schönberger 2013, p. 29)

Big data is poised to reshape the way we live, work, and think. A worldview built on the importance of causation is being challenged by a preponderance of correlations. The possession of knowledge, which once meant an understanding of the past, is coming to mean an ability to predict the future. The challenges posed by big data will not be easy to resolve. Rather, they are simply the next step in the timeless debate over how to best understand the world. (Cukier & Mayer-Schönberger 2013, p. 39)

Once seen, we can work with their nature, rather than struggle against it. Massive copying is here to stay. Massive tracking and total surveillance [are] here to stay. Ownership is shifting away. Virtual reality is becoming real. We can't stop artificial intelligences and robots from improving, creating new businesses, and taking our current jobs. It may be against our initial impulse, but we should embrace the perpetual remixing of these technologies. Only by working with these technologies, rather than trying to thwart them, can we gain the best of what they have to offer. I don't mean to keep our hands off. We need to manage these emerging inventions to prevent actual (versus hypothetical) harms, both by legal and technological means. (Kelly 2016, p. 5)

Access to reliable and meaningful data is a consistent barrier for social sector organizations interested in applying AI methods and capabilities. ... The data challenges faced by economic empowerment and equality and inclusion propos-als illustrate the difficulty in collecting large amounts of data from vulnerable populations that are often more transient, highly sensitive to privacy, and less likely to participate in the formal economy. ... In sectors where data already exists but is not easily accessible, organizations that own data have an opportu-nity to invest in data-sharing partnerships and responsible open-sourcing to allow other stakeholders to utilize this data. In these cases, it will be important to consider privacy and security risks as well as potentially harmful use cases before sharing datasets broadly. In more data-sparse sectors, funders can help finance data collection. Funders and policymakers could leverage their resources and influence to support the collection and sharing of data, where appropriate. (Google 2019, pp. 16–17)

The first two excerpts are taken from a well-known article about big data that gave the impetus for the best-selling book *Big Data: The Essential Guide to Work, Life and Learning in the Age of Insight* (2013), written by renowned journalist Kenneth Cukier and Oxford University professor Viktor Mayer-Schönberger. The third one is taken from *The Inevit-able: Understanding the 12 Technological Forces That Will Shape Our Future*, by Kevin Kelly, a prominent techno-enthusiast and the founding executive editor of *Wired* magazine. The fourth one is an excerpt from Google.org's report on the hundreds of applicants to its 2018 'AI for Social Good' funding competition. This passage provides an overview of the relationship between datafication and the social good, as it has been illustrated by media scholars Magalhães and Couldry (2020) in a recent article on big tech and data colonialism. We have chosen these excerpts because they are representative of how we tend to look at datafication and frame its relation to justice.

The first two extracts are illustrative of how we often depict the phenomenon of data-fication as something disembodied and, above all, identical across the globe. While the authors are making a general point about the enormous changes brought about by this process, the problematic implications of frequently evoking 'the world' when making these claims are twofold. First, the world that is evoked is often associated with, and equated to, the United States of America, or to the characteristics of the social settings of Euro-America. Second, there is a risk of offering homogenizing reflections about a sup-posedly uniform world, instead of addressing the most important point, that is precisely how datafication (as well as data justice's meanings and practices) unfolds differently in the many, highly unequal worlds that compose our planet. The third excerpt adds the trope of 'inevitability' to the mix, depicting some of the most debated injustices associ-ated to datafication (surveillance, tracking, loss of jobs) as something that we simply cannot halt, but must start accepting and coexisting with. The last quote is illustrative of how big tech sees the social good and therefore can illuminate how datafication con-structs of justice. As it has been carefully explained by Magalhães and Couldry (2020), this line of thinking is problematic for various reasons. It frames the shortage of data as a 'barrier' that endangers the feasibility of social good, justifying the call for 'funders and policymakers' to use their 'resources and influence' to construct data sets about 'vulner-able' populations (Google 2019, p. 17). Further, it glosses over concerns for privacy and security and safeguards for the vulnerable. Finally, there are no references to the individ-ual abilities needed to understand these possible breaches, nor to the unequal conditions that frame this capacity.

From these lines, it is hard to grasp the complexity of how datafication is shaped by the encounters with different cultures and understandings around the Earth. It is also hard to understand how the inevitability in its current unfolding represents a social con-struction of the powerful, not an unchangeable condition. The ways in which we envi-sion and enact data justice are incessantly shaped by humans and by contrasting power forces that reclaim different types of thinking, doing and imagining data, as this book extensively illustrates. Many of these understandings and practices are constantly being forged within the socio-political configurations of the so-called Global South, assuming different characteristics from the ones that we usually attach to datafication in the Global North. However, even though most of the world's population lives in the Global South, key debates around datafication, democracy and social justice are still largely focused on 'Western' contexts and concerns, and processed through the conceptual prism of the Global North (Arora 2016, 2019a, 2019b). This phenomenon, it has been argued elsewhere, can be considered a form of 'data universalism' that 'tends to assimilate the heterogeneity of diverse contexts and practices and to gloss over differences and cultural specificities' (Milan & Treré 2019, p. 324). This kind of universalism can be better under-stood as the last heir of a protracted historical trajectory of technological determinism and communicative reductionism. These tendencies largely disregard the ways in which different populations around the world appropriate technologies – and consequently data – for their own needs and through the prism of their specific cultures, traditions and worldviews. Hence, data universalism tends to flatten the heterogeneity, plurality and richness of both contexts and cultural specificities. It casts datafication and data justice as phenomena that unfold inevitably and homogeneously across the world.

But the *universalism* in 'data universalism' should also be understood in light of Žižek's reflections (n.d.). The Slovenian philosopher and cultural critic argues that the universality presumed by Western liberalism does not only consist in the fact that its values are seen as universal because they would hold supposedly for *all* cultures. Instead, this universalism should be intended in the more radical sense that people in the West participate in the universal dimension *directly*, since they are allowed to bypass their social position. Conversely, an African or Latin American author, by virtue of a generic particularity, is foreclosed from writing in the cosmopolitan voice that is taken for granted by intellectuals in Europe or North America, and an additional explanation or a justification is always required. Data universalism erases past and peripheral imaginations of globalization (Ferdinand, Villaescusa-Illán, & Peeren 2019) and obfuscates the recognition that the prevailing vision of the capitalist and calculable globe is merely one among many possible ways in which the global has been and might be articulated. As prominent anthropologists Comaroff and Comaroff (2012) have argued, the West has always had the tendency to look at the non-West – now more commonly referred to as the Global South – as an exotic place of parochial wisdom, unrefined knowledge and 'unprocessed data'. To counter this view, we need to firmly situate contemporary dynamics of datafication and data justice within the historical trajectories of modernity. In line with Comaroff and Comaroff (2012), we should look at modernity as a composite of multiple, permanently contested significations, materializations and temporalities that have coalesced in the great aspirations of liberalism, the 'politico-jural edifice of democracy' (2012, p. 6). Western modernity has provided the knowledge underlying colonialism, and later global financial capitalism. These historical processes have often subjugated, excluded, marginalized and devalued the knowledge, and the specific ways of knowing of the Global South. In the present momentum, unyielding global dynamics of data extraction and accumulation are accelerating, intensifying and aggravating these processes, pushing us to interrogate the distinct data politics that traverse both the Global South and the Global North. As pointed out by sociologists Engin Isin and Evelyn Ruppert (2019), we now live in an emerging and unprecedented global data empire. Decolonial scholars Mignolo and Walsh (2018) have illustrated how different local histories, embodied conceptions and practices of decoloniality can enter into conversation, building understandings that cross geopolitical locations and colonial differences. Similarly, reflecting on how data justice is lived and shaped beyond the West can help us to contest the totalizing claims and political-epistemic violence of modernity. More specifically, it can foreground both its *relationality* and *vincularidad*. The former notion refers to the fact that the struggles around data and social justice across diverse geographical latitudes and involving diverse populations are all deeply interconnected. The latter term is intended as the awareness of the integral relation and interdependence among all living organisms with territories and the cosmos. This means that expressions of data (in)justices can only be grasped in relation to the tragic environmental consequences of neoliberal capitalism, as we make clear in the introductory and concluding chapters. Seeing all these experiences in a relational way challenges the totalizing claims inherent in critical data studies, privileging instead the pursuit of connections, conversations and correlations between contexts, experiences and visions.

In the next sections, we continue our journey outlining six preliminary observations that can orient our de-westernizing gaze. We then delineate and reflect on four dimensions in the de-westernization of data studies: academic cultures, issues, cases and analytical frameworks. We conclude by connecting our reflections to key components in the debate over contemporary global sociology. In doing so, we illuminate key facets of the powerful, evolving notion of data justice.

De-Westernization: Assumptions, Conditions and Meanings

As film scholars Bâ and Higbee have pointed out, we can think of de-westernization as both an ongoing process and an intellectual shift that challenges and repositions 'the West's dominance (real or imagined) as a conceptual "force" and representational norm' (2012, p. 3). The definition of this concept is not straightforward, as the phenomenon comprises different meanings, dimensions and analytical perspectives. Central to this process is a critique of the dominant influence of Western academic research and knowledge. Sri Lanka-born communication scholar Gunaratne has referred to it as the 'oligopoly of social science powers' (2010, p. 474), which include in his view the US and the UK but also France, Germany, Japan, the Netherlands and Italy as a second tier. Other scholars, such as American sociologist Immanuel Wallerstein, have similarly divided the world into centre, semiperiphery and periphery to describe existing power relations and inequalities (Wallerstein 2004). This oligopoly of powers defines to some extent an existing 'European universalism' (Gunaratne 2009) that, according to Gunaratne and other scholars, entails a culturally-bound worldview based on ideas of the Greek and the Enlightenment periods. This can lead to biases in the selection of topics, research frameworks, methods and data interpretation that will be filtered through a Western axiology, epistemology and ontology. In this process, indigenous literary and philosophical traditions and worldviews risk being disregarded, and Western contents, visions and conceptualizations uncritically applied. It might sound rather evident (at least to some scholars), but it is worth pointing out that the meanings and the factors driving calls for de-westernization are genuinely different in the West/Global North and in the rest of the world. Every analysis on the issue of de-westernization should begin by specifying that communication research in Africa, Asia, the Middle East and Latin America tackled questions about the intellectual origins of conceptual frameworks, topics, ideas and research questions much earlier than in the West. So, as Latin American media scholars Waisbord and Mellado (2014) incisively point out, de-westernization is somehow a specific preoccupation of the West, because outside its borders this process has often been conceived as a necessary manoeuvre to reorient intellectual work against academic Eurocentrism. De-westernization is an intellectual shift with countless meanings and a debate that is in no way limited to the field of communication and media studies, but that profoundly pervades social sciences and humanities. This chapter does not in any way aspire to fulfil the herculean task of disentangling the complexity of this debate. However, any attempt at de-westernizing data studies should start from the recognition that meanings, motivations, needs and contexts of de-westernization are historically determined. In other words, we should not fall into the trap of thinking there is a universal conception of de-westernization, and that the epistemological and ontological preoccupations that animate this debate are somehow only afflicting the West.

It is also important to remember that the need to de-westernize is grounded in the acknowledgment that the Global South demands to be apprehended, addressed and explored in *its own right*, not as some kind of doppelgänger of the Global North. In other words, there is no so-called 'Euro-American original' (Comaroff & Comaroff 2012). Following directly from this point, we need to look at the Global South not as 'tracking behind the curve of Universal History, always in deficit, always playing catch-up' (Comaroff & Comaroff 2012, p. 12), but instead as a space where novelty, creativity and technological innovation have always thrived (Mutsvairo 2018). Even more, in the South, 'radically new assemblages of capital and labour are taking shape, thus to prefigure the future of the global north' (Comaroff & Comaroff 2012, p. 12). The assumption that the Global South is always a left-behind with respect to the developed northern hemisphere is not only inaccurate, but also, as Professor of Spanish and Latin American Cultures Hilda Chacón underlines, 'demonstrates a biased and subalternizing premise about the south that is issued from the centres of power – usually located in the north' (2019, p. 12). This is especially true with regards to scientific research and technological developments, as media historians have frequently remarked (Medina 2014).

Another key aspect we should consider in our de-westernizing endeavour is that every attempt to generate connections and establish conversations among different ways of engaging with data needs to seriously consider the complexity of both the Global North and the South. This means that we should resist the temptation to provide Manichean accounts that downplay the importance of ground-breaking scientific and technological advancements in the North, or romanticize Indigenous knowledge, eradicating conflict and tension from the history of technological engagements in the Global South. Instead, both the North and the South, along with their ways of thinking and their interconnections, should be critically engaged with as they are both part of what Colombian anthropologist Arturo Escobar calls the *pluriversal* (Escobar 2018). Instead of replicating worn tropes, stereotypes and myths, we should strive to understand and do justice to the complexity of the social world and the richness in the ways of thinking, sensing, believing, doing, living and appropriating data in the different contexts that comprise both the North and the South. These are not monolithic blocs whose histories, traditions, cultures and ways of understanding and living data can be unified and easily interpreted. There are nuances, differences and similarities that need to be carefully dug out: our job is to bring them to light in all their intricacy. Furthermore, the de-westernization of data studies should be aligned with the broader programme of decentring social theory (Arora 2019b; Connell 2014) and have the ambition to advance towards a truly global social theory for our age (Bhambra, Medien, & Tilley 2020). Global sociology resists universalism in its tendency to homogenize cultural differences, but strives to find solutions to global problems such as social inequality, violence, oppression and racism (Hanafi 2020). This point will be further developed in the concluding section of the chapter. Finally, it is important to conceive the de-westernization of data justice as a contribution not only to epistemic diversity, but also to epistemic justice, that is the active struggle to assure that different ways of knowing are appraised, respected and preserved. Accordingly, its aim should be not simply to voice otherness, but also to include a key component of affirmative action that takes inequality, oppression and injustice seriously and seek to concretely operate against them.

Four Dimensions in the De-Westernization of Data Studies: Cultures, Issues, Cases and Theories

This section is concerned with what elements are being de-westernized, under which circumstances and with what consequences in the field of (critical) data studies. Waisbord and Mellado (2014) have fleshed out the idea of de-westernization in four key dimensions: academic cultures, the subject of study (issues), the body of evidence (cases) and analytical frameworks (theories). In what follows, we apply and discuss these dimensions in relation to critical data studies and the conversation around data justice.

We can consider academic cultures as the network of interrelated and explicit beliefs about the practice of teaching and research and the social significance of these practices (Ringer 1992), including 'the way scholars distinguish themselves in terms of their own personal characteristics, professional experiences, dedication to teaching versus research and their scientific production' (Mellado 2011, p. 366). In line with what Waisbord and Mellado (2014) argue, it is key to scrutinize the dynamics of de-westernization of academic cultures, particularly if standards and shared practices prevalent in the United States and in European countries increasingly define expectations and principles across data studies research at a global level. While one cannot talk of a single 'Western academic culture', it could be argued that the values of specific Western academic cultures have become somehow dominant (Mellado 2011). For example, based on their review of Europe-based journals and European academic conferences in media and communication studies from 2010 to 2016, Ganter and Ortega (2019) demonstrate that European media studies nurture a scholarly practice of talking about Latin American contexts rather than including voices from within the continent. The two scholars conclude that a critical implementation of de-westernization would require more geographically diverse editorial boards, greater international cooperation and comparative accounts to capture diversity in regional contexts. Similarly, Demeter (2019), in his study of more than 400 career paths of communication researchers from the Global South, found that it is almost impossible to become an internationally recognized scientist in communication research without Global North capital, and that the network of international education is quite similar to the network of international collaboration. These findings are echoed by the critical insights of the recent #CommunicationSoWhite movement and the @citeblack-women Collective that demonstrated how non-White scholars continue to be widely underrepresented in publication rates, citation rates and editorial positions in communication studies (Chakravartty et al. 2018). Even specific data on the composition of the data studies academic community are lacking, various scholars have repeatedly lamented the overabundance of US-centric perspectives that tend to replicate the same distortions and limitations that afflict media and communication studies. This also connected to the issue and the several problematic implications of the *de facto* imposition of English as the *lingua franca* in academia (Suzina 2020). Brazilian media scholar Ana Suzina has noted (2020) that English functions as a sterilization filter that prevents knowledge from non-English speakers to be published, shared and debated. This issue also permeates data studies and the debate over data justice. While initiatives such as the 'COVID-19 from the Margins' blog and book (Milan, Treré, & Masiero 2021) purposely adopt multilingualism to amplify voices from the Global South and empower them in their own terms, the English language reigns, often unchallenged, in the majority of contexts and academic cultures where data justice issues are addressed. This has serious implications in terms of the actors that are involved and get to have a say in these conversations, as well as the ideas that are debated and the insights that can be gained.

The 'issues' dimension refers to reassessing and expanding the ontological horizons of data studies and conceptions of data justice. This implies bringing attention to issues that might be absent in the analytical radar of Western scholars but are instead relevant in the non-Western world. The aim is to expand the research agenda and probe the conventional analytical parameters of Western-based scholarship. It also includes covering data-related phenomena that are not contained by specific countries and regions of the world and exceed conventional geopolitical boundaries. The 'cases' dimension relates instead to the expansion of the body of evidence in critical data studies and the need to consider non-Western cases and experiences to produce more complex, nuanced and stronger conclusions. This dimension directly engages with the necessity to travel beyond data universalism, abandoning (or at least significantly scaling back and nuancing) universalistic pretentions based on a narrow slice of cases and contexts. There is a strong need to include evidence from several cases and experiences in the Global South and promote a transnational dialogue around common theoretical and empirical questions informed by this global evidence. However, inclusion of several cases from around the world – as Waisbord and Mellado (2014) caution – is not enough. There needs to be in-depth cross-cultural engagement with common questions and conclusions. Often times, we are presented with rather superficial 'world tours' that only guarantee a display of variety, but do not provide a reasoned and critical synthesis of common issues, trends and directions. In the field of data studies, the expansion of the body of evidence has been intimately connected to the analysis of issues understudied or absent in the West. These dimensions are thus difficult to separate, as they are closely coupled. In fact, the study of a new issue is typically related to the investigation of a specific case that illustrates it: therefore, these two dimensions are considered together in the following lines.

To illustrate the relation between these two aspects, it is helpful to look at two recently published special collections of articles (Masiero & Shakthi 2020; Rao & Nair 2019) that address the complexity of the Indian national biometric identification programme Aadhaar. In these two special issues, several authors dissect the functioning of the colossal Indian identification scheme from various perspectives, casting light on issues of digital identity, biometrics, coded citizenship, data curation, population management, surveillance operations and governance. In so doing, they illuminate a significant case from the Global South, while at the same time they reflect on key issues that are context-specific to India, fleshing out other concerns that are common to similar experiences around the globe. The Digital Development Working Paper Series, edited by Richard Heeks from the Global Development Institute at the University of Manchester, also provides a venue for the unfolding of several insights and analyses of issues and cases of the Global South. These include the study of the impact of datafication on informal urban settlements in South Africa (Sutherland et al. 2019) and Peru (Albornoz, Reilly, & Flore 2019), as well as reflections on the characteristics of data-related injustices in Iran, India, Colombia, and in other realities of the Global South. As the first pandemic of the datafied society, Covid-19 has spurred many reflections on the social, cultural, political and economic consequences of this global crisis in relation to social justice and datafication. This has also implied a look at the specificities of responses in the non-Western world along with the ways in which data systems have been affected during this emergency. In addressing the implications of Covid-19 for data justice, a recent edited collection of the Global Data Justice project (Taylor et al. 2020) investigates the ways in which technologies of monitoring infections, information and behaviour have been applied and justified during the emergency, including their side effects and the diverse forms of resistance they have been faced with. The book also comprises dispatches that discuss cases from Argentina, Brazil, China, Ghana, Japan, Jordan, Kenya, Mexico, Uganda, and other Global South scenarios. The platform 'COVID-19 from the Margins', launched at the beginning of May 2020, is a multilingual blog platform whose aim has been to amplify voices and narratives on the pandemic from social groups and individuals at the margins, who are frequently invisibilized by mainstream coverage and policies. The blog has published dozens of contributions from the Global South, from countries as diverse as Brazil, Mexico, Indonesia, China, Iran, South Africa, Malaysia and India. It has covered issues of perpetuated vulnerabilities and inequalities, datafied social policies, data activism and grassroots solidarity at the time of the pandemic. The many contributions survey the social, economic, infrastructural and redistributional consequences of COVID in relation to the datafied society.

In doing so, they foreground how various forms of data injustice are experienced by communities at the margins and which practices and visions of data justice are shaped in the peripheries of the world. Further, this platform establishes connections and build bridges with similar situations of exclusion, marginalization and oppression in the Global North. The key contributions of the blog platform generated an open access book featuring 75 authors writing in five languages (Milan, Treré & Masiero 2021). All these examples point to a growing focus within the broad area of data studies on both issues and cases from the Global South, in an attempt to illuminate the several elements that constitute data justice in a truly global perspective.

The dimension of analytical frameworks refers to the foregrounding of theoretical perspectives and conceptual frameworks original to the global South that are absent in critical data studies in the West. It also addresses the need to cultivate indigenous theories and philosophical traditions. These theories can be better equipped to reflect specific conditions and understandings of non-Western communities, since they are embedded in cosmovisions and infused with interpretations from specific contexts, local cultures and worldviews. An example of this is Indigenous Data Sovereignty (IDS), which emerged as both an important theme and a framework in the last few years. This concept deals with the right of Indigenous peoples to control data from and about their communities and lands, articulating both individual and collective rights to data access and to privacy (Rainie et al. 2019; Walter 2020). This notion challenges dominant discourses and current approaches to data ownership, use and licensing that often see Indigenous Peoples as the unwilling targets of policy interventions. These populations are frequently left with little or no say over the collection, use and application of data about them, their territories and cultures. Hence, Indigenous Data Sovereignty draws attention to the issue of power and justice in relation to data processes and interrogates the post-colonial dynamics that lie within data agendas. It sheds light on various forms of Indigenous self-determination over their institutions, resources and data systems, and cautions against the mounting threats of data-related risks and harms. The notion of data and technological sovereignty has also inspired projects in the Global North, constituting the basis for a more democratic engagement of citizens with technologies and data systems in European cities like Barcelona. The Ethics Digital Standards of the Barcelona city council defines it as 'the decision-making and self-management powers of an individual or legal entity over the information thereon held by a third party, making the former also responsible for the use and consumption thereof'.[1]

Decolonial and post-colonial theories have been particularly favoured by critical data and artificial intelligence (AI) scholars to account for the colonial mechanisms of power that traverse contemporary data relations and explain processes of data extraction and exploitation. This strand of research does not exclusively represent an original contribution from the South, nor does it always emerge from the populations directly affected by data injustices. However, it signals the growing relevance of viewing the impact of data dynamics (on both the Global South and the North) through the critical lens of coloniality, decolonial and post-colonial theory.[2] Within this corpus, scholars foreground the power asymmetries inherent in contemporary forms of data commodification (Thatcher, O'Sullivan, & Mahmoudi 2016). Others advance conceptual lenses that scrutinize the coloniality of technological power through data. They examine data-centric epistemologies as an expression of the coloniality of power and exemplify how they impose 'ways of being, thinking, and feeling that leads to the expulsion of human beings from the social order, denies the existence of alternative worlds and epistemologies, and threatens life on Earth' (Ricaurte 2019, p. 351). Others (Couldry & Mejias 2019) illustrate the colonial continuities of extraction and exploitation of land, labour and relations through data infrastructure, and postulate a new social order where data relations enact a new form of data colonialism. This new form of colonialism relies on the exploitation of human beings and the capitalization of life through data, just like historical colonialism appropriated territory and resources and ruled subjects for profit. Migration researcher Mirca Madianou (2019) has demonstrated how this colonialism affects specifically the humanitarian response to the refugee crisis. Others have focused on algorithmic colonialism and how it influences the allocation of resources, as well as having an impact on social, cultural and political behaviours, discriminatory systems and the ethics discourse (Mohamed, Png, & Isaac 2020). In relation to the African context, Ethiopian-born cognitive scientist and critical race scholar Abeba Birhane (2020, p. 389) writes: 'while traditional colonialism is driven by political and government forces, algorithmic colonialism is driven by corporate agendas. While the former used brute force domination, colonialism in the age of AI takes the form of "state-of-the-art algorithms" and "AI driven solutions" to social problems'. The notion of data empire has been put forward by sociologists Engin Isin and Evelin Ruppert (2019), who have shown that this empire functions through assemblages of actors, arrangements, technologies and logics that are transversal and not confined to a given territory (Isin & Ruppert 2019). While data's empire differs from modern Euromerican empires – the two scholars maintain – it inherits their logics of government, establishing both novel mechanisms of power and principles of knowledge.

The strongest contribution of this corpus of research consists in its ability to bring to the fore of data studies the continuities in the forms of exploitation, accumulation, extraction and injustices that connects modern digital infrastructures to the colonial past and present. Moreover, there are many potential connections that link these analytical reflections to other studies that advocate the need to decolonize methodologies (Smith 2012). As design justice researcher Costanza-Chock (2020) emphasizes, the context in which research problems are conceptualized and designed, as well as the implications of research for its participants and communities, needs to be problematized as well. This could forge a stronger relationship between indigenous researchers and academics addressing social issues within the wider framework of self-determination, decolonization and data justice. Some issues have also been pointed out. In a widely cited article, decolonial scholars Tuck and Wayne (2012) insist that decolonization is not a metaphor and that the metaphorization of decolonization and its recent extension to other realms is depriving the concept of its power. For these scholars, this extension of the concept disguises the simple and brutal realization that decolonization will require a change in the order of the world (Fanon 1963). While scholars adopting this lens in relation to data systems are typically careful not to overstretch its semantic applicability, a constant epistemic vigilance should be applied. This will help to avoid what sociologist Leon Moosavi has called the 'decolonial bandwagon and the dangers of intellectual decolonization' (2020, p. 332). It is important to keep track of the core tenets and real value of decolonization in order not to dilute its analytical power, systemic critique and political potential. In a similar vein, Tallinn University Fellow Stefano Calzati (2020) has criticized Couldry and Mejias's articulation of data colonialism (2019) for its 'conceptual essentialism', which according to him tends to disregard the historical-materialist roots of both datafication and colonialism. The two authors have responded to such critique (Couldry & Mejias 2021), remarking that the reliance on general conceptual frameworks does not erase local specificities in the unfolding of – and resistance to – datafication. Others have pointed out that it is almost impossible to conceive colonialism without addressing the violence, the brutality and the dispossession that this coercive process has generated throughout the centuries (Segura & Waisbord 2019). In response to this observation, Couldry and Mejias (2021, p. 11) have further elaborated the differences between historic and data colonialism. The two scholars maintain that while physical violence plays a lesser role in the latter, 'it involves new modalities of oppression' that will 'have fundamental long-term impact' (2021, p. 12). Finally, adopting a decolonial approach should not come at the expense of historical particularity. As decolonial philosopher Pappas has pointed out, one of the most obvious limitations of this conceptual framework is that 'it tends to lump the history of countries and people with different histories subjected to different sorts of exploitation and manipulations and not always by the same colonizers [...]. There is a danger that coloniality is colonizing all other categories of analysis of concrete injustices' (Pappas 2017, p. 7). For instance, as outlined by anthropologist Sareeta Amrute (2019) in her keynote on tech colonialism, the 'over-reliance on the issue of *data* colonialism obscures the complicated welter of colonial relationships that cut across technological infrastructures and the imaginaries of person, place, and power that accompany them'. According to Amrute, this includes 'the material extraction of minerals, and the specific place of ex-colonial countries and still-colonized populations within the relations of power that cut across tech worlds'. In sum, while decolonial lenses are contributing a great deal to make sense of data-related injustices, it is key to remember, in line with Mignolo and Walsh (2018), that we should not look at decoloniality as a new paradigm or mode of critical thought. Instead, we should rather conceive it as a way, option, standpoint, analytic, project, practice and praxis. This means that there is not a singular way to look at data justice through a decolonial lens. The application of more general frameworks that can establish connections at a more global scale should coexist with the analysis of (and intervention into) context-specific injustices.

A final analytical framework intersects with notions of pluriversal knowledge, the South(s) and the margins. The Big Data from the South Research Initiative (BigDataSur), a space for the de-westernization of the ways in which we think about datafication, surveillance and AI, was launched in 2017. BigDataSur brings together researchers, activists and practitioners united by the urgency to critically examine the intersections between data, technology and the plurality of South(s) that comprise our world. At the heart of the Initiative lies an understanding of the South(s) not merely as a geographical marker (Milan & Treré 2019), but as a plural, multi-layered place of (and a proxy for) resistance, subversion and creativity. Paired with this understanding of the South(s), the Initiative has been informed in its de-westernizing efforts by the notion of 'the margins'. This idea has been used to capture the multiplicity and variety of the several voices that have been neglected within the mainstream narratives of the COVID-19 pandemic (Masiero, Milan & Treré 2021; Milan, Treré & Masiero 2021). Inspired by Colombian citizen media scholar Clemencia Rodríguez, the margins are conceived by the Initiative as 'a shortcut to speak of complex dynamics of power inequality' (Rodríguez 2017, p. 49). They constitute sites of struggle where the challenges of datafication unfold in unpredicted ways, challenging conventional understandings regarding the meanings and the implications of data systems. The plural notion of the South(s) and the lens of the margins represent two powerful prisms through which we can unsettle the universal character of datafication and re-evaluate our conceptual repertoire. Their plurality, multiplicity, openness and unexpectedness, together with their situatedness and context-specific nature, allow us to complexify data universalism. Through these lenses, we can make sense of the variety of concrete data-related injustices that unfold across the world and illuminate the circumstances of the oppressed, marginalized and the new 'data poor' (Milan & Treré 2020) that are progressively emerging in our societies. Law scholar Chinmayi Arun, an affiliate of the Berkman Klein Center of Internet & Society at Harvard University, argues that:

> this inclusive definition of the South as a plural entity is worth holding on to since it accounts for the rights and priorities of the many populations excluded from our current thinking about AI. It forces us to understand that the concerns raised by the South are varied, and it helps to think about different populations of the South within their own context. (Arun 2019, p. 5)

Similarly, Singh and Guzmán (2021), from the Data & Society Institute, maintain a concept of the 'Global South' as referring concomitantly to four elements: a geographical site, a method to explore a set of practices, a metaphor for harms engendered by capitalism and colonialism, and the resistance to such harms.

Further, these ideas allow us to establish connections with the data-related dynamics of domination and resistance that animate the Global North, where growing forms of data injustice, invisibility and poorness are on the rise. De-westernizing the field of data studies through the South(s) and the margins triggers a reflection on the peripheries of the world and the global nature of inequality and injustice. This can help relate vulnerable populations in both the South and the North, instituting fruitful relations with recent critical approaches to data and digital technology. These include seeing data through intersectional feminism (D'Ignazio & Klein 2020), critical race theory (Ali 2017; Amrute 2016; Benjamin 2019; Cave & Dihal 2021; Gangadharan & Niklas 2019) and environmental data justice (Vera et al. 2019) – just to name a few. These lenses also reso-nate with the enactment of the ontological politics of Latin American social movements fighting against extractivism, from whose struggles emanates the pluriverse. This term has been employed to characterize a world consisting of many worlds, each with its own ontological and epistemic grounding (Escobar 2018). As the Colombian anthropologist Arturo Escobar illustrates, this kind of resistance brings to life different possible futures. From these futures, the radical social transformations that are urgently needed to address the current planetary crises can emerge. The conceptual constellation of big data from the south and the margins questions the European epistemology upon which modernity is founded, thus engaging with/in decoloniality 'in order to foster a pluriverse of alterna-tive knowledges' (Mumford 2021; see also Milan & Treré 2021), 'a move that is not seem-ingly the core purpose of data colonialism' (Mumford 2021).

Conclusion: How do we Connect Global Sociology and Data Justice?

In an attempt to counter data universalism and complicate the debate over data justice, this chapter has outlined the contours of the de-westernization of data studies, focus-ing on academic cultures, issues, cases and theoretical frameworks. In doing so, it has illustrated how datafication is always rooted in local histories of adoption, opposition, appropriation and dysfunctionality (Mignolo 2003). The chapter has outlined prob-lems, practices and people whose work is key to understand datafication and data justice beyond data universalism. It has become clear that a growing number of voices is starting to address, articulate and understand how data (in)justice unfolds in the plurality of the South(s) constituting our world. These voices intend to undo the singularity and linearity of the West, challenging dominant narratives and ideologies of technological develop-ment. They reflect on how coloniality continues to work to negate, disavow, distort and deny knowledges, subjectivities, world sense and life visions (Mignolo & Walsh 2018). This is accompanied by a critique of Western academia for exercising a monopoly over the conditions of knowledge that determines commonly acceptable forms of intellectual work and the implications this has for critical data studies. In our de-westernization efforts, we have warned against any kind of essentialism in the critique of Western schol-arship (Khiabany 2003). There is not a single, easily identifiable and stable intellectual framework or tradition that defines the Global North or the Global South: cultures are and have always been the result of multiple encounters and hybridizations. We should thus resist crafting binary oppositions that could lead to Orientalist and/or Occidentalist perspectives, flattening precisely the plurality of ideas and difference in understandings that this process aims to bring to light and safeguard. As Waisbord and Mellado (2014) remark, de-westernization should be guided by a hybrid, dynamic and open vision of academic knowledge where undemocratic conceptions of intellectual sovereignty and intellectual parochialism should be avoided.

In closing the chapter, it is important to recall a recent essay that discusses how global sociology can move forward, written by the president of the International Sociological Association, professor Sari Hanafi. In this essay, Hanafi (2020) outlines five key operations, all of which are relevant to the conversation around data justice that we explore in this book and in this specific chapter. The first key feature is the necessary dialogue between different national sociologies. He writes: 'Global sociology should bring some complexity, nuance, precision, and caution towards any sweeping a-historically and apolitically universalized concepts that deflect attention from the historical-structural heterogeneity of our world. This is a call for *constructing a more appropriate theoretical framework* for understanding the mix of micro and macro that characterizes the global situation today' (Hanafi 2020, p. 14, original emphasis). This dialogue seems particularly urgent for critical data studies and for data justice particularly. The second element is related to the need to reconcile the local and the universal. As we have argued in this chapter, data universalism, intended as an erasure of local specificities and knowledges that frames the data encounters as inevitable and homogeneous processes, should be transcended. However, the struggle for certain universal concepts seems necessary. This, as highlighted by Hanafi (2020), should be guided by three conditions: (a) that the concept is the outline of a quasi-cross-cultural consensus and not the universalization of values from the Euro-American context; (b) that it is not a teleological concept, but it is grounded in history and thus inherently open-ended; (c) that its universality is conceived as an imaginary, not as a model. According to this view, we should look at data justice not as a model, but as an imaginary that is transformed into a workable model in a given context in line with what Nancy Fraser called a 'field of multiple, debinarized, fluid, ever-shifting differences' (1997, p. 25). Another element is the need to link knowledge production at the international and local levels. This means that publication in English – that we discussed as the *lingua franca* of critical data studies – is a necessary condition for conversation at the global level. Yet, this should be accompanied and strengthened by publications in multiple local languages, as the experience of COVID-19 from the Margins exemplifies. The fourth feature linked to global sociology is the need to accompany social movements in their struggles for social justice. This aspect connects to the pluriversal knowledges that are needed to (re)build more just societies and that emanate from social movements and forms of resistance across the world. These global knowledges can fuel new imaginaries of data justice outside the boundaries, limitations and beyond neoliberal capitalism. Lastly, the fifth element of a global sociology lies in its ability to capture the fears and desires of the present moment. As we have seen across this chapter, data justice should always be attentive to the evolution of concrete socio-political developments and proactive in fighting injustices on the ground. In the words of anthropologist Azadeh Akbari (2020, p. 17), 'without accounting for the experiences of people in the countries of the Global South, no collective framework of data justice can be drawn. Data injustice lies in an uneven matrix of injustices and any discussion about it cannot neglect either the topology of injustice or its intersectional nature'.

Notes

1 https://ajuntamentdebarcelona.github.io/ethical-digital-standards-site/glossary/0.1/glossary.html
2 For space reasons, in this chapter we cannot cover other frameworks that have also established a connection between technology, imperialism and colonialism, such as Kwet's 'digital colonialism' (2019), Toupin's 'anti-colonial hacking' (2016) or Syed Mustafa Ali's (2016) work on 'decolonial computing'. For a more extensive review of the 'decolonial turn' in data and technology research, including a discussion of the differences between the converging strands of digital/data/techno-colonialism, please see Couldry and Mejias (2021).

4

DATA HARMS

By Joanna Redden

A key element in debates about data justice has been towards investigating, documenting and politicizing data harms. At the Data Justice Lab we have been maintaining a Data Harm Record since 2016. The idea behind the Record is that we can learn much about the transformations happening as a result of datafication as well as the nature of these transformations and their implications, by paying attention to how people are being adversely affected by these changes. The approach is informed by a recognition of the value and importance, particularly in relation to our capitalist societies, of paying attention to how sociotechnical transformations impact on people's rights, life-chances and well-being. There is now widespread consensus that datafication brings opportunities and risk. The Data Harm Record begins from a different position, one that sees a discourse of risk as problematic and even enabling. To use a discourse of risk is to suggest that people *may* be negatively affected by datafication and presents harm as a *future* prospect. In contrast, the Data Harm Record documents how people and society more broadly are *already* being negatively affected by algorithmic systems. The Data Harm Record collates examples published in academic journals, news articles and by civil society organizations. The examples identified and listed are wide-ranging and extensive (Redden, Brand, & Terzieva 2020, Redden 2018b).

The dictionary definition of harm links it to physical and material injury now or in the future, and also to damages and adverse effects. Solove and Citron (2016) extend the concept of harm to understand how people are being negatively affected by data systems. They argue that we must also understand harm as 'impairment' or as setting the interests of a person, community or society back. Conceptually, we can understand data harm as meaning that a person, community or society is worse off as a result of a data-related practice (Citron & Pasquale 2014). The term 'data harms' is used throughout this chapter, but it is important to recognize that in many cases the examples presented in the Record can be better understood as data violence or algorithmic violence given the levels of destruction (Hoffmann 2020; Onuoha 2018).

This chapter draws on examples from the Data Harm Record and presents a taxonomy of these harms with a view to facilitating discussion. Our goal is to demonstrate the pervasiveness of these harms in order to gain a better 'big picture' appreciation of where we are heading so that we may decide collectively how we need to change course. While taxonomies can aid with analyses, they can also obscure understanding through a failure to attend to the qualitative aspects of people's lived experiences. To counter this, we have also included qualitative details that relay specificity as well as people's stories in what follows. As we go on to discuss in later chapters, understanding and evidencing these harms is central for highlighting the urgent need for political mobilization and action.

A Data Harm Record

The Data Harm Record is a record of injustice. Across the Data Harm Record are examples of commercial uses of algorithmic systems that have led to exploitation, discrimination, losses of privacy due to data breaches, and physical injury. We find data being used in political campaigning in ways that has aimed to disinform and manipulate opinions and behaviour. In terms of government uses of algorithmic systems, we list examples of errors and bias that lead to a wrongful denial of services, and that negatively impact life-opportunities and access to needed resources. Harms are occurring at the individual, community and societal levels.

The Data Harm Record is, of course, not a record of all harms that have occurred. We are limited by time, resources and language. The record documents the accounts we found published up to July 2020. There is ongoing and important work investigating data harms globally. For example, Divij Joshi (2020) unpacks algorithmic harms in India. Two former Data Justice Lab Fellows, Ira Anjali Anwar and Carolina Onate Burgos are investigating data harms in India and Latin America. Below we outline a brief taxonomy of data harms intended to draw attention to the range of uses and applications, particularly across commerce, politics and governance. While this is the focus of this chapter, we also recognize that harms also occur in relation to applications by civil society organizations, humanitarian organizations and in the area of health and medicine. It is also important to note that the categories used in the taxonomy are not neatly self-contained, as is often the case with taxonomies.

The range of examples detailed across the Data Harm Record reinforce our need to address the fact that the problems identified are not simply the result of biased data-sets or algorithms not working as intended; instead, the harms identified are connected to the inequality and power imbalances that pervade our societies. The harms detailed below are manifestations of the structural violence that is rooted across our commercial, governmental, societal and political processes. Finally, the Data Harm Record is not meant to disempower readers. We know about the examples highlighted in the Record because of the time and resources of researchers, community organizers, lawyers, journalists and political activists to render these systems more visible, to seek redress for the harms detailed and to try to prevent harms like this from occurring again. The Record is meant to underline that the way technologies are developed and implemented is not inevitable. Rather, it is important to see technologies as sites of struggle (Eubanks 2011). To do so is to recognize that there are competing values, politics and visions informing these struggles. Paying attention to where these struggles are occurring makes it more apparent that our shared futures are undetermined.

A Data Harm Taxonomy

Table 4.1 A Data Harm Taxonomy

Exploitation
Discrimination
Loss of privacy
Surveillance, control and physical injury
Manipulation
Exclusion from necessities for life
Injustice

Exploitation

World Privacy Forum's Pam Dixon was among the first to raise concerns about how data brokers were collecting highly personal data and using it to sort and categorize people so that perceived vulnerabilities could be capitalized upon (Dixon 2013). Data brokers collect information about people and then package it into content that can be sold to others, for example by compiling lists that can be used by companies to target advertising. The staggering amount of data being produced by us online, through our use of digital tools and our engagement with 'smart' technologies, fuels this multibillion-dollar industry. The problem is that people often do not know that the data they produce as they use a dating site, for example, is being vacuumed up by data brokers. In her testimony to Congress in America, Dixon details the troubling practices she uncovered when trying to find out just what kind of information about people was being collected, combined and sold (Dixon 2013). She reported finding data brokers selling lists of rape victims, addresses of domestic violence shelters, people suffering from genetic disease and struggling with addiction. In 2015, the American Federal Trade Commission reported that it had charged a data broker with illegally selling the financial data of those applying for payday loans.

Another way that behavioural data has been used is to limit or restrict access to credit. Researchers have documented how one man had his credit rating reduced because the credit card company determined that people who used their card at similar locations had a poor repayment history. In this way, the credit card company was risk assessing the individual based on the behaviour of others who shopped at similar places. This has been referred to as 'creditworthiness by association' and involves using behavioural data to socially sort and make predictions about individuals based on the behaviour of others (Hurley & Adebayo 2016).

Discrimination

Researchers and journalists have published numerous accounts of algorithmically-driven systems that discriminate. Of particular concern is how data-driven processes reproduce illegal redlining practices. Such practices, historically, involved discriminating against communities by denying communities access to things like insurance or the housing opportunities afforded to others. Redlining has also involved making people who live in particular communities pay more for services. Differential access and pricing were often based on ethnicity and class, and location was used to facilitate the process. Redlining was made illegal across democratic countries. Despite this, researchers are now identifying algorithmic redlining. The black-boxed nature of algorithmic processes makes these practices difficult to identify and challenge (Pasquale 2015).

Researchers have identified that redlining played a role in the sub-prime financial crisis of 2007/08 (Rosenblat et al. 2014). Data collected about people was used by banks to promote sub-prime loans to African American and Hispanic communities. For example, the American Department of Justice reached a settlement with the Wells Fargo Bank after alleging that the bank had pushed African American and Hispanic borrowers into more risky and expensive sub-prime loans (Newman 2014). Researchers have demonstrated that in America, Black homeowners were disproportionately affected by foreclosure as a result of the sub-prime crisis. Black homeowners in Washington DC were found to be twice as likely to lose their homes as compared to whites with similar income (Baptiste 2014). The sub-prime crisis and the targeting of African Americans has been linked to a collapse of Black wealth in the United States (Potts 2012). Targeting low-income communities with predatory loans continues as investigators find data brokers selling lists of those deemed financially vulnerable to those offering payday loans (Office of Oversight and Investigations 2013). Lists being sold were called things like 'Tough Start: Young Single Parents' and 'Ethnic Second-City Strugglers'. Madden et al. (2017) note that many low-income people are particularly vulnerable to exploitive and discriminatory targeting practices because research shows they are more likely to rely on their mobile phones for internet access. In this way, as argued by Newman (2014), inequality is compounded by information inequality as companies have the ability to know more about people and use this information for targeting while individuals have limited ability to find out how their data is being collected and used.

Targeting communities with higher costs for services has also been identified. Julia Angwin, Surya Mattu and Jeff Larson (2015) identified several examples of predatory pricing. They identified that tutoring packages were more costly in ZIP codes with large Asian populations and high incomes. The company offering the tutoring package said that the pricing difference was not intentional, but instead the product of an algorithm that was 'unintentionally' discriminating. Similarly, in 2012 the *Wall Street Journal* found Staples showing different prices on its website for people based on their location. The prices were lower for people in higher-income neighbourhoods and higher for people in lower-income neighbourhoods. Another investigation by Angwin, Larson, Kirchner and Mattu (2017) found car insurance companies charging higher insurance rates for those living in neighbourhoods populated by minorities versus white neighbourhoods with similar accident and risk rates. In short, Angwin et al. found that contrary to insurance company claims, the data did not support the rates being charged to those living in minority neighbourhoods. Cost matters, particularly when you are struggling on minimum or just above minimum wage and depend on your vehicle to get to work. In places with no or poor public transport, as with many rural communities and cities in North America, access to a vehicle is essential for work. *ProPublica* found people foregoing other necessities because of the high cost of car insurance. Investigators also found discriminatory car insurance pricing affecting even affluent minority neighbourhoods, with comparable drivers paying more in an affluent minority neighbourhood than those with similar profiles in a white suburb.

Automated systems have been found to reinforce discriminatory practices. In 2015, Facebook suspended the accounts of Indigenous Americans because the algorithm the company was using did not recognize their names as real. In response, those who had their accounts cancelled had to spend much time producing ID to prove their identities and have their accounts reinstated. Facebook has also faced criticism for enabling advertisers to target and exclude based on ethnicity and gender. Another investigation by *ProPublica* found that companies were able to purchase ads through Facebook that would enable them to target and exclude people based on gender and ethnicity. Landlords were able, through this process, to target different groups of users with housing ads and to exclude Hispanic or African American users (Angwin et al. 2016).

Automated hiring tools have been found to discriminate on the basis of gender, ethnicity and health. In 2019, it was reported that Amazon stopped using an internally developed recruitment tool after finding that the algorithm was ranking applications with the word 'women's' lower, as well as those who graduated from all women's colleges (Friedman & McCarthy 2020). Researchers have raised concerns about HireVue, a company that provides AI video systems to aid with interviews and the assessment of candidates. The system analyses speech patterns, tone of voice, facial movements as well as other details in order to make recommendations about job candidates (Whitaker et al. 2019). As argued by Jim Fruchterman and Joan Mellea (2018), the HireVue system discriminates against people who have disabilities which affect facial movements and their voice. A 2019 report noted that at that time more than 100 employers were using the system. AI Now's Meredith Whitaker calls the system, which claims it can determine which candidate is best for a position based on an analysis of facial expressions and voice, 'pseudoscience' and a 'license to discriminate', particularly as the those who are judged by the system have little ability to challenge it. Cathy O'Neil (2016a) has raised concerns about the way these automated hiring systems can incorporate questions of mental health and personality tests. Further, Sánchez-Monedero, Dencik and Edwards (2020) have demonstrated how attempts by corporate providers to try to mitigate the bias embedded in their recruitment systems leads to more problems, including the neglect of intersectionality, lack of accountability and failure to adhere to country-specific legal obligations.

Joy Buolamwini's research has demonstrated that facial recognition technologies have problems identifying people with darker skin. Buolamwini and Timnit Gebru's (2018) tests of facial recognition systems found misrecognition was tied to skin colour and gender, with darker skinned females being the group of people most misclassified. The American Civil Liberties Union tested Amazon's Rekognition system on members of Congress and found that mismatches were common and also that people of colour in Congress were two times as likely to be misidentified as a potential criminal than their white colleagues.

The use of these technologies is particularly threatening to people of colour. As noted by the ACLU's Jacob Snow:

> An identification – whether accurate or not – could cost people their freedom or even their lives. People of color are already disproportionately harmed by police practices, and it's easy to see how Rekognition could exacerbate that. A recent incident in San Francisco provides a disturbing illustration of that risk. Police stopped a car, handcuffed an elderly Black woman and forced her to kneel at gunpoint – all because an automatic license plate reader improperly identified her car as a stolen vehicle. (Snow 2018)

As argued by Buolamwini and Gebru (2018), these systems become even more problematic the more they are integrated into governmental processes. Misidentification due to the use of facial recognition technology has already led to wrongful arrest and detention. Nijeer Parks is one of the people who has been wrongly accused of a crime he didn't commit due to the use of a facial recognition system which misidentified him. He spent 10 days in jail and US$5,000 in legal costs before the case was dismissed due to a lack of evidence (Hill 2020). As a result of mounting pressure from across civil society, some companies and government agencies are making the decision to pause or cancel their use of facial recognition systems.

These examples reinforce Oscar Gandy's (1993, p. 16) observation that 'the poor, especially poor people of color, are increasingly being treated as broken material or damaged goods' in our datafied societies. They also underline David Lyon's description of datafication as a means to socially sort and as a process laden with assumptions about people's value (Lyon 2002). Sasha Costanza-Chock (2020) argues that we need to pay attention to the way norms, values and assumptions are embedded in sociotechnical data-driven systems and how the use of these systems reinforces harm and inequality. The examples of harms caused by uses of data systems outlined thus far betray a predatory logic, one which seeks to profit by learning about people's vulnerabilities and trying to use these to manipulate behaviours. The examples highlighted above also demonstrate that racism, sexism and class bias are informing harmful practices. Moreover, the systems discussed thus far create systems of advantage and disadvantage (Crenshaw 1989; Hoffmann 2019). While those in minority neighbourhoods pay more for car insurance, those in white neighbourhoods pay less. Facial recognition technologies have high error rates, but get things wrong far more often for people of colour, which leads to more criminalization. Why is it that corporations have been able to engage in such problematic practices unchecked? Why were these systems put to use before careful impact assessments? Here too a logic of predation becomes part of the answer. As discussed in Chapter 1, through their position as monopolies, some of the major tech companies implicated in harms are able to exert political power that is used to try to limit regulation and oversight.

Loss of privacy

The staggering number of data breaches every year suggests that as companies and government bodies strive to collect ever more data, they are not matching this enthusiasm with the effort required to protect this data. McCandles and Evans' (2021) online visualization presents a record of the world's biggest data breaches and hacks. There are 30,000 examples in their visualization. Just some examples include the Facebook hack that led to the publication of the personal details of more than 500 million users from 106 countries. Experian exposed the personal data of more than 220 million citizens. In 2019, Suprema's Biostar, which is used by government agencies, defence contractors and banks, left millions of personal records vulnerable because they were found unprotected and unencrypted. This included biometric data, usernames and passwords (Taylor 2019). Government exposure of sensitive information has included a 2016 Swedish government data breach that left undercover operatives vulnerable, a 2019 UK government database breach that exposed the personal information of more than 1 million people and India's Aadhaar breach that exposed the personal information of more than 1 billion people.

As argued by Citron and Solove (2018), data breaches are significant because of the risk they pose of future injury relating to identity theft, fraud or reputational damage. Harm also occurs in real time, given the anxiety that is caused as people worry about how they may be negatively affected by a data breach. Those with low income and limited resources stand to be more negatively affected by data breaches because they do not have the ability to hire legal representation and any sudden loss of income or errors that result from identity theft can be disastrous. Sarah Dranoff (2014) notes that identity theft can also lead to wrongful arrest, loss of access to essential services and harassment by collection agencies.

The sheer magnitude and prevalence of data breaches across corporate and government sectors raises legitimate questions about whether these organizations can be trusted with the personal data they are collecting and also how seriously some of these organizations are taking their responsibility to protect the data they hold. Many companies do not invest enough in data security and regulators often lack the resources to oversee company security practices and compliance (McGeveran 2019). The fact that some companies, like Facebook, are repeatedly exposing the personal data of users betrays a recklessness that is dangerous.

Surveillance, control and physical injury

An extractive logic underlies the increasing practice of companies to use data systems to monitor and manage the behaviour of their employees. Employers are now demanding the ability to collect the health and biometric data of workers (Mateescu & Nguyen 2019). There are reports of companies taking photos of workers every 10 minutes through their webcams as well as screenshots to come up with a 'focus score' (Solon 2017). Some employers are encouraging their female employees to use family planning apps. Diana Diller was paid US$1 a day by her employer to use a pregnancy tracking app called Ovia, which recorded details about her body, medications, baby's medical data, location and more. While the company says it uses the data in aggregate form, experts worry about the impact of potential data breaches and how such personal data will be used by employers and insurers (Harwell 2019). Such breaches have already occurred with Fitness apps. This kind of breach can be used to track people in real time and can also reveal sensitive health information. Some companies are going further than wearable tech and opting to encourage employees to implant smart microchips under their skin so that behaviour can be tracked. Unlike wearable devices, these chips can't be taken off and give employers access to data about their employees at all hours of the day (Metz 2018). Esther Kaplan's (2015) work investigating the impact of datafied workplace monitoring details how this is leading to physical injury as workers try to do more than they are physically capable of because of the sense of being watched and evaluated continuously.

Manipulation

Over the last few years, a great deal of attention has been devoted to trying to better understand how data tools are being used to manipulate information systems and voters. Algorithmically-driven and automated systems lead to harm in this area as the information that voters need to make decisions is corrupted, which can lead to misinformation as well as the disruption of social and political processes. As people rely ever more on social media for information, this issue becomes more pressing across countries. Researchers have found examples of bots spreading false information, amplifying dangerous content and being used in ways that harass or silence voices (Woolley & Howard 2016).

The Cambridge Analytica scandal of 2018 brought public and political attention to the way companies are collecting personal data about people in order to profile them and influence their behaviour. Through the reporting of Carole Cadwalladr and whistle-blower Christopher Wylie, we learned how Cambridge Analytica had used the data of 80 million people to build a profiling system for political advertising to influence opinion and behaviour. Concerns are being raised about the lack of accountability of these practices. This data is used to target particular demographic groups or communities with tailored messages, and as this is done on social media platforms such as Facebook, we do not know who is being targeted by what kinds of messages. For example, we know that Cambridge Analytica was involved in political campaigning in the run-up to the Brexit vote and the 2016 American election. The ability of people to post 'dark ads' for political purposes undermines the transparency and accountability required to ensure fairness in democratic processes. Investigations into the use of dark ads finds that they were used to try to manipulate opinion, amplify fear and supress votes. Concerns have also been raised about how social media platforms can be manipulated by external forces to undermine domestic stability. Reviews of the 2016 American election led to Facebook admitting that 3,000 ads posted during the election were purchased by groups linked to Russia, and that these ads focused on divisive social issues. Google and Twitter have also testified that ads were purchased on their platforms by Russian operations.

Exclusion from necessities for life

Government agencies around the world are increasingly making use of algorithmic systems to provide access to services and benefits, to risk assess people and to inform decision-making in the areas of policing, law and immigration and for fraud detection. This datafied turn by governments is leading to much harm, as is evidenced by the following examples.

Margaret Hu (2015) has demonstrated how automated data matching systems are leading to the wrongful blacklisting of people. Being blacklisted can affect the ability of people to be hired for work, prevent people from travelling and, in some cases, lead to wrongful detention and deportation. Hu uses the E-Verify System to demonstrate how these harms occur. This system claims to be able to use statistical algorithms and its access to multiple databases in order to verify identity or citizenship. Employers use the system to determine if someone is legally able to work. The system is unreliable because the data it relies on is unreliable. Research into the system by the American Civil Liberties Union (2013) demonstrates that people born in a different country, people with multiple surnames and women who change their name after marriage are far more likely to be falsely flagged. The problems are compounded by the fact that low-wage workers who are flagged because of a spelling error in their name often do not have the time, legal expertise or resources to navigate the bureaucracy required to correct misinformation (Rosenblat et al. 2014). Hu's work also details how errors can lead to unlawful detention and deportation. She has described how the Prioritized Enforcement Program, a data-sharing program used by the Federal Bureau of Investigation (FBI), the Department of Homeland Security (DHS) and law enforcement agencies, has made errors. She reports that Immigration and Customs Enforcement may have wrongly detained about 3,600 US citizens because of faulty information (Hu, 2015).

Hu argues that these two data systems assign guilt through inference. People's fundamental rights – the idea that we are all innocent until proven guilty – are turned upside down by systems like this when government authorities presume the algorithmic system is right and assign guilt without requiring further investigation (Alston 2019). It is important to recognize that anyone who has experience with algorithmic detection systems will know that error is common. Therefore, automating detection systems must be recognized as a political choice, one that has embedded within it ideas about the value of people – who deserves due process and who does not.

In 2019, the Australian government finally conceded that its automated debt recovery system was flawed after years of activism and political mobilization. In November 2020, the government agreed to pay AUS$1.2 billion to settle a class action lawsuit brought by citizens who were negatively affected. It has been reported that 400,000 Australians will share in extra compensation for the harms they experienced. The story starts in 2016 when the Department of Human Services and Centrelink, which manages social security payments in Australia, changed the way it identified if people had been overpaid their benefits. The new method meant fortnightly earnings could be used to estimate annual earnings. This is a problem for many who work seasonally, are precarious or part-time workers, are students, or who have poor health because of the way the income of people in these circumstances fluctuates. The automation of the system was another key change. Previously when a person was flagged as being overpaid benefits, a human would investigate to ensure the system was right. In 2016, this step was removed and those flagged by the system were automatically sent debt notices. At one point, the system went from sending out 20,000 debt notices a year to 20,000 a week. Further, it became the responsibility of those receiving the debt notices to prove that the system was wrong. This was a significant challenge because it was difficult for those affected to find out more information about their case. Individuals reported spending hours on the phone trying to speak with a Centrelink officer. There were widespread errors. During a Senate hearing, one social service organization reported that one quarter of the debt notices it investigated were wrong. People's lives were destroyed. For people already living paycheque to pay-cheque, or struggling with health conditions, being hounded by debt collectors created intense stress and anxiety. Asher Wolf is one of the activists who challenged the system and organized the 'Not My Debt' campaign. She has described the system, labelled 'Robodebt', as an 'algorithmic weapon of calculated political cruelty' because of the negative impact it had on those falsely accused and because of the way it disproportionately targeted 'the unemployed, disabled people, single parents, care-givers, casual and gig economy workers' (Wolf 2021).

A similar case occurred in Michigan, in the United States. In that state, the government stopped using an Integrated Data Automated System only after pressure from the federal government and a lawsuit. As with the Robodebt scandal, there has been much critical media coverage, community mobilization and government review of the MiDAS system. The damage the system caused to people's lives was well documented, including coverage in *Time* magazine. This coverage details how the lives of Lindsay and Justin Perry were devastated by an accusation of unemployment fraud that was made in error. The couple were wrongly fined US$10,000 and tried to dispute the charges but could not get anyone to address their concerns. The couple had their tax returns seized, their vehicle repossessed and were forced to file for bankruptcy. Years later the state admitted it had been wrong and reversed the charges, but the damage had already been done. The money that was returned went to bankruptcy lawyers. Lindsay Perry has said that because of the bankruptcy the couple cannot 'get a mortgage, lease a car, or rent an apartment on their own for themselves and their three children' (De La Garza 2020). It was later concluded that 40,000 people in Michigan were wrongly accused of fraud because of a data system that was 'error-prone' in combination with too little government oversight (De La Garza 2020).

In Little Rock, Arkansas, the government changed the way homecare hours were calculated. It used to be the case that a homecare nurse would assess how many homecare hours each person required. In 2016, this changed as the Department of Human Services decided that an algorithmic system would assess need and make the decision about how many homecare hours each person would receive. Homecare nurses could administer the necessary questionnaire and enter the data into the algorithmic system, but they were not able to challenge the decision made by the algorithm (Lecher 2018). For many, the new system led to a drastic cut in hours, which led to tragedy as people saw their quality of life attacked. As just one example, the drastic cut in homecare hours meant people with mobility limitations were left to languish in their beds for extended periods. Some people were no longer able to remain in their own homes. Legal Aid of Arkansas's Kevin De Liban began investigating the algorithm on behalf of clients who wanted to challenge the new datafied system. Through legal pressure, he was able to access the algorithm, which enabled him to identify major problems with it, for example that it didn't accurately recognize conditions like cerebral palsy and diabetes (De Liban Interview 2018). Legal challenges continue, with some success, but the Department of Human Services continues to invest in trying to make better algorithms instead of addressing the values and assumptions being embedded in their practices.

Privacy International raises concern about how ID systems can be used in ways that prevent people from their rightful access to necessary support, including food, fuel, work and education. In India, Aadhaar data system errors are being linked to deaths as people are left without access to food and other essentials to live (Biswas 2018; Ratcliffe 2019). These errors can be linked to a name not matching as it should or a fingerprint not registering. The Aadhaar identification database contains biometric data for 80 per cent of India's population (Dixon 2017). More and more government services now require the use of the system to access services. For example, in 2018, the BBC reported finding many people in the village of Jharkhand not being able to access the food they were entitled to because their ration cards had not been linked to their biometric ID numbers. One woman reported travelling 35 km to a nearby town to submit the necessary forms, paying a bribe to have the data linked and still finding the system was not working. The BBC reported finding that 60 out of 350 food ration recipients in just one village had their access discontinued after failing to link their cards to the system on time (Biswas 2018).

In the United States, Virginia Eubanks (2015) details how automating welfare services in Indiana, Florida and Texas has devastated the lives of thousands while costing taxpayers millions. The errors related to automated systems, which, in these cases, meant that people lost access to Medicaid, food stamps and benefits. As a result, families were thrown into crisis and people were hospitalized. For example, in 2006, the state of Indiana's Family and Services Administration signed a contract with IBM to automate its public assistance eligibility processes. The US$1.3 billion contract was cancelled three years later following errors as thousands of people were wrongly denied assistance, documents were lost and wait times got longer and longer. The state took the case to court and after a long battle were eventually awarded damages by the Indiana Supreme Court.

In addition to cruelty, the examples of harm across these governmental examples brings to the fore administrative and bureaucratic violence (Graeber 2015; Spade 2011). The ideological underpinnings of this violence were explored more in Chapter 2 on Data and Governance, but here it is important to stress that the use of data by governments in these cases suggest how these systems distance the state from the people it is supposed to serve as well as how data systems are being used to exclude and block access to the services it is supposed to provide. Here too we find an extractive logic, as with the Robodebt case in Australia and the MiDAS case in Michigan, where systems known to be error-prone are maintained for years and tap those living in precarity for money on the basis of wrongful automated assessments.

Injustice

There are increasing challenges to the use of predictive technologies for policing and sentencing because of the biases embedded in these systems. In response to community concerns, journalists at *ProPublica* investigated a predictive system used to aid decisions about sentencing and bonds. The system was supposed to predict the likelihood that someone would reoffend. The *ProPublica* team investigated the accuracy of these scores and found them to be 'remarkably unreliable in forecasting violent crime'

(Angwin et al. 2016). They also found that the system was biased: it was much more likely to wrongly flag Black defendants as future criminals than white defendants. Others have found similar types of bias in predictive policing systems. Kristian Lum and William Isaac (2016) have noted that because predictive policing systems rely on historical data, in practice what they predict is where arrests will happen, not necessarily where crime is occurring. If vagrancy and other nuisance crimes are included in predictive policing models, this contributes to bias as it leads to an over-policing of poor communities, which leads to more arrests and, in the process, creates a feedback loop of injustice, sending police back to these same communities over and over again (O'Neil 2016b). Lum and Isaac employ drug use as an example to illustrate how bias works in practice. They note that while population-level data sources indicate that drug use is fairly evenly distributed across communities, drug-related arrests are more likely to happen in communities with higher BIPOC (Black, Indigenous, and people of colour) and low-income populations. Their study of predictive policing tools found them to target Black people at twice the rate of people who are white. They also find that low-income households are targeted by police at much higher rates than higher-income homes.

Amnesty International's study of the London Met Gang Matrix demonstrated how this system, which was designed as a risk management tool, discriminates against young Black men. In some cases, young Black men are being labelled as a risk for nothing more than the kind of music they listen to. Their study found that 78 per cent of those listed in the matrix were Black despite police data showing that less than 30 per cent of those behind violent crime are Black. Amnesty International's director has said: 'The entire system is racially discriminatory, stigmatising young Black men for the type of music they listen to or their social media behaviour, and perpetrating racial bias with potential impacts in all sorts of areas of their lives' (cited in Dodd 2018). Having your name on the gang matrix can affect what opportunities are afforded to you and lead to stigmatization as the red flag label follows individuals throughout their interactions with the state from housing to education. Being labelled can also affect how family members are treated. For example, one family was threatened with eviction because a young man living in the home had been wrongly labelled as a gang member. At the time the family received the threat, the young man in question was studying at Cambridge University.

Conclusion

The Data Harm Record demonstrates that people are already being negatively affected by datafication and that harms are wide-ranging and pervasive and are the result of corporate and governmental actions. The Data Harm Record is a record of injustice and also a means of diagnosing the kind of datafied societies in which we now live, as well as the fact that our shared future will be even worse if action is not taken. Throughout the Record we see a lack of fairness, inequality and a violation of people's rights, including their right to health, liberty, dignity and privacy. The datafied practices identified include: (a) targeting people based on inferred vulnerabilities for the purpose of exploitation,

(b) discriminatory social sorting in ways that disproportionately disadvantage on the basis of ethnicity, gender, sexuality and income, (c) increased surveillance and control of labourers, in some cases leading to physical injury, (d) data breaches that threaten livelihoods and can lead to increased anxiety and identity theft, (e) the manipulation of information and targeting of voters in ways that undermine democratic processes and sow social division, and (f) the automation of government systems which are preventing people from accessing the necessities of life and leading to wrongful and discriminatory persecution in ways that destroy lives.

When these harms are presented in sequence, as done here, the cruelty of datafication is unmistakable, so too is the predatory logic that pervades these systems. Whether it is targeting African Americans with sub-prime loans or putting into use a debt compliance system that is prone to error, we see across the Record a repeated recklessness with people's lives. We also see datafication being used to extract money from those who have the least of it. In addition, the new uses of wearable tech and workplace monitoring, including the implanting of microchips, demonstrates how surveillance and population management are an intricate part of the systems leading to harm. The political uses of data systems present worrying examples of information warfare. Finally, we must contend with the callousness evident across these examples of harm.

Politically, the Data Harm Record and the taxonomy of harms presented throughout this chapter demonstrate that the pillars of our democratic systems are not enough. People are challenging data harms and seeking redress, often through the use of law and through organizing (Hearn 2022; Richardson 2019). In many of these cases, investigative reporting has led to greater awareness and debate. The problem is that redress takes years and, in the meantime, lives are destroyed. The Record points to multiple and intersecting levels of inequality and that marginalized communities are more negatively affected than other groups. The Record demonstrates that there are differing levels of accountability for socially-sorted citizens (Eubanks 2018; Lyon 2002). The Record points to the changing power dynamics linked to processes of datafication as citizens need to spend a lot of time and energy to uncover how the systems that are negatively affecting them work, and also that getting access to necessary information is difficult, if not impossible, in some cases. Our democratic institutions at present are not equipped to oversee and hold to account many of the data systems being implemented.

Technical solutions are not going to fix or prevent the kinds of harms identified throughout the Record and in this chapter (Gangadharan & Niklas 2019; Stark, Greene, & Hoffmann 2021). As argued by Anna Lauren Hoffmann (2018), in the face of such continuous and widespread harm, to focus on technical solutions is to enter into a 'continual game of technical whack-a-mole'. We can reform our laws to better protect people, but legal protections tend to focus on individual actors and redress, and are employed only after harms have already happened (Hoffmann 2018). Tackling data harms will require addressing the social and cultural violence that is embedded in our social, political and economic systems (Hoffmann 2020).

5
DATA AND CITIZENSHIP

By Arne Hintz

As we discussed in the previous chapters, the ways in which we are governed – as a society and as individuals – are increasingly based on the collection and processing of personal and behavioural data. Data analytics situate us in society and they affect the relation between those that analyse – including the government and the state – and those who are analysed – us. They therefore implicate our role as citizens.

Citizenship as a concept and practice denotes our formal belonging to a community and the rights, duties and rules that come with it, such as the freedoms and restrictions to move within and across state territories. Yet it has also been used more widely to address our capacity to act and intervene in matters of that community, and it is therefore a notion of power, agency and participation. Citizenship, understood in this broader sense, is about how we are situated in, and interact with, our social and political environment.

A concern with questions of citizenship thus addresses the systemic, societal and political dimensions of datafication that are at the heart of a data justice perspective. It considers both the reconfiguration of state–citizen relations that emerges from practices of profiling, categorizing and scoring people through an ever-increasing amount of data-points and the agency of citizens in shaping these relations through activism, civic engagement and the development of data literacy. Moreover, a focus on data justice invites us not to limit our interest to the individual acts of citizens but to situate these in broader transformations of authority and social justice in a datafied world.

This chapter unpacks the notion of citizenship, explores how its different components are affected by datafication and discusses how both the conceptual and practical tenets of citizenship can be reasserted in the context of a data justice agenda. We will begin by examining traditional understandings of citizenship that define the citizen through their membership of a nation-state as well as the more recent concept of digital citizenship that focuses on the self-creation and self-assertion of citizens as active participants in society through digital acts and the use of digital tools. Then we will investigate how these forms of citizenship are transformed in datafied environments as data analytics increasingly determine how we are assessed as citizens, what rights we enjoy and what restrictions we face, but also what means are available to us to participate and intervene. This has significant implications for core practices and understandings of democracy as the data-driven management of state–citizen relations clashes with the accessibility of the state for civic participation. The democratic effects of datafied citizenship will therefore be explored before, finally, we examine the ways in which the roles of citizens can be enhanced in a datafied society, focusing on questions of data literacy and on new models for civic participation in decisions about the use of data analytics in the governance of society.

Citizenship as Status and Practice

According to its most established understanding, citizenship denotes the formal relation between a person and a nation-state. It is a notion of belonging and of membership to a political community, formalized through documents such as the passport and typically received at birth. Formalizing the relation between the state and the individual, it determines the rights (such as voting) and obligations (such as taxation) of the individual, as well as the individual's access to and share in the state's collective resources (Marshall 1950; Tilly 1997; Turner 2009). Historically, this focus on the legal status of citizens was most clearly pronounced in the Roman (or liberal) model of citizenship, which emphasized citizens' freedom to pursue their private interests within the context of the state, and the protection they enjoyed from interference by state authorities, other powers and other individuals, while the Greek (or republican) model foregrounded the participation of citizens in public affairs and in the institutions of public administration, and thus in the creation of the rules, laws and decisions that govern them (Walzer 1970). Both traditions have affected modern understandings of citizenship, which fuse the provision of state protection with (to varying degrees) the participation of citizens in the community's political, social and economic processes (Bellamy 2008). Yet both share a focus on the state as the core institution for determining citizen rights and duties.

This narrow conception has been challenged and, as a result, widened. Critics have highlighted the exclusionary nature of citizenship, leading to concepts such as 'feminist citizenship' (Lister 1997) as a pluralist idea of the citizen that is rooted in difference. The territorial focus of citizenship has been questioned by 'postnational' (Soysal 1994), 'transnational' (Bauböck 1994) and 'cosmopolitan' (Linklater 2002) notions of citizenship that account for processes of globalization, the rise of non-state organizations and the growing role of transnational configurations of authority as well as changing forms of belonging and affiliation that spread from the national to local and regional communities and to transnational diasporas (McNevin 2011). Further, the rise of neoliberalism and the increasing primacy of the economic domain over the political (Mouffe 2000) has led to the emergence of a 'citizen-consumer' (Clarke et al. 2007), who is politically passive and interacts with society mainly as a consumer of privatized goods and services (Turner 2017). These critiques demonstrate that classic reference points of organizing belonging are being challenged, political communities are witnessing transformations and new claims for inclusion are being made.

Moving further beyond the centrality of belonging, recent scholarship has emphasized the acts of citizens in developing their own position in society, thus conceptualizing citizenship as practice, rather than status. Understanding citizenship as 'expression of agency' (Lister 1997, p. 38) points our attention to the ways in which people constitute themselves as citizens (Isin 2012) and 'do citizenship' (Zivi 2012). It begins with the citizen as an active figure, not with the nation-state as grantor of a privileged status (Clarke et al. 2014). The concept of 'digital citizenship' serves as a prime example for this performative and engaged approach as it explores how people generate their own role as citizens through 'digital acts' (Isin & Ruppert 2015). Digital protest and online campaigns, citizen journalism, digital culture, and a range of other practices of online collaboration and networked production all constitute such digital acts that allow digital subjects to engage with their social and political environment and contribute their voice to questions of public concern. Scholars who have advanced our thinking of digital citizenship have celebrated the participatory potential of digital infrastructures and online practices (Mossberger, Tolbert, & McNeal 2007) that may 'democratise civic and political participation and facilitate social inclusion' (Vivienne, McCosker, & Johns 2016, p. 8) and recognize people as 'active narrators of their individual lives' (Couldry et al. 2014, p. 615). This resonates with observations on social media uses of young people who 'write themselves and their communities into being' (boyd 2007, p. 14) as well as previous analyses of how participation in older, non-digital media, such as community radio and video activism, can generate recognition, self-actuation and community-building, and thus construct active citizenship (Rodríguez 2001). Understood as a form of do-it-yourself citizenship (Ratto & Boler 2014), digital citizenship thus has an intrinsic connection with citizen empowerment, implies a democratizing trend in state–citizen relations and points to a power shift from the state to citizens.

While the concept differs from traditional state-centred citizenship models in its normative objectives, institutional context and performative character, it also refers to, and generates, different kinds of community. Classic reference points for citizenship, such as national borders and formal organizations, are de-emphasized and complemented by a wider range of often looser and more fluid affiliations. Digital citizenship points to a fragmentation of the public sphere into multiple publics and a loss of cohesion from traditional bonds. Instead, the individual of the digital age is 'a composite' (Isin & Ruppert 2015, p. 12) of a variety of cultural, social, political and geographic affiliations, and operates in an environment of changing social configurations. Digital social contexts have given rise to fluid organizational forms that have been conceptualized as, for example, 'networked individualism' (Rainie & Wellman 2012), 'smart mobs' (Rheingold 2002) and 'connective action' (Bennett & Segerberg 2014) in which the public sphere becomes divided into diverse sets of what Dean (2001) calls 'cybersalons' based on interests, tastes, political affiliations or geographic communities, but not necessarily national membership. Public and private activities may become intertwined in what Papacharissi (2010) termed 'private citizenship' as seemingly private acts in online communities may have public political effects, and civic engagement is often shared with entertainment and a wider set of (private) motivations. This form of citizenship comes along with a transformation of social structures from masses and collectivities to 'a variety of atomized actions' (Papacharissi 2010, p. 131) which are collaborative and interactive but lack the stability of life-long national affiliation or other traditional organizational processes.

The Citizen as Data Profile

The pervasive tracking of our personal and behavioural data has significant implications for both the formal understanding of citizenship as belonging to a nation-state and the performative perspective of empowerment through digital citizenship. As a growing part of our online and offline lives is monitored and analysed, new categories of citizenship as well as new methods for assessing our performance as citizens are emerging, which leads to transformations in how citizenship is impacted and understood.

We may start our exploration by considering a traditional feature of status-oriented citizenship: national borders. Border control has seen a particularly substantial expansion of data analytics, including digital registration processes, biometric data collection and the exploitation of a vast range of data sources, including social media profiles and mobility tracing. This extensive datafication, as Metcalfe and Dencik (2019) note, 'augments borders significantly; both the management of physical external borders and the dispersal of borders across and within societies'. In other words, 'with big data comes "big borders"' (Ajana 2015, p. 13). This suggests that data extraction enhances the contours and restrictions of traditional forms of citizenship and strengthens status-oriented understandings. Far from considering performative, self-organized and empowering citizen acts, the application of digital infrastructures in this example advances the management of people's movements by the state and thus expands the control over, rather than by, populations. Yet the border case also shows how traditional citizenship categories are complemented by other mechanisms in treating people distinctly and in allowing, or restricting, their rights and activities. In the context of contemporary mass migration, 'data functions to systematically stigmatize, exclude and oppress "unwanted" migrant populations' (Metcalfe & Dencik 2019, n.p.) as refugees are particularly targeted by data tracing and comprehensive monitoring whereas other forms of trans-border movements receive different responses. The distinction in 'wanted' and 'unwanted' populations is thus solidified through data analytics and incorporated in the wider datafied governance of people as data collected for border control is shared with databases regarding other state functions, such as welfare provision and criminal justice. The practices and implications of citizenship are thereby reorganized as different ways of sorting populations overlay traditional separations according to national status.

In a context of pervasive data collection, this national status may even be (temporarily) altered, as the revelations by whistleblower Edward Snowden demonstrated. A key factor in determining the legality of surveillance practices by the US National Security Agency (NSA) is whether an item of communication – or data – is sent by a US citizen or a foreign national, with the law allowing for the detailed monitoring of the latter but restricting surveillance of the former. This means that determining the origin of communication, and thus the nationality of the (often anonymous) sender, is crucial for the decision on what level of surveillance is allowed. According to the Snowden leaks, this origin is established by analysing different components, including the infrastructure that is used (e.g. phone number, IP address), the data and metadata that is produced (e.g. the language in which the email is written) and the regular communication practices of the sender (e.g. their degree of interaction with people inside and outside the US). If the origin of the communication is deemed to be foreign, according to these criteria, and thus not a US citizen, the email, message or phone call can be legally surveilled. National citizenship thereby becomes determined by, and dependent on, communications data. A US citizen who appears to be a foreign citizen based on the analysis of their data is consequently treated as a foreign citizen. Cheney-Lippold (2016) refers to this designation as *jus algoritmi*, in contrast to classic legacies of *jus sanguinis* (family-based citizenship) and *jus soli* (location of birth). *Jus algoritmi* is 'a formal, state-sanctioned enaction of citizenship that distributes political rights according to the NSA's interpretations of data' (Cheney-Lippold 2016, p. 1729). As a consequence, it 'functionally abandons citizenship in terms of national identity in order to privilege citizenship in terms of provisional interpretations of data' (p. 1738). These interpretations sometimes align with a citizen's formal nationality, and sometimes become detached from it. *Jus algoritmi* is therefore an identity that we are assigned through data analysis, but not necessarily one that corresponds with our passport, that we identify with, or that we create for ourselves.

Beyond such alterations of traditional features of citizenship, the use of data has transformed state–citizen relations more regularly and thus perhaps more profoundly. As government and the public sector increasingly identify, profile and categorize individuals, and segment populations for distinct treatment and targeted interventions, data-based 'social sorting' (Gandy 1993; Lyon 2015) has advanced the opportunities for the state to manage populations. The most comprehensive and most widely-discussed system to date has been the Chinese Social Credit Score, which integrates the rating of citizens' financial creditworthiness with a wide range of social and consumer behaviour to assess people's overall trustworthiness and allow, or deny, services accordingly. The system awards points for what is regarded as good behaviour (such as community engagement and donations to charities) and deducts points for negative behaviour (such as traffic offences or spreading online 'rumours'). Citizens with high scores receive privileges, such as fast-track promotion at work or access to good schools and housing, while those with low scores are restricted from, for example, certain forms of travel (Hvistendahl 2017). The score categorizes the citizenry and assigns distinct services and privileges – as well as punitive measures – across different bands of the score. It combines data from, for example, online consumption, use of services, legal, financial and educational records, and social media activity, and it is based on a public-private partnership, with the government having enlisted major tech companies, such as Baidu, Alibaba and Tencent, to develop relevant databases, provide user data and incorporate the system into their services (Lv & Luo 2018). While the social credit score has been criticized in the West as a 'digital totalitarian state' (The Economist 2016) and a 'tool for social control' (Chin & Wong 2016), it points to an emerging trend of applying data analytics in the public sector of a wider range of countries (Fullerton 2018; Jefferson 2018).

The use of data analytics, scoring systems and the segmentation of populations is increasingly adopted to inform security measures, provide services and devise policy in areas such as education, child welfare and housing. Practices of scoring and predictive risk assessment that are applied in the democratic 'West' and have led to significant controversies include predictive policing, criminal justice, welfare systems and child protection (Angwin et al. 2016; Eubanks 2018; Redden, Dencik, & Warne 2020; Trottier 2015). Research by the Data Justice Lab has shown how the use of predictive analytics has become normalized across a wide range of public services and government institutions (Dencik, Hintz et al. 2018). While these applications differ regarding their implementation, purposes and impact, they demonstrate a growing practice of assessing behaviour, needs and risk through the combination of extensive datasets in 'data warehouses' that seek to get 'the golden view' of citizens (Dencik, Redden et al. 2019). Systems of categorization, risk assessment, social sorting and prediction inform specific actions by the state and thereby evaluate citizens' activities and status (see also Chapter 2 on Data and Governance).

While citizens are thus subject to fine-grained assessments of their conduct and lives, they typically have no knowledge about how, when, where, by whom and for what purpose they are scored, categorized or segmented. The Chinese Social Credit Score (or, more accurately, the various pilots and platform-based scores that exist at the time of writing this book) provide people with a final score figure but remain obscure about how that figure was calculated and what data sources are used, leading to significant uncertainty among citizens (Ma 2022). None of the data score systems analysed in the UK include a means for people even to know their score, let alone how it was generated (Dencik, Hintz et al. 2018). This corresponds with the black-boxed nature of data processes, which has been one of the core critiques of systems of datafication (Pasquale 2015). It means that citizens are assessed according to criteria they do not know about, with consequences that remain obscure to them, and thus without a means to interrogate the purposes and practices of data uses, nor to object, challenge or resist. Citizens are positioned as recipients of data-based administrative measures but not as participants or co-creators in decisions that govern their lives.

As the example of the Chinese Social Credit Score demonstrates, the information that is used for scoring systems and other forms of data analytics increasingly combines a variety of data from financial and business transactions, police and criminal justice data sources, social and cultural life, personal networks, etc. Consumer profiling has incorporated a wider range of life data to introduce, for instance, socially-oriented judgements into financial decision-making processes – for example, an analysis of people's mobile phone use, or the creditworthiness of their social media friends (Dixon & Gellman 2014). The platform economy has predicted consumption patterns based on a variety of social, cultural, health and other data (McCann, Hall, & Warin 2018). Data brokers collect thousands of attributes for each citizen or household based on both commercial and noncommercial data sources (Christl 2017). Similarly, government uses of data analytics have drawn from data collected for commercial purposes and provided by data businesses, such as data brokers and financial credit agencies. Companies like Experian have provided categorization and segmentation services to the public sector that assess citizens based on information from this wider range of sources. So while practices of consumer scoring have migrated into the realm of citizenship (McQuillan 2019), the actual data by which our past and future actions are evaluated have incorporated consumer data, too. The rise of the 'citizen-consumer' (see above) is thus enabled and supported, and it is constructed, in part, outside established categories of citizenship and civic rights.

This wide range of data sources does not mean that the basis on which citizens are judged and assessed is accurate. In comparison to the complexity of human existence, data systems are simplistic and reductionist, and they cannot take into account the full variety of human motivations, experiences and identities (Costanza-Chock 2018). Life is messy, contradictory and often unpredictable, and so are the digital practices of citizens that create data traces and lead to data-based categorizations and scores. Those scores may be formed, for example, by online shopping that we do for other people or tactical behaviour that emerges from the knowledge of being monitored. The data that results from these actions will always be decontextualized and, in many cases, inaccurate. Data analytics may thus construct patterns where none exist (boyd & Crawford 2012). While data traces increasingly 'are made to speak for and about us' (Barassi 2020a, p. 141) and 'build stories about who we are' (p. 140), those narratives may easily be misleading and, at best, reductionist. Not only *jus algoritmi*, as noted above, but the regular adoption of data-based social sorting is thus based, in part, on categorizations or 'stories' that we may not recognize or identify with. As Barassi (2020a) notes, this has particularly severe implications for children being born into the datafied age as the narratives about their identities and their growth into future citizens are built even before birth, based on data about their families, living conditions, etc., and they will be judged in their role as citizens by a multitude of data-points that they have no control over and that may misrepresent, and obstruct, their development as citizens. Yet while these consequences for citizens-to-be are particularly stark, they demonstrate the general challenges for citizens in a context where self-control over data is limited and misrepresentation by decontextualized data sources is endemic. We are constructed as data subjects (Cheney-Lippold, 2017) but based on criteria that do not necessarily correspond to lived experience and may thereby severely alter our relation with the state as well as the institutions that we engage with as citizens. As Couldry and Hepp (2017, p. 212, original emphasis) note, 'when governments' actions, *whatever* their democratic intent, become routinely dependent on processes of automated categorization, a dislocation is threatened between citizens' experience and the data trajectory on the basis of which they are judged'.

Data-based sorting of citizens – or, as we have called it elsewhere, 'citizen scoring' (Dencik, Redden et al. 2019, n.p.) – reorders the contours of citizenship, 'shaping the deserving and undeserving, the risky and the vulnerable, and, ultimately, the terms upon which access to and participation in society might occur'. It thereby changes traditional factors of citizenship as a nation-state-related status, and it provides a particularly stark contrast to the ideas of digital citizenship. Although datafication emerges from the digital environment of our everyday lives and builds on 'digital acts', it shifts our attention from the performative and empowering dimensions of digital citizenship to the management of populations through data analytics. The effective use of online tools, which was previously seen to have democratizing effects, now renders digital citizens transparent to those institutions with the means to collect and analyse data. As, at the same time, these institutions maintain obscurity over the practices and extent of data-based governance, the response by digital citizens has not been one of empowerment, but rather of 'digital resignation' (Draper & Turow 2019), in which they are aware of being monitored and assessed through data but know little about how this is done, by whom and with what kind of consequences, and how to oppose and resist it. From this, it follows that data-fied citizens are not primarily constituted through their own actions, but through the analysis of data brokers and state institutions, and their agency is significantly limited.

The emerging power relations of the datafied age are between those who provide personal and behavioural data (digital citizens) and those who own, trade and control it (data businesses and the state). The state as purveyor of traditional forms of citizenship is thereby empowered as data analytics provide vastly enhanced possibilities to understand, predict and control citizen activities and assign people their societal position based on data traces. This is the case, particularly, in a context of dispersed and individualized social structures that provide challenges for a comprehensive regulation of the citizenry by state authorities. Monitoring and profiling the 'atomized actions' (see above) of populations allows the state to address a fragmented reality and create a new and governable collectivity. As a result, the datafied citizen becomes a monitored, managed and supervised citizen (Hintz, Dencik, & Wahl-Jorgensen 2019).

Datafied Citizenship and Democracy

These developments pose severe challenges for democracy as they affect the role and capacity of the citizen as the sovereign in a democratic society. If algorithmic systems of governance are changing who and what is made visible and calculable (Amoore 2020), the institutionalization of citizen scoring and other classification systems means that citizens are becoming increasingly transparent and subject to management techniques they have no knowledge about. More than merely assessing citizen activities, algorithmic and automated systems allow for the steering and nudging of citizens, and thus offer significant means of control (Cardullo & Kitchin 2019). As the example of the social credit score demonstrated, citizens can be incentivized to engage in behaviours which government regards as desirable. Concern for one's own score and the advantages that come with increasing it may lead citizens to refrain from public critiques of government policies, stick to mainstream news sources, or 'clean' their social networks from controversial followers (Ma 2022). But even without a comprehensive scoring system, choices regarding people's health, pastimes and finances, to name but a few examples, will be affected by the pervasive tracking of behaviours and activities and the possibility that such behaviours might have detrimental implications for the availability of social services, insurances or employment. Citizens are thus guided and disciplined in (more or less) prescribed ways towards acceptable avenues of activity and engagement (Fourcade & Gordon 2020).

As scholars like Rob Kitchin have highlighted in their critical interrogation of debates around the 'smart city', these avenues are primarily those of consumers. Inhabitants of the smart city and the broader digital citizenry, as Cardullo and Kitchin (2019) argue, can typically choose from different service options in the marketplace of providers, test new offers, provide feedback and, perhaps, suggestions. This however is a long way from the more comprehensive democratic scenario of assigning to the citizen the role of proposer, co-creator or decision-maker, and thus of someone who contributes to steering the state. It implies a tokenistic form of civic participation as citizens occupy 'a largely passive role, with companies and city administrations performing forms of civic paternalism (deciding what's best for citizens) and stewardship (delivering on behalf of citizens)' (Cardullo & Kitchin 2019, p. 814). The authors position this understanding of citizenship in a neoliberal governance rationality that limits citizen voice and involvement to market values of choice, thus connecting with the concept of the 'citizen-consumer', which we have already encountered in this chapter. The dominant notion of the 'user' suits this reductionist model as citizen agency and autonomy focus on the application of provided solutions. All this limits the space for democratic engagement and shrinks the role of the citizen in governing society, and it transforms how citizenship is constituted in democratic societies. If the citizen gains rights primarily through acting responsibly and moving along the paths desired by government and the business sector, this involves a significant shift from the focus on civil, social and political rights that have traditionally been associated with citizenship (Graham et al. 2019).

These rights place the citizen in relation with the state and with fellow citizens, and they thus express the collective nature of both citizenship and democracy. Citizens are inevitably connected with others and with the state through their being citizens; they are part of a collectivity and, ideally, they engage actively with it. However, algorithmic systems have been used to advance personalization and individual solutions. On social media platforms, they have tailored advertising and news to what they assess as our specific interests; on shopping and consumption platforms, they provide recommendations and calculate prices according to our specific user profiles; and as a citizen score, they assign public services and state interventions according to our specific (calculated) needs and characteristics. The reconstitution of public services as personalized transactions is particularly relevant in this respect, as it demonstrates a shift from a generalized 'public' based on mutual experiences and common foundations to customized and automated relationships between the individual and authorities. Citizens are assessed as individuals, their problems and challenges are treated as specific to them and emerging from their individual acts and choices, and remedies and government responses therefore target the individual (as opposed to, say, broader social, political and economic challenges that society may be facing). Data-driven personalization leads to individuation, rather than collective citizenship; it neglects that our roles and preferences as citizens are developed in interaction with others; and it entrenches a focus on individual responsibility and personal culpability, rather than collective approaches to societal challenges (Andrejevic 2020).

This is underpinned by the focus of data analytics on identifying and measuring 'risk'. Risk management has emerged as a new 'paradigm' of public administration (Yeung 2017) and has become the predominant lens through which citizen activities are observed and assessed in a datafied context. Yet such risk is typically identified at the individual, not the societal, level, and the consequences of risk are equally individualized. As data analytics are applied to score, rate and categorize individuals and households regarding the risks they pose, for instance, for child safety or fire hazards, the explanatory focus of these systems is diverted away from structural causes, such as issues of inequality, poverty or racism. As the burden of responsibility for social ills is shifted on to individuals, the citizen becomes both the cause of and the remedy for societal challenges.

The predictive capacities of algorithmic data processing lie at the core of risk management. Scoring and other forms of data analytics use information about past events to predict future behaviour. This allows for the effective management of citizens and identification of, as well as response to, risks. For example, predictive policing attempts to analyse the record of past crimes and police interventions to predict and pre-empt future transgressions, and citizen scoring (as well as commercial and financial scoring) calculates future behaviour based on past acts. This practice has led to multiple experiences of discrimination and misidentification, but what is particularly relevant for our discussion here is that it creates a static image of society. It posits that what happened before will happen again. It implies that datafied citizens, assessed through predictive analytics, will not change and evolve through social interaction and changing living circumstances, and, perhaps more importantly, that they do not possess the agency to shape and affect their societal environment. Predictive forms of governance leave little space for change and for civic agency, and they are therefore inherently undemocratic. Democracies – at least, in their ideal type – are dynamic, governed by changing political formations and guided by the changing preferences of citizens. They are affected by the ongoing development of norms, cultures, social practices and economic circumstances, and by the political struggles of citizens, communities and a variety of social sectors. The transformation of governance into a system of social management based on prediction and pre-emption contradicts this fundamental quality of a democracy and, as a consequence, shapes a different form of a datafied society, just like it shapes datafied citizenship.

Predictive analytics, moreover, allow for the shaping of citizens in the way that was outlined at the beginning of this section. It is a proactive form of governance that requires pre-emptive measures to manage a citizenry and steer it along predicted paths. Through nudges, incentives or more forceful interventions, the course of citizens' lives is moved (or interrupted) if the prediction leads to results deemed undesirable. The sovereign that is, in a democracy, supposed to steer and oversee the course of government is thus guided, its actions pre-empted, and ultimately controlled.

As a result of the democratic challenge of datafication and automation, scholars like Mark Andrejevic have called for the re-democratization of our increasingly datafied societies. Employing the notion of 'data civics', he highlights the problematic role played by data infrastructures in a democratic society and identifies datafication as a political phenomenon that requires broader political responses. Rather than solving societal problems at the level of 'systems engineering', new democratic arrangements are required for the collection and use of data (Andrejevic 2020). From a similar perspective, scholars have drawn connections between the current challenges of datafication and older, non-digital struggles, such as for the right to the city (Currie, Knox, & McGregor 2022). Constituted by the demand for democratic control over the resources for, characteristics of and access to urbanization, the right to the city is a radial concept of citizenship that calls for the collective design of urban life. As a basic infrastructure of daily life that is shielded from democratic participation and intervention, datafication and automation pose similar problems, and approaches such as data civics call for similar strategies.

They resonate, not least, with a data justice approach to the challenges that emerge with datafication. Rejecting the fetishized focus on 'big data' as the level of discussing and resolving contemporary societal problems, and critically interrogating data-oriented solutions to data harms (such as 'data ethics'), it explores the social, political and economic contexts of datafication. A central concern for data justice is the manifestation and concentration of power in the political and economic sector, which shapes data infrastructures and their uses. Concerns about the latter therefore need to be tackled at the political, economic and social level in order to, in Andrejevic's words, 'directly address the political question' (Andrejevic 2020, p. 562). For the democratic challenge of datafication, this means that mechanisms of participation not only need to be established in the digital realm and through digital means, but also that a democratization of political decision-making more broadly is required. If datafication undermines citizen agency, and thus core democratic principles, questions need to be asked not just about data systems but about the interests and forces that advance their implementation.

Active Citizenship, Literacy and Participation

How, then, can re-democratization be achieved? How can citizen agency be enhanced and reasserted in the datafied society? While any answer to these questions will have to consider the political-economic context of datafication (see Chapter 1), the experiences of digital citizenship offer some interesting starting-points for practices that may address the disempowering nature of datafied citizenship. Building on online activism and other forms of digital civic engagement that have been prime components in the construction of digital citizenship, 'data activism' has applied digital social and political involvement to the datafied age. In exploring alternative forms of data gathering, analysis and visualization to advance the goals of civic initiatives and social movements, and in using data for empowerment and political change, data activism aims to 'bring democratic agency back into the analysis of how big data affect contemporary society' (Milan 2017, p. 153). Revisiting and updating the practices of digital citizenship, it reclaims the agency of citizens that is at risk in datafied societies (see Chapter 7). As part of the wider field of data activism, datafied subjects have challenged and negotiated the prominence of data collection and analytics through practices of technological self-defence. Tools and methods for providing secure digital infrastructures for active citizens have proliferated, ranging from encrypted chat- and email-communication to anonymous web browsing and to a multitude of privacy guides and security suites, complemented by public debate and training at 'Cryptoparties', and encompassing 'numerous digital rights and internet freedom initiatives seizing the moment to propose new communication methods for activists (and everyday citizens) that are strengthened through encryption' (Aouragh, Gürses, & Rocha 2015, p. 213).

These approaches correspond with a growing interest in 'data literacy' to complement earlier forms of media and digital literacy, and its inclusion in debates on (digital) citizenship. Data literacy seeks to 'articulate the set of skills required to have agency in a datafied world' (Pangrazio & Sefton-Green 2020, p. 214) and enhance 'the desire and ability to constructively engage in society through and about data' (Bhargava et al. 2015, p. 8). Just as earlier definitions of digital citizenship have emphasized citizens' competence in negotiating and applying digital tools (e.g. Mossberger et al. 2007), data literacy originates from a perceived need to develop skills and has, at times, found itself in tension with a more critical approach that explores the underlying political economy, ideologies and power relations of data infrastructures. Its emphasis has tended to be placed 'on technical literacy [...] and still disregards the need to address deeper structural issues of inequality' (Fotopoulou 2020, p. 2). However, this latter approach is increasingly recognized as necessary to consider the 'complex and opaque' nature of digital infrastructure (Pangrazio 2016, p. 169) and 'develop critical thinking about the online ecosystem [to] empower people to become active citizens' (Carmi et al. 2020, p. 5). In proposing the concept of 'critical big data literacy', Sander (2020, p. 2) has emphasized citizens' need 'to understand and critically reflect upon the ubiquitous collection of their personal data and the possible risks and implications that come with these big data practices', which necessitates both an understanding and citizen-driven scrutiny of the systemic and structural levels of data collection, analytics and automation. This perspective demonstrates a data justice approach by emphasizing the need for critical understanding of the societal, political and economic underpinnings of data-based inequalities, awareness of power structures and biases, and empowerment towards practical intervention into the workings of the datafied society. Highlighting a data literacy approach that prioritizes proactive citizen participation, Carmi et al. (2020, p. 5) have used the concept of 'data citizenship' in their call to raise citizens' abilities for 'understanding and being able to challenge, object and protest contemporary power asymmetries manifested in datafied societies'.

While critical understandings of the infrastructures and processes of datafication, and of strategies to challenge them, are crucial preconditions, an active form of citizenship in the datafied society would require possibilities for actual intervention and for meaningful participation at the systemic and institutional level of data-based governance. If datafication has affected the core pillars of citizenship, shifted state–citizen relations and impacted the roles of citizens in democracies, the reassertion of citizens in guiding, overseeing and deciding upon datafication would be paramount. The democratization of datafied governance systems is at stake, and thus democracy itself in a context of pervasive datafication of the state. Neither data literacy nor forms of online participation that have been at the core of debates around digital citizenship may be sufficient to address this systemic challenge. Scholarship on democratic innovation, on the other hand, offers helpful insights on participatory mechanisms that can advance citizen voices and citizen-based decision-making outside and beyond classic electoral procedures (Goodin 2008; Patriquin 2020; Smith 2009). Participatory models, such as citizen juries, citizen assemblies and public dialogues, have emerged as prominent methods to address

key challenges of contemporary societies. While distinct in their specific implementation (i.e. their size, goals, policy focus, etc.), these initiatives all bring together a small
selection of the population for deliberation on important social issues (Escobar & Elstub
2017). Amounting to what some describe as a 'deliberative wave' (OECD 2020), these
practices have enjoyed growing popularity.

These methods have increasingly been applied to questions of data and artificial
intelligence (AI). In the UK, recent participatory and deliberative events have included
a citizens' summit on the use of data in the health and care sector, citizens juries on
applications of AI in criminal justice, recruitment and healthcare, and a citizens' biometrics council on the use of facial recognition technology, to name just a few examples.
Several of these initiatives were commissioned by major oversight and advisory institutions, such as the Royal Society and the Information Commissioners Office, and are
thus closely related to policy development. As 'institutional arrangements that enable
democratic processes of deliberation and participation' (Andrejevic 2020, p. 565), they
resonate with the call for 'data civics', as discussed earlier.

Initiatives like these may not automatically generate increased citizen agency and
participation as the perceived need for governments to legitimize policy – and, in this
case, the roll-out of predictive analytics in the public sector – may limit their power to
meaningfully affect decision-making and lead to 'engagement-washing'. Therefore, civil
society pressure is important in campaigning for proper participatory decision-making
and in advancing 'citizen audits' to address the lack of transparency, accountability and
democratic legitimacy that continues to characterize the roll-out of data-based decision-
making in government (Reilly 2020). Together, these approaches have created a nascent
trend towards the democratization of datafication.

Conclusion: Datafied Citizenship between Participation and Control

As we have examined in this chapter, datafication has significant implications for the
relations between the state and the people, and thus for the concept and practice of citizenship. In adding tools to the state's arsenal for gaining detailed knowledge about citizens, predicting their future behaviour and enabling a more fine-grained administration
of public services, it leads to a power shift in state–citizen relations towards enhancing
government capabilities in managing the citizenry. This might manifest itself in tighter
border regimes, the segmentation of populations and the assessment of individuals
through data scores, or by assigning new citizenship categories altogether. The concept
of digital citizenship, which has become a prominent means for understanding people's
position as political subjects in digitized environments and which focuses on the performative self-enactment of citizens through digital acts, is thus under siege. Rather than
creating their own societal roles, digital citizens are persistently monitored and profiled,
integrated into new modes of citizenship according to the data that is collected about
them, and their citizenship is thereby constituted through data analysis by new (the data
economy) and traditional (the state) institutions.

Citizenship is thus shifting in the ways it is provided, enacted and secured. Even in the traditional understanding of citizenship as status, established frameworks of rights and obligations intersect with new categories in which citizens are positioned and which affect their opportunities and life-chances. Moreover, datafication limits citizens' agency, as its practices and consequences largely remain unknown to people, who have little ability to interrogate and challenge the use of their data. Algorithmic forms of governance emphasize the individual, at the expense of the citizen's role in a collective realm, and support the configuration of the 'consumer-citizen' who may select from different service options but whose role in co-creating society is severely diminished. All this raises significant challenges for democratic processes as it means that the sovereign who is supposed to steer the course of government is weakened and restricted.

Yet, as we have seen, an understanding of this democratic deficit is emerging and, with it, new forms of civic engagement and participation. Deliberative methods, civil society initiatives, data literacy and data activism open up a further dimension of datafied citizenship in which people intervene into the systems that assess and categorize them and develop new democratic practices to ensure participation and accountability. Citizenship in a context of datafication may thus traverse and combine contradictory dimensions of the active and empowered, as well as the monitored and controlled subject. It points to the need, though, for considering classic political practices in both its manifestation and the reassertion of citizens as political subject. It requires us to 'go offline' if we want to understand the characteristics of citizenship as well as the models of democratic innovation that may advance participatory decision-making. The debate on citizenship thereby anchors datafication in the power dynamics of state–citizen relations, foregrounds questions of political participation and offers an important building-block for a data justice perspective.

6

DATA AND POLICY

By Arne Hintz

The increasingly central role of datafication in the economic, political and social dimensions of contemporary life and its various implications and potential harms raise the question of the limits of data collection and use – and thus of the legal and regulatory framework of datafication. What rules exist to regulate how data about people and communities is collected, processed and used? How are these rules created, based on whose interests and what norms and ideas? Do they effectively protect datafied citizens from data harms? And what would be necessary components of a data justice policy framework?

Data policy has been emerging together with the datafication of society. Yet while technological innovation and implementation have moved ahead rather quickly, the development of an appropriate regulatory environment has been lagging behind. Long-standing laws and policies have been reinterpreted, regulatory vacuums have been filled by self-regulation of internet companies, and newer laws have often had contradictory objectives and consequences. While some recent legislation facilitates data collection by internet companies and data use by the state, other policies demonstrate increased attention towards user protection and citizens' control over data that affects them. A consistent legal and regulatory framework is not (yet) in existence in most jurisdictions. We can observe a nascent trend towards enhancing and protecting a more active role of citizens in the data ecology, but also the continuation and expansion of data collection by platform businesses and government, complemented by rapidly developing and no less contradictory industrial policy surrounding artificial intelligence (AI) and the internet of things (IoT).

From a data justice perspective, the ways in which legal and regulatory regimes may address data harms and protect as well as empower datafied citizens are particularly relevant. However, this specific vantage point invites us to explore the wider context, underpinnings and implications of data laws. How does data policy interact with other areas of the law to affect social justice? What ideas, ideologies and social constructs underpin current regulatory frameworks, and what are the impacts of these on users, citizens and communities? How are data policies developed, which social actors and forces are able to influence them, and whose interests are therefore reflected in them? A data justice perspective will thus investigate the meanings, contexts and implications of data law, with a particular view on how policy affects social justice. While it is interested in the core concerns of data collection that have often revolved around questions of privacy and surveillance, it articulates a broader agenda that explores how people are treated and positioned in society through data, what systemic changes occur in this respect, and how regulatory frameworks may affect such changes.

This chapter provides an entry-point into these developments and debates. It begins by interrogating current regulatory frameworks that shape, constrain and advance control over personal data by the state, internet platforms, citizens and affected communities. To that end, it considers current trends in, particularly, surveillance and data protection law that impact the control that data subjects have over the terms of their datafication. However, it also questions and problematizes the focus on individual approaches that we see in predominant legal constructs and frameworks. If data is a social relation, and this relational aspect drives the social value as well as the potential harm of datafication, an emphasis on the individual data subject will likely lead to a severely limited consideration of contemporary data challenges. This, then, points to the need for a social approach to data policy as well as public, collective and democratic forms of governing data production. Finally, an institutional perspective on data policy highlights the power-related context of datafication and leads us to consider the actors, interests and norms that affect the rules of datafication. Policy is thus regarded as a struggle between competing interests, norms and discourses, and the chapter will unpack some of these to explore the discursive and power-related context in which current data policy is being developed. While each of these various dimensions would require a more thorough investigation to fully explore their roots and impacts, the chapter outlines and connects these debates to assemble relevant building blocks for a data justice perspective on data policy.

As legal and regulatory frameworks differ from country to country and from region to region, choices inevitably need to be made regarding the national and regional vantage point of a discussion on data policy. The examples and cases highlighted in this chapter therefore consider, primarily, the jurisdiction that the Data Justice Lab is situated in – the United Kingdom (UK), as well as its larger neighbour, the European Union (EU). However, they will be contextualized in wider policy developments and express broader trends that can be observed in other contexts.

The Data Regulation Ecology

Key pillars of the regulatory framework for data collection and analysis have included data protection legislation and rules that allow or constrain data collection and sharing by both government and internet businesses. However, the law has been slow in catching up with the development and implementation of technology, and so the policy environment has, for a long time, relied on interpretations of older rules. In the UK, for example, the Data Protection Act of 1998 was adopted long before the recent rise of IoT and algorithmic forms of governance, yet it formed a cornerstone of rules for data collection, access and sharing until its revision in 2018. The Telecommunications Act of 1984 offered the Secretary of State substantial interception powers in communications networks, and the Intelligence Services Act of 1994 provided the legal basis for the surveillance activities by GCHQ, the British intelligence agency, long before the widespread use of the internet and of social media. Some laws were updated, for example, the Regulation of Investigatory Powers Act (RIPA) of 2000, which was as amended by the Data Retention and Investigatory Powers Act (DRIPA) of 2014, but often in the interest of expanding state access to user data. DRIPA allowed a Secretary of State to authorize the interception not only of the communications of a specific individual but of wide-ranging and vaguely defined types of data traffic in bulk. The Data Protection Act, too, included substantial exemptions for the protection of 'national security' and the prevention or detection of crime (Hintz & Brown 2017).

In response to major scandals, such as the revelations by whistleblower Edward Snowden in 2013, and resulting pressures from different stakeholders, such legislation has been reviewed and reformed in many countries. For example, the UK Investigatory Powers (IP) Act of 2016 constituted a new and comprehensive framework for state-based data collection which updated previous legislation, although it confirmed, legalized and expanded existing practices of security agencies. The Digital Economy (DE) Act of 2017 added rules on, for example, data sharing between government departments and required further data collection and storage by online platforms. Together with the Data Protection Act of 2018, these have been examples for governments attempting to catch up with the rapid development of data infrastructures.

National rules, institutions and processes have been embedded in regional and international policy, such as the European Convention for the Protection of Human Rights and Fundamental Freedoms (ECHR), which was incorporated into UK law in the Human Rights Act 1998. Article 8 of the Convention guarantees everyone's 'right to respect for his private and family life, his home and his correspondence' (Council of Europe 1950). More recently, the General Data Protection Regulation (GDPR) has been a prominent example for a regulatory framework that applies to the entire European Union. 'Directives' adopted by the European Commission, such as the Data Retention Directive of 2006, are not automatically applicable but have to be implemented by all member states and thus, still, have far-reaching consequences for national law. The Data Retention Directive required telecommunications services to collect and store the 'metadata' of online communication, such as who communicates with whom, at what time and from what IP address. It was revoked in 2014 by the Court of Justice of the European Union but was effectively continued by the UK government at the national level when it adopted DRIPA. Following a legal challenge, this Act was ruled unlawful by the European Court of Justice in 2016 (Hintz & Brown 2017). Such direct interactions between the national and regional level no longer apply to the UK since it left the European Union in 2020–21 but continue to be a core feature of the law in other European countries as well as countries participating in other intergovernmental associations. Generally, these examples demonstrate the fluid nature of policy and the various national and international influences to which it is subject.

Despite (and prior to) recent efforts to update relevant data policies, the data extraction industry of platforms, data trackers and data brokers has largely emerged in a context of self-regulation where tentative interpretations of user consent have formed the core of data-oriented restrictions. In some jurisdictions, platforms and apps are required to seek acceptance from users for the ways in which these companies track their browsing habits and use their data. For example, the EU Directive on Privacy and Electronic Communications of 2002 (and amended in 2009) required 'explicit consent' from those who visit websites for the installation of 'cookies' that may identify, track and profile them. However, this model of user consent has, in practice, required people to agree to the comprehensive collection of their data if they wish to partake in digital life through the most widely used platforms and services. The model places the burden of privacy protection on the individual and 'merely legitimises the extraction of personal data from unwitting data subjects' (Edwards & Veale 2017, p. 49).

As the law has been catching up with technological development, the most current iteration of data policy is AI policy – a set of regulatory debates and regimes that address challenges emerging with the deployment of artificial intelligence and similar data-driven technologies. These include, among others, questions of safety, support for research and development, and impacts on labour and social justice (Calo 2017). It is often underpinned by a strong focus on industrial policy due to the perceived economic and geo-strategic value of AI. The European Union has seen a flurry of AI policy initiatives since 2017–18, consisting of communications, resolutions, white papers, guidelines and plans, often with the goal to boost technological capacity. 'Shaping Europe's Digital Future', according to the digital strategy by the European Commission from 2020, will involve the development of a European data economy to 'make sure the EU becomes a role model and a leader for a society empowered by data' (Niklas & Dencik 2020).

Regulatory Trends: A Tale of Two Policies

The emerging regulatory environment for data collection and use is affected by different trends, with often contradictory effects on citizens. On the one hand, legislative frameworks allow for an ever-increasing collection of data on people, particularly by the state, while on the other hand, the collection and use of some specific types of data are restricted through data protection rules. In the following, we will illustrate these trends through two prominent examples.

Despite high-profile scandals such as the Snowden revelations, many countries have expanded the legal frameworks for data collection, typically justified with security considerations in light of terrorist threats. The UK Investigatory (IP) Powers Act of 2016 is a particularly far-reaching case. As comprehensive legislation to combine the previously fragmented rules for communications interception and data collection by state agencies, it addresses a wide range of surveillance practices. While it opens up many of the traditionally secret surveillance measures to public scrutiny and oversight, it confirms, legalizes and expands existing practices of state-based data collection and analysis. These include both targeted and 'bulk' interception of communication, that is, wide definitions of data types that can be scooped up; the mandatory communications (or meta-) data retention by Internet Service Providers (ISPs) and telecommunications operators (including platforms) and the requirement to make it available to authorities upon request; and 'computer network exploitation' (i.e. hacking by state agencies into servers and devices). It also introduces the requirement for ISPs to capture 'internet connection records' (effectively, people's browsing habits), which are then accessible by a range of government institutions. The law offers an extensive framework for government agencies to collect data about people and render citizens transparent to the state (Hintz & Brown 2017). As noted above, it has been complemented by the Digital Economy (DE) Act of 2017, which mandates data collection on user behaviour by private sector entities on certain types of platforms and facilitates data-sharing between government departments as well as between government and private companies (Hintz & Brand 2019). This data transfer typically takes place without citizens' knowledge and consent, and it exemplifies the growing interaction between public and private data operations, such as the use of commercial data aggregation tools in the public sector (Dencik, Hintz et al. 2018).

Meanwhile, and in apparent contradiction to the trend of extended data collection, data protection rules have been strengthened in some jurisdictions, leading to stricter regulation of, particularly, the data-related activities of the internet industry and commercial platforms. The most prominent case is the EU General Data Protection Regulation (GDPR) of 2018, which limits the use and sharing of personal data by companies and offers new directions for providing citizens with some control in the context of new challenges that have emerged with datafication. In restricting data uses, it mandates purpose limitation of data collection and processing, that is, it requires that personal data must be collected for specific and explicit purposes and cannot be used for a wider variety of objectives that it was not intended for. Further, it limits the processing of sensitive personal data (i.e. personal data revealing racial or ethnic origin, political opinions, religious or philosophical beliefs, as well as genetic, biometric and health data) and it addresses the increasing practices of automated decision-making by prohibiting decisions 'based solely on automated processing'. While this may not affect those uses of data analytics in the public sector (see Dencik, Hintz et al. 2018, as well as Chapters 2 on Data and Governance and Chapter 5 on Data and Citizenship) which support (rather than replace) human decision-making, it serves as a safeguard against transforming such processes into exclusively automated decisions about citizens and their lives.

In addition to such protective measures, the GDPR has advanced a whole set of regulations that enhance people's control over data that is collected about them and that affects them. These include the right of access to personal data and data portability that allow users to move their data across services, thereby facilitating the switching from one service provider to another; and it makes new forms of automated and algorithmic decision-making more transparent by assigning citizens a right to explanation and to challenge the outcomes of algorithmic decisions. Further, the GDPR expands and refines the notion of consent by defining it as an ongoing and actively managed choice, rather than a one-off compliance box to tick. It requires consent to be actively obtained by internet services and gives users the option to withhold or withdraw at any moment.

The GDPR reflects an emerging recognition that citizens require some form of protection from data harms and they lack the ability to exert control over data that is collected about them. This has also been adopted by national policy discourse, for example the UK government's 'Digital Charter' from 2018, which includes the provision that 'personal data should be respected and used appropriately', and concerns regarding the collection and analysis of personal data have underpinned discourses on data ethics and institutional development, for example the creation of the 'Centre for Data Ethics and Innovation' (CDEI). However, the policy environment that provides the context to these efforts remains highly contradictory. While it recognizes citizens' needs for controlling (some) data and enhancing (some) citizen rights, the collection of personal and behavioural data by the private sector and, particularly, the state continues with relatively few restrictions. The processing, application and use of citizens' data may be subject to more specific regulations, but that has not prevented the ever-more detailed and fine-grained collection and extraction of data.

The Problem of the Informed User and Data Individualism

From a data justice perspective, the GDPR includes many components that a citizen- and justice-oriented regulatory framework may need to entail. Rules on purpose limitation, the collection of sensitive data and automated decision-making would be essential for addressing privacy concerns, reducing data harms and tackling the increasing automation of state–citizen relations. While the implementation of these principles has encountered many challenges and the specific composition of the GDPR has drawn substantial criticism (e.g. Edwards & Veale 2017; Wachter, Mittelstadt, & Floridi 2017), the norms that it expresses may constitute a significant step towards a set of rules that are oriented towards a data justice agenda. Similarly, the quest to advance people's control over data and equip citizens with the means to enact their rights and become knowledgeable and capable actors in a datafied society provides a significant change to state–corporate–citizen relations that are too often characterized by 'digital resignation' (Draper & Turow 2019) by disempowered data subjects. The goal of advancing 'user choice, user control and consumer empowerment' (Article 29 Working Party 2016), as formulated by the Article 29 Working Party, an independent European working group that dealt with privacy and data protection before the adoption of GDPR, would thus address an important imbalance in data relations and a key problem for a datafied future.

However, the approach of user empowerment means that the requirement for user protection and (in the case of the right to explanation and challenge) the burden of proof are placed on the 'data subject', that is, the individual citizen. Enhancements to data portability, the need for consent and the right to explanation provide citizens with important tools, but these may have limited meaning if citizens lack the knowledge and capacity to enact them. As Edwards and Veale (2017, pp. 66–67) note, 'individual data subjects are not empowered to make use of the kind of algorithmic explanations they are likely to be offered [...] individuals are mostly too time-poor, resource-poor and lacking in the necessary expertise to meaningfully make use of these individual rights.' With regards to the improved requirement of consent, this may lead to a 'consent fallacy' in which users are provided with the illusion of choice while being forced (or enticed) to agree to the transfer of their data. The right to receive an explanation for the collection and processing of data, similarly, may create a 'transparency fallacy' as an explanation alone is likely not meaningful enough to confer much autonomy 'on even the most empowered data subject' (ibid., p. 67). Particularly, that is the case if this right is limited 'to a general explanation, rather than a right that would allow individuals to obtain an explanation for a particular individual decision that affects them' (Kaltheuner & Bietti 2017, p. 15).

The idea of the 'informed user' has been at the heart of regulatory frameworks for a while and is further emphasized, rather than critically reviewed, by regulations such as GDPR. While the role of active citizens in the datafied society is an important concern (see the chapters addressing questions of citizenship and activism in this book), the dominant construct of user empowerment as guideline for policy conceals that rights to access personal data require a level of understanding and engagement by the citizen that is currently not realistic. Rather than strengthening the role of the citizen, it may obscure actual power relations and imbalances that keep citizens at a severely disadvantaged position. This critique of the informed user connects with earlier concerns, formulated from a data justice perspective, regarding predominant responses to state surveillance (Dencik, Hintz, & Cable 2016). The practice of self-protection and self-defence against privacy violations through the use of encryption and anonymization tools has pointed to a useful tactical arsenal but placed the onus of addressing systematic and pervasive surveillance on the individual and transferred a societal problem to the realm of individual lifestyle changes. The emergence of a data justice perspective has been intrinsically linked to a critique of the reduction of societal challenges to individual responses, and this applies to the underlying principles of data policy as well.

The emphasis by contemporary data protection rules, such as the GDPR, on 'personal data' highlights a further dimension of the problematic focus on individualism in data policy. Advancing user control through measures such as data portability typically applies to data that an individual has explicitly provided to a data controller, such as a platform, but excludes combinations of this data with data from other sources or providers (such as information about the individual that the platform may have acquired from a data broker), as well as information inferred from this data, that is, interpretations that the platform may conduct to categorize and profile their users. Moreover, it does not necessarily include the vast range of behavioural data that is now collected by platforms and other parts of the data industry and that is at the core of 'surveillance capitalism' (Zuboff 2019). This may encompass the activities of users on platforms, such as Facebook clicks and likes, responses to advertising, times of accessing a site, writing style, mood analysis and detailed analyses of other actions by the user. Interpretations of this kind of data, and combinations with the user's personal data, other data sources and the data collected about other users, are generated by the platform (or other data businesses) as part of its own data processing and therefore remain the property of the system that generates them, rather than the data subject (Edwards & Veale 2017, p. 67). Such interpretations of, inferences from, and combinations of data have become particularly valuable for both the private and the public sector in profiling, categorizing, rating and scoring both consumers and citizens (Dencik, Hintz et al. 2018). Predictive analytics, behavioural targeting and risk assessment are built on the relational aspects of shared features and common patterns of behaviour of data subjects, and thus on their belonging to, and interaction with, groups (Viljoen 2020). Moreover, inferences may circumvent GDPR rules regarding the processing of sensitive personal data as they can gain unobservable (and potentially sensitive) data about a person from pieces of observable (but 'non-personal') data. The risk scoring in the criminal justice system in the US, where a wide range of (largely non-sensitive) data-points has led to racial bias, may serve as a prominent example (Angwin et al. 2016).

The focus on the informed user, individual responsibility and on personal data thus have significant problems addressing the societal impact of datafication and are insufficient foundations for data policy. Most importantly, they point to the limits of individual approaches to regulating data. Data typically denotes a relation to others, and the individual's place within a broader collective, from which they can either be distinguished or to which they belong. This is the case even for 'personal' data, but even more so for the wider range of inferred and derived data. Data, in that sense, is valuable primarily in relation to others, which is particularly apparent in the case of categorizations, rankings and 'risk scores' produced by data analytics companies and used, among others, by public services. Such evaluations compare citizens and consumers with each other and allocate resources based on the results. As noted previously in this book, they sort people, prioritize recipients of services or of state interventions, or develop connections of 'relevant' friends and followers whose content should be pushed more than that of others. Further, if a data subject's online communication, 'friending', and service use in the platform economy inevitably connects them with other users, they affect the data inferred about those users – for example, the characteristics of their social network, their cultural and political environments, and potentially their personal credit score or the 'risk' they pose according to police or social services. My personal and behavioural data affects the outcome of data analytics that are conducted about others and may change the way they are profiled, categorized or prioritized. Data, then, is never entirely 'individual'.

Most data laws and regulations, however, consider the individual, rather than the relational and population-level characteristics of data, as well as individual harms. They thus reduce the problem of datafication to individual effects and propose individualist remedies which are not well suited to address the impacts of population-oriented data collection and analysis. Digital privacy law may serve as a particular case in point that contemplates individual data harms but is not designed for addressing the relational effects of data. Proposals to advance individual ownership and commercialization of personal data by allowing citizens to sell and trade 'their' data as part of the broader data economy (Lanier 2013) do not address this problem either. As Viljoen (2020) notes, the structural flaw of data individualism concerns not just existing data law but most efforts of policy reform. Those current debates 'center on how to secure greater data subject control, more robust protections for data subject dignity, or better legal expressions of data subject autonomy' (Viljoen 2020, p. 9). An account of data social relations, on the other hand, would focus 'on how to balance the overlapping and at times competing interests that comprise the population-level effects of data production' (ibid.).

Institutional Responses: Data Stewardship

In the current data environment, the individual user is confronted by the data collection and analysis interests of the major powers of the state and the digital economy. Strengthening the data subject by reasserting their individual control over personal data as well as the terms of their datafication may alleviate some of the harms which they are currently facing and may reduce some of the power imbalances that characterize current data interactions. However, it is unlikely to resolve these problems as even the theoretical but impractical concept of a fully informed user will be structurally disadvantaged in comparison with corporate and governmental institutions with their vast resources and data-related capabilities. Further, as noted above, an individual approach to data is not able to address the relational aspects that generate value and constitute the core of contemporary forms of data-driven governance. If that is so, it will not be sufficient to empower individuals in handling their data and confronting major data collectors. In order to properly address the relational and collective characteristics of data, as well as the power imbalances in the process of datafication, policy approaches may need to consider alternative institutional arrangements in governing data and its various implications. What is needed, then, are institutional responses that constitute 'far more collective, democratic modes of ordering this productive activity' (Viljoen 2020, p. 4).

A variety of different models, concepts and proposals have emerged that offer collective and institutional responses which mediate the relation between the individual data subject and powerful actors collecting and processing data. Data trusts – perhaps the most prominent model – are inspired by the idea of fiduciary and charitable trusts (Winickoff & Winickoff 2003). They are based on the private administration of data about many data subjects, with the goal of enforcing and strengthening the latter's rights. Data trusts might use, process and share data if that is in the interest of the data subject and properly governed to ensure accountability. An ethical and trustworthy foundation regarding the benefits, accountability, oversight and sanctions is thus crucial (O'Hara 2019). While decisions about data use are delegated to the fiduciary, individuals can extend or withdraw their support and involvement. Different forms of stewardship have been proposed, ranging from independent non-governmental institutions to statutory bodies operating independently of government and to sector-specific data trusts (Mulgan & Straub 2019; The Royal Society 2017). From a data justice perspective, the model of data cooperatives may be particularly interesting as their governance and ownership structures are most explicitly grounded in the participation of members (and, thus, data subjects), allowing for democratic decision-making and an immediate connection with the collective interests of members (Ada Lovelace Institute 2021). Yet all the different iterations of data trusts share the importance of constituting an intermediary between data providers (the citizen) and the major data processors of the digital economy and the state.

However, they also express an ambition of combining the protection of data subjects from data harms with the goal of maximizing the social benefits that population-level data can provide. Data trusts and cooperatives pool data by individuals or organizations for the benefit of their members and seek to curate data in the public interest. They are thus informed by an understanding of data as a public good (Morozov 2015). As such, though, they face the challenge of negotiating the trade-off between the protection of their members and the wider sharing and use of these members' data resources. How they might prioritize these often-conflicting goals will depend on their structure and objectives.

A different form of data stewardship that is increasingly the subject of data policy debate and faces this very challenge, is data localization. In a world in which the economic value of data is centralized among large (and mostly US-based) internet companies as well as the countries (mostly in the Global North) that host them, requirements for the localized storing and processing of data collected from citizens of a particular country or members of a particular community, can serve to decentralize control over data and distribute the economic benefits from data processing more evenly. As such, it can serve to alleviate unequal power relations in both the digital economy and digital geopolitics. Calls for data localization – and thus for removing the control over data from a heavily concentrated data industry – have emerged in many countries, and certain types of data are required to be localized in jurisdictions as different as Australia, Nigeria and Russia (Browman 2017). In Europe, the GDPR does not explicitly advocate for data localization, although its strict requirements limiting the transfer of personal data to non-EU countries may certainly encourage it. But a more forceful agenda of 'technological sovereignty' is emerging here, too, as part of the recent European digital strategy and AI policy debates, and it includes the goals of advancing European control and ownership of data infrastructure as well as building 'European data spaces' – sector-specific data repositories (Niklas & Dencik 2020).

In its most prominent incarnation of 'data nationalization', the concept of data localization has been criticized as a pretext for increased access by national governments to data that otherwise would be processed outside national boundaries and jurisdictions. It may advance surveillance by governments with few legal restrictions and safeguards to protect the data rights of citizens (Hintz & Brand 2019). Localization policies at municipality level, on the other hand, may offer avenues for enhancing citizen control over data without transferring further power to national governments. Experiments in cities such as Barcelona and Amsterdam have advanced the benefits of decentralization while reducing the risk of data-based harms that may emerge from concentrating data-processing power at state level.

Such developments approach a form a community ownership of data that considers the collective nature of data while recognizing the need to protect vulnerable communities from data exploitation and discrimination. The concept of indigenous data sovereignty has been a prime example for this approach. Based on the need to both preserve and develop their cultural heritage, traditional knowledge and traditional cultural expressions, indigenous communities have formulated programmes for the right to maintain, control, protect and develop their intellectual property over these and, more broadly, over data that is collected about them (Kukutai & Taylor 2016).

The approaches outlined here differ according to their scope and thus their focus on either specific communities or the wider public. Some conceive citizen data as a public resource (or infrastructure), while others emphasize its role for citizen and community empowerment. However, they all seek to advance public goals, as opposed to private profit, and advocate for public governance rather than private, commercial or individual control. They offer avenues for developing institutional responses to represent both the collective dimension of data and the social benefits of population-level data, and they allow citizens to meaningfully determine what data is collected and how it is used. In providing people with a voice in decision-making over data and the collective interests that accumulate over data production and processing, they constitute forms of democratic governance and lead to what Viljoen (2020) has described as 'data as democratic medium'.

Discourses, Norms and Interests

Whether these kinds of institutional developments are initiated, how they are implemented, and which legislative and regulatory trends prevail depends, not least, on the social forces that advocate for particular options and shape the discursive environment in which policies emerge. As media scholar Des Freedman reminds us, communication systems are 'purposefully created, their characters shaped by competing political interests that seek to inscribe their own values and objectives', which means that policy debates are 'an arena in which different political preferences are celebrated, contested, or compromised' and a 'battleground in which contrasting political positions fight for material advantage [...] and for ideological legitimation' (Freedman 2008, p. 3). In order to understand how policy is constructed, we therefore need to interrogate who seeks to influence policy processes, what capacities they have to affect the policy debate, what their interests are, and by what predominant ideas and ideologies these interests are informed.

Returning to one of the cases that we explored earlier – the UK Investigatory Powers Act – we can observe an assemblage of actors and interests that all tried to pull the development of a new law in different directions. Mobilized by the Snowden revelations, civil society organizations and campaign groups exerted significant pressure by organizing public debates, lobbying legislators and expanding their membership. A coalition – Don't Spy On Us – combined this advocacy work towards a common campaign. Having previously been shut out of debates on national security, the post-Snowden era allowed them to contribute their expertise and perspectives to the considerations over the new law, and they managed to occupy a significant discursive space (Hintz & Brown 2017). In addition, internet companies were increasingly vocal in their criticism of large-scale data collection. Concerned about the implications of the Snowden revelations for user trust in their services, they focused more attention on data security and user privacy and advocated for policy reform. This introduced tensions into the relationship between governments and the corporate sector and weakened, to some extent, the powerful collusion between government and internet business (Wizner 2017).

Further, reviews by several institutional actors with relations to the UK government, such as the Independent Reviewer of Terrorism Legislation and the Royal United Services Institute criticized the existing legal framework as 'undemocratic' (Anderson 2015, p. 13) and demanded change, while at the international level, the United Nations Special Rapporteur on Freedom of Expression and Opinion condemned pervasive data collection (Kaye 2015). Moreover, frequent interventions of courts demonstrated the role that judicial systems and court decisions have played in policy reform. Campaign organizations such as Privacy International, Liberty and Amnesty International, successfully challenged British surveillance practices at the Investigatory Powers Tribunal (IPT) and the European Court of Human Rights and, in some cases, were successful. Court decisions regarding the illegality of previous forms of state surveillance were instrumental in requiring policy change that led to the development of the IP Act.

While all these efforts impacted the new law, an alliance of the UK government, particularly the Home Office, which was responsible for its development, and security agencies managed to steer the IP Act towards an expansion, rather than a reduction, of surveillance capacities. Existing connections and close access to policy-makers proved to be vital, and the counter-narrative provided by these actors resonated with the public or, at least, neutralized public concerns over undue state surveillance (Hintz & Brown 2017). At a time when public debate was dominated by terrorist attacks and security anxieties had superseded the surveillance concerns raised by Snowden, the alleged need for strengthening security agencies in order to enhance public safety proved to be a successful argument. It was underpinned by strong public relations efforts by leading government representatives and intelligence agencies – for example, GCHQ Director Robert Hannigan calling social media networks 'terrorists' command and control networks of choice' (Hannigan 2014) – as well as a dominant media narrative that dismissed the revelations about extensive surveillance and supported the government line (Wahl-Jorgensen, Bennett, & Taylor 2017).

This example shows us how data policy is often embedded in a discursive struggle between a variety of stakeholders. Civil society campaigns and digital rights advocacy were largely unsuccessful in this case, but other instances of digital policy development have demonstrated that they can have a decisive influence (for example, in defeats of restrictive intellectual property legislation and in campaigns for net neutrality, see Sell 2013). Normative claims lie at the core of these efforts. As the debate around the IP Act demonstrated, dominant sectors of the state successfully established 'security' (or rather, a specific understanding of national security) as a prominent benchmark which came to dominate norms of citizen rights and people's control over data. The latter, meanwhile, formed the context of the GDPR and this narrative proved convincing despite strong industry efforts to water down the regulation. Business interests have used 'innovation' as the frame for guiding data policy and arguing for reduced restrictions to data uses, and this approach has resonated with government and has underpinned efforts against restrictive rules on data collection (Hintz & Brand 2019).

In this context, 'data ethics' has emerged as a prominent normative approach to guide datafication and frame data use in both public institutions and the private sector. While it picks up concerns over citizen protection and data harms and proposes, as a result, the responsible treatment of data, its underlying premise is that data collection as such is justifiable or even required, and it offers an alternative to legislative restrictions, which resonates strongly with the proponents of 'security' and 'innovation' norms (Wagner 2018). Unsurprisingly, data ethics frameworks have been popular among scholarly, business-oriented and governmental debates and have informed the development of new institutions, such as the UK Centre for Data Ethics and Innovation, whose task is to develop norms and guidelines on data use.

Discourses around ethics have been particularly prominent in the emergence of AI policy and have been accompanied by the notion of trust. In EU policy documents on AI, the goal of developing strong AI industries is often accompanied with the need to secure the trust and confidence of citizens in the use of AI applications. Concerns around ethical and human-centric approaches to technology thus become an integral part of strategies of innovation and industry development. They are consistently highlighted (see Niklas & Dencik 2020) but subsumed under the primacy of industrial policy and presented (although not always explicitly) as a necessary step towards business growth and AI deployment. The case of AI, moreover, is particularly interesting as it brings together not just industrial and ethical goals but also geopolitical strategies. AI has become a primary battlefield of global competition between the US and China, and EU policy aims at joining these major powers in creating successful AI-based economies. While ethical concerns and social justice-oriented development may enter this struggle as factors of competitive advantage, their role as fundamental policy objectives is limited.

We should note, moreover, that a social justice agenda does not necessarily encompass an agreed catalogue of measures and goals but is itself affected by competing approaches. As noted above, the individual user remains the dominant focus of data protection efforts and the underlying norms include individual privacy, non-discrimination and transparency. Much less attention has been assigned to social and economic rights, such as the right to work, social security, healthcare or education, even though they are at the core of societal tensions surrounding developments in datafied governance and AI (Alston 2019). While they feature prominently in some debates on technological development, they rarely guide policy development or policy reform agendas where individual freedoms offer a less controversial focus that does not challenge core interests of the digital business sector.

Overall, these multiple considerations of goals and principles point us to the significance of the normative context of data policy. Non-binding normative and discursive frameworks can guide the development of legislation and provide an important environment for a debate on what should, and should not, be done. They affect the range and legitimacy of available regulatory options. Data justice considerations constitute a growing discourse but compete with other understandings of policy needs and goals. The protection of citizens and the enhancement of their control over data have become strong narratives, as the GDPR and other policy initiatives have demonstrated, but they still need to assert their place against goals of national security and economic innova-tion. In contemporary debates over datafication, these different objectives struggle for prominence, and a clear primary benchmark has not necessarily emerged.

What these normative struggles reiterate, moreover, is that datafication is not neutral. It is closely connected with competing interests by different societal sectors. As previous chapters in this book have shown, it can lead to business opportunities, a redistribution of wealth and economic inequality, as well as to discrimination, domination and punish-ment. Competing narratives about policy needs are underpinned by material interests and by struggles over social justice that predate the datafied society.

Conclusion: Towards Data Justice Policy

Current data policy developments construct a contradictory picture. On the one side, the collection of data by both commercial and state actors and data-sharing across different institutions and agencies are expanding. Laws like the IP Act allow for a wide range of surveillance and interception methods, and there is little appetite among policy-makers for restrictions to the collection of personal and behavioural data. Some necessary limita-tions are increasingly recognized but they mainly concern the use of data through data protection rules and normative data ethics frameworks. The debate on ethical data use and on citizen protection through GDPR-type rules may thus turn attention away from the questions on, and risks of, excessive data collection. As the UK example demon-strates, efforts to strengthen data protection and expand citizen control over data can exist alongside intensified data exploitation.

On the other hand, the increased attention towards the need for protecting citizens against data harms and advancing control by citizens over data cannot be dismissed. Fuelled by data-related scandals, such as the Snowden revelations and the Cambridge Analytica case, there is growing recognition that datafication requires regulatory limi-tations. The most prominent component of this is the empowerment of the citizen to take informed decisions in a datafied environment. The GDPR seeks to enhance citi-zens' active role in different ways, from the right of access to personal data and to data portability to new consent requirements and a right to explanation. These mechanisms are complemented by restrictions to the exploitation of people's data, including the principle of purpose limitation, restrictions to profiling and limitations to automated decision-making.

From a data justice perspective, these principles and rules offer useful starting-points. At their core, they point to the need for citizen-centric regulatory frameworks and focus on the question of where control lies regarding the data that is collected from and about citizens. Does it rest with the citizen, or with platforms and other internet companies, or with government institutions?

However, as we have seen, a regulatory framework that centres on the construct of the 'informed user' is deeply flawed and will encounter severe limitations. Further, a focus on individual rights, capabilities and protections does not account for the collective and relational dimension of data. Data policy therefore requires a reconceptualization from securing individual rights to recognizing and institutionalizing collective ordering. From data localization policies to data trusts and data cooperatives, new concepts and institutions for organizing data are being shaped and imagined. From a data justice perspective, such a collective response to datafication is essential, not just to effectively address data harms, but to democratize approaches to dealing with the challenges of the datafied society and to address the power imbalances that characterize it.

Finally, the development of data justice policy cannot be separated from the need for a supportive normative and discursive environment. Even the increasingly acknowledged principles of citizens' rights and control continue to compete with dominant normative frames of 'security' and 'innovation' and are struggling, often enough, to assert their place in the context of relevant ideas that inform policy-making. Collective approaches to datafication have hardly been noticed yet in policy debate. Data policy, thus, is a discursive endeavour as much as a legal.

7

DATA AND MOVEMENTS

By Emiliano Treré

An NGO creates a map of people affected by COVID-19 to reflect the needs of marginalized people who are not covered by official statistics. A social movement orchestrates a protest on Twitter where several accounts use the same hashtag simultaneously to get it to trend. An organization launches a campaign to ban the deployment of facial recognition technologies in a specific sector. These are all examples of activists' engagement with data and algorithms to pursue social and political change, often referred to as data activism. This chapter explores how social movements and civil society organizations appropriate data to enhance social justice. It illuminates the forms of agency and social change that are being imagined and enacted in the datafied society, arguing that data activism represents a key component of data justice. The chapter starts by defining the meanings of data agency and data politics. Then, it explores the mutual shaping between data and movements through the concepts of ecologies, infrastructures and imaginaries. Through key examples of activists' appropriation of data and algorithms to enhance social justice (counter-data action and algorithmic activism/politics), it subsequently zooms in on the dynamics, opportunities and challenges of data activism. In the current struggle around data, this chapter demonstrates that activists are contributing not only to reorient the course of datafication, but also to challenge the inevitability of its application at a more structural level.

Social Movements, Data Agency and Politics

As contemporary thinkers have stressed – and as this book extensively illustrates – data and algorithms are profoundly reshaping social relations and politics, and the power that digital platforms and data systems exercise is rapidly becoming more pervasive and threatening. Harvard professor Shoshana Zuboff (2019) argues that data collection and the deployment of predictive algorithms by tech industry corporations represent a means of behavioural modification that can render human behaviour not only completely predictable and manageable, but also automated through a 'digital order that thrives within things and bodies, transforming volition into reinforcement and action into conditioned response' (Zuboff 2019, p. 378). Yet, the focus on the increasingly central role of data and algorithms feeding commercial platforms should not prevent us from recognizing that data always represents a contested, shifting terrain of conflicting powers, negotiations and interpretations. We should thus resist the tendency to reassert 'monolithic accounts of power that tend to downplay or exclude audiences and the significance of the lifeworld' (Livingstone 2019, p. 171). Critically addressing the immense economic, social and political power exercised by tech companies should thus be accompanied by the exploration of which forms of agency, resistance and social change are possible in the age of datafication. As communication scholars Velkova and Kaun (2021) have remarked, people are not merely passive victims of algorithmic power, as some contemporary accounts tend to portray them.

Collective behaviour and social movements are two of the most powerful forces that drive social change. Protest movements have, throughout history, influenced major societal, cultural and political shifts. Recognizing their role and understanding their dynamics is thus key to illuminating how data is envisioned and enacted in the struggle for a more just society. Its role is especially important in the face of rising inequality, injustice and in the context of the environmental crisis that we are currently experiencing. Furthermore, social movements are central to our understanding of technological experimentation and innovation. Throughout history, activists have demonstrated how to appropriate technologies in ways that differ from the intentions of their creators and fulfil their social justice objectives. With their creativity and limited resources, they have also been at the forefront of the creation of independent media infrastructure for the dissemination of alternative content (Barranquero & Treré 2021). At the same time, they have constituted privileged environments for the development and diffusion of counter-hegemonic social imaginaries. Protest movements constitute spaces where different ways of thinking about democracy, equality and justice emerge and where radical ways of using technology are envisioned, experimented with and enacted. It is therefore pivotal to reflect on the ways in which movements appropriate data and react to datafication. Contemporary social movements and activist formations show us that social actors are able to resist, subvert, repurpose data and algorithms to envision alternative social imaginaries and foster different objectives around data, seeking to build a more just society. But the fact that data and algorithms are mobilized for social justice constitutes only one aspect of the ongoing struggle around the datafication of society. The engagement with data to enhance social justice often does little to actually challenge the premise of datafication (Hintz, Dencik, & Wahl-Jorgensen 2019). Hence, this chapter will address the use of data by social movements as both *repertoires* and *stakes* (Beraldo & Milan 2019), showing that data activism constitutes a key component of data justice.

Reflecting on the meanings and implications of everyday experiences of datafication, critical data scholar Helen Kennedy has written that 'data activism thus requires the possibility of agency, yet there is little scope for agentic engagements with data in the visions of datafication provided in much data studies scholarship' (Kennedy 2018, p. 21). While data studies are awash with accounts portraying the dystopian consequences of data systems, the study of people's engagements, appropriations and experimentations with datafication are still rare. However, if we want to understand how data systems can be changed, repurposed, or even dismantled, we need to look at agency, intended as 'the ability of social actors to variably engage with and react to the context in which they are embedded that empowers them to change their relation to structure' (Milan 2018, p. 512). Another definition of agency will further clarify this point.

Media scholar Nick Couldry (2014, p. 891) defines it as 'the longer processes of action based on reflection, making sense of the world so as to act within it', emphasizing the centrality of reflexivity. Moving to the contested field of data, we can define data agency accordingly as the users' 'reflexive ability' to make data work to their own needs. This ability resides not only in the hands of elites, big business, governments and corporations. Protest movements, small-scale organizations and a plethora of grassroots and alternative actors can also produce, gather and analyse data in ways that enhance the agency of the public, contributing to imagine, shape and enact diverse 'data worlds'

(Gray 2018). Studies on data agency (Couldry & Powell 2014), data activism (Milan 2017) and everyday practices of 'living with data' (Kennedy 2018) converge in underlining that the analysis of top-down processes of datafication is just one side of the story. Different actors can make sense of data 'from below' and appropriate them to advance social justice and try to change the world. Datafication should thus be understood as a two-fold process of collecting, analysing and profiting from data about users while at the same time of feeding such data back, enabling them 'to orient themselves in the world' (Kennedy, Poell, & van Dijck 2015, p. 1). In this book, we have seen how data is being deployed widely for surveillance purposes by governments and corporations. Yet, community groups, small organizations and activist collectives are also leveraging the possibilities of datafication, pursuing objectives and fulfilling needs that are very different from those of 'big brother's uses of Big Data' (van Dijck 2014).

From the above reflections, it appears clear that data and algorithmic systems are battlegrounds of contrasting forces, and that data agency can be exercised from above and from below by various actors and for contrasting purposes. This is particularly true if we examine data agency in the realm of politics, exploring what Ruppert, Isin and Bigo (2017) have termed 'data politics'. As the three authors explain, 'data politics is concerned with the conditions of possibility of data that involve things [...], language [...], and people [...] that together create new worlds' (Ruppert et al. 2017, p. 1). It designates 'both the articulation of political questions about these worlds and the ways in which they provoke subjects to govern themselves and others by making rights claims' (p. 1) and is 'concerned with not only political struggles around data collection and its deployments, but how data is generative of new forms of power relations and politics at different and inter-connected scales' (p. 2). Data and politics are therefore inseparable, and data is shaping the dynamics of our very democracies in multiple ways, raising issues in relation to governance, sovereignty, freedom, autonomy and justice that we have helped to chart throughout this book.

Expanding on this definition and building on the notion of 'contentious politics' by social movement scholars Tilly and Tarrow (2015), critical data scholars Beraldo and Milan (2019) have recently introduced a differentiation between two kinds of data politics. The former, the 'institutional politics of data', refers to the top-down effects of datafication on groups and individuals. The latter, the 'contentious politics of data', denotes instead 'the bottom-up practices embodied and promoted by individuals and groups' (Beraldo & Milan 2019, p. 4). More specifically, with contentious politics of data, the two scholars refer to 'the multiplicity of bottom-up, transformative initiatives interfering with and/or hijacking dominant, top-down processes of datafication, by contesting existing power relations and narratives and/or by re-appropriating data practices and infrastructure for purposes distinct from the intended' (p. 2). Hence, contentious data politics is the realm of all those practices that envision, engage and appropriate data to enhance social justice and seeks to change our society.

Both data and algorithms can be appropriated and mobilized by social movements and collectives that can leverage the power of data to shape a more just society. As we will see in the next sections, this can be accomplished by integrating data and algorithms into the contentious repertoire of social movements and civil society actors, or through questioning the premise and the need to deploy data systems in the first place. These two interrelated aspects, it will become evident, cast data activism as a constituent element of data justice.

The Mutual Shaping between Data and Movements: Ecologies, Infrastructures, Imaginaries

When looking at the relationship between data and movements, it is key to remember that activists' engagement with data is part of broader, multifaceted activist media ecologies (Treré 2012, 2019). This means that in their protest activities, activists and civil society actors engage daily with a rich spectrum of multiple devices, formats, platforms and technologies. These media technologies can be analogue and digital, old and new, conventional and alternative. They can range from leaflets, flyers and posters to social media platforms, emails and online forums, from mobile phones and radio transmitters to wi-fi antennas and servers. Practices of data activism are inserted and intersect with activists' wider contentious repertoires. We should therefore look at them not as a replacement for other kinds of activism, but rather as a set of hybrid dynamics that often coexist and integrate more traditional forms of activism. This means that from the perspective of social movement actors and activist collectives, tactics of data activism often appear as new tools to be added to the palette of already available resources used to protest, mobilize, campaign, organize and spread information. Data activism itself should also be regarded not as a monolithic process, but rather as a continuum of practices. These practices span from counter-data actions to civic hacking, from litigations to obfuscation techniques, from algorithmic activism to the construction of radical autonomous infrastructures for activists. Data activism is a complex phenomenon that is comprised of a wide variety of actors, technologies, formats, infrastructures and tactics that vary greatly across contexts and cultures.

To map this wide variety, social movement and data scholar Stefania Milan has located activist engagements with data on a continuum between 'pro-active' and 're-active' forms of data activism. Proactive data activism mobilizes new datasets to promote social justice, whereas reactive data activism challenges algorithmic control by the state, corporations and elites (Milan 2017). The former type refers to 'projects taking advantage of the possibilities for civic engagement, advocacy, and campaigning that the datafication of social life brings about' (Beraldo & Milan 2019, p. 4). Proactive data activism comprises activists who appropriate open data to promote social justice and broaden participation in decision-making and conflict resolution processes through leveraging socially-distributed information systems (Gutiérrez, 2018). Examples cover case studies as varied as: the revision of DNA kits in relation to rape cases in the United States thanks to 'Ending the Backlog' (O'Connor 2003); the legal work of forensic organizations in the creation and managing of databases like Ciencia Forense Ciudadana and Data Cívica in Mexico (Sastre Domínguez, & Gordo López 2019); open data movements, civic hacking, hackatons and transparency initiatives (Baack 2015; Schrock 2016); the Info-Amazonia network of environmental activists promoting data transparency in the Amazonian region (Gutiérrez 2018). For some scholars, this kind of activism stretches as far as including direct participation initiatives for the citizenry through information systems and digital platforms such as LiquidFeedback, Democracia 4.0 and DemocracyOS (Sastre Domínguez, & Gordo López 2019). The latter type of data activism identified as 'reactive' refers instead to individuals and civil society organizations that resist 'the perceived threats of massive data collection, often by way of technical fixes' (Beraldo & Milan 2019, p. 4). This type of data activism reclaims agency in the face of increasing dataveillance and oppressive algorithmic control by governments and the corporate sector. Examples include: tactics of obfuscation of industrial data collection (Brunton & Nissenbaum 2011); the development of autonomous Web services, apps, tools and infrastructure that protect people's privacy and digital rights (e.g. Austistici/Inventati in Italy, Sindominio and Lorea in Spain, Riseup, etc.); the deployment of open-source software for enabling anonymous and censorship-resistant communication like TOR and Freenet; and forms of counter-data action (Currie et al. 2016; Dalton & Thatcher 2014) to contest, resignify and resist claims and understandings related to dominant datasets, including counter-mapping strategies. Beyond these helpful distinctions, scholars have also interpreted data journalism as a form of data activism (Gray & Bounegru 2019) focusing on practices of assembling data and investigating datafication. Another area that brings to the fore the importance of data activism in connection to social justice is the framework of environmental data justice (EDJ) (Vera et al. 2019) that counter 'extractive logics' sustained by the matrix of domination described by Black feminist scholar Patricia Hill Collins (1990) as the interrelated forces of white supremacy, heteropatriarchy, ableism, capitalism, settler colonialism and other forms of oppression (see also Costanza-Chock 2020).

Further, the engagement of social movements with data brings to the fore two interrelated elements that largely define contemporary digital activism: the importance of the infrastructure and the relevance of social imaginaries and visions attached to them. The first element, as clarified by Beraldo and Milan (2019), foregrounds the prominence and the productive and deeply political role of infrastructure and material arrangements. Data activism is enabled and constrained by the limitations of the data infrastructure (Gutiérrez 2018) and can leverage the production and collection of various kinds of data to confront existing power relations (Elmer, Langlois, & Redden 2015). Across history, social movements have always engaged with media infrastructure to suit their own needs and political objectives (Milan 2013). In this context, media infrastructure should be understood as 'things and also the relation between things' (Larkin 2013, p. 329), evoking 'a sense of intentional, structured, and *material* organization that is designed and implemented with a political aim and to a political effect' (Maeckelbergh 2016, p. 281, original emphasis). Through their practices, activists can either reinterpret and repurpose existing networks, artifacts and infrastructure, or they can create autonomous alternatives to communication systems and networks (Milan 2013). The former case involves the engagement with digital networks and social media which were developed with the aim of profit under capitalism but can be appropriated by movements to advance social justice and challenge the pillars of the same system from which these platforms originate (Gerbaudo 2017). The latter case comprises examples like the creation of community radios and wi-fi networks, the deployment of autonomous cell systems, independent media centres like Indymedia, or grassroots internet service providers (ISPs). These autonomous infrastructures embed different values and political understandings from those feeding corporate platforms. They are built to serve the movements that created them and respect their principles and rights.

The second element that is foregrounded by activist engagements with datafication is the relevance of social imaginaries and political visions (Barassi 2015; Treré 2019) that are ascribed to (and inscribed into) different conceptions of data activism (Lehtiniemi & Ruckenstein 2019). The construction of more just data futures hinges on our capacity to imagine ways of using data systems differently to nurture social justice and political participation. Imagination should be understood here as a social, collective and creative force that inspires and motivates action. Across history, protest movements have been pioneers in reimagining the values and the practices of society and in the art of prefiguration, that is the enactment in the present of the desired world of the future. Prefiguration is indissolubly linked to communication and carried out through the technological infrastructures and technologies that are available in a given historical context. Yet, data activism should not be merely confined to a reappropriation or reimagination of data, but should also be thought as a challenge to the premise of using data systems in the first place. To further clarify this last point, it is helpful to mobilize the useful distinction introduced by Beraldo and Milan (2019) between 'data as stakes' and 'data as repertoire'. In the former (data-oriented activism), data are the 'main stake in a hypothetical claim-making agenda' (p. 6). In the latter (data-enabled activism), they are instead incorporated within the repertoire of action of social movements and activists (Tilly 2008), 'alongside other more traditional forms of protest and civic engagement' (Beraldo & Milan 2019, p. 6). This double articulation casts data activism as a component of data justice that includes both a reorientation of datafication for the improvement of our society and the questioning of its deployment and applications.

Scholars have exposed the problematic assumptions and decisions in relation to race, gender, status, class and the various forms of oppression and discrimination that are enshrined and aggravated by these systems (see, among others, Barocas & Selbst 2016; Eubanks 2018; Hargittai 2020; Hintz, Dencik, & Wahl-Jorgensen 2019; Noble 2018; O'Neil 2016b). At the same time, a growing number of movements and organizations (Algorithm Watch, the Algorithmic Justice League, the Ada Lovelace Institute, Data for Black Lives, etc.) are focusing on data as stakes, developing forms of activism that highlight the damaging effects of platform power and the several biases that are often reproduced by data systems and the proprietary algorithms of digital platforms. This has led to a questioning of the deployment of these systems at a more structural level, contributing not only to reorient the course of datafication to fulfil social justice needs, but also to challenge the necessity and inevitability of its application.

In the next sections, we shed light on how activists are repurposing data and algorithms to fulfil their social justice objectives, analysing two central expressions of data activism. We first explore the evolution in the datafied age of practices of mobilizing statistics for social change (e.g. so-called statactivism; Bruno & Didier 2013), that is counter-data action and, more specifically, counter-mapping. Then, we focus on the expansion of the contentious repertoires of social movements (Tilly & Tarrow 2015) that are progressively engaging with algorithms in their social justice struggles.

Counter-Data Action

The notion of 'counter-data action' has been coined by critical geographers Dalton and Thatcher (2014) to refer to acts of resistance to hegemonic datasets and originates from the two scholars' work on critical geographic information systems (GIS). Drawing on their work, Currie et al. (2016) address counter-data action as an act of data appropriation in which individuals intervene to contest the truth of a dataset and build their own metrics (Currie et al. 2016, p. 4). Counter-data actions represent the most recent manifestation of what social movements scholars have traditionally called 'statactivism'. This term was coined by political scientists Bruno and Didier (2013) by merging the words *statistics* and *activism* to indicate the mobilization and creation of statistics for social change purposes. Bruno, Didier and Vitale (2014, p. 198) have explained 'the double role of statistics in representing as well as criticizing reality'. Statistics have always represented a contested terrain since statistical tools are key in 'producing a shared reading of reality' (Bruno, Didier, & Vitale 2014, p. 200). Forms of collective action across history have differently relied on numbers, variables, indicators and measurements to expose, denounce and criticize power. Counter-data action embraces a variety of actions and practices. Examples include Conroy and Scassa's critique of the data collection model for sexual assault reporting developed in Philadelphia, and their proposal of a more reliable and just model (Conroy & Scassa 2015). Another example is the hackathon analysed in Currie et al. (2016) in their study of counter-data action and civic data in Los Angeles County. Researchers, citizens and members of the community were invited to participate in this collective activity 'to identify the limits and challenges present in police officer-involved homicide data and to propose new methods for deriving meaning from these indicators and statistics' (Currie et al. 2016, p. 1). Another illustration is the counter-data action of a grassroots affordable housing advocacy group (Westside Atlanta Land Trust) in Atlanta, documented by Meng and DiSalvo (2018). As the two American scholars point out, 'the inaccuracy of the county data produced a space that WALT members were able to act within, to challenge the completeness and veracity of the county data, and then to realize and subsequently express their situated knowledge and capacity to collect data themselves' (Meng & DiSalvo 2018, p. 2).

Counter-data mapping[1] denotes a subset of counter-data action. It represents a significant form of activists' engagement with data that displays how social actors can contest forms of data marginalization and oppression by creating their own counter-maps, counterplots and subaltern data mapping. Harris and Hazen (2006, p. 115) define counter-mapping as 'any effort that fundamentally questions the assumptions or biases of cartographic conventions, that challenges predominant power effects of mapping, or that engages in mapping in ways that upset power relations'. Through counter-data mapping, activists rethink key elements involved in mapping, unveiling its underlying social and political construction. Through this process, they reveal the injustices that are concealed or magnified through the mapping process. These injustices can be attached to various elements that constitute maps, from the sources of data to the selected geographical regions and the inherent interpretations in the construction, explanation and visualization of the data (Evangelista & Firmino 2020). Data activists can imagine, envision and enact alternative counter-mapping representations, realities and outcomes.

To better understand the connection between counter-data mapping and data justice, we need to investigate the colonial legacy of mapping and consider that data collection in the form of mapping is a practice that dates back to the 15th century. This practice is connected to issues of power and domination as cartographers acted on behalf of their imperial powers to assemble data on Indigenous populations in order to extract their resources and at the same time 'reinforce their worldviews and status' (Willow 2013, p. 872). As critical media professor and activist Dorothy Kidd (2019) has shown, these dynamics have been particularly visible and intense in the context of Canada, a settler colonial state founded on extractivist economies and the dispossession of Indigenous peoples. In this context, maps were deployed during the 19th century as a disciplinary technology in the management of dispossession. Today, as Kidd demonstrates, oil and natural gas industries have perfected these cartographic practices that are still widely applied in both domestic and international operations. But at the same time, Indigenous first nations have used counter-mapping tactics as part of their complex repertoire of contention to fight against extractivist projects. To show continuities and disruptions with the past, Kidd compares the use of counter-mapping in two cycles of Indigenous resistance to oil pipelines, that is, the deployment of counter-mapping by the Dene and Inuit during the 1970s and its current use within the Unist'ot'en and Secwepemc anti-pipeline campaigns. The scholar shows that practices of Indigenous counter-mapping provide key lessons for a more comprehensive understanding of data justice. More specifically, Kidd's analysis illustrates 'how counter-mapping by itself can never be substituted for long-term political organizing' (Kidd 2019, p. 967). Furthermore, building on data activist and scholar Sasha Costanza-Chock, Kidd demonstrates how counter-data mapping strategies 'provide examples of data activism fused within larger projects of redistributive, transformative and restorative justice, which optimize their liberation and not the capitalist market' (Costanza-Chock 2018, n.p.). This example displays the need to always locate forms of data activism within a wider framework of data justice. Social movements' engagements with data are inserted within pre-existing social conditions, complex protest cultures, contention repertoires and more established ways of organizing politically. The importance of counter-maps in decolonizing geographies has been stressed beyond the case of Canada (Radcliffe 2022). For instance, in Brazil, Indigenous people are mapping by group the numbers of 'Indigenous people who have lost their relatives' (Emergencia Indigena 2020) to counter forms of data colonialism (Ricaurte 2019 – see Chapter 3). Their maps are rendering visible Indigenous people living in urban centres who are often not counted in Indigenous data by colonial structures. Other scholars have mapped social justice initiatives in Latin America to understand the repertoires of pandemic collective action (Duque Franco et al. 2020).

The COVID-19 pandemic offers a paradigmatic case for exploring the contested terrain of data mapping, shaped on the one side by the contrasting narratives of institutional data mapping by governments and the establishment, and on the other side by the contentious maps of data activists, tech collectives, social movements and communities on the ground. Governments frequently deploy data visualizations and maps that include cases, trends and fatalities to influence public behaviour. These visualizations are not exempt from issues. For instance, they are often based on non-comparable data types across countries, varied reporting criteria and timeframes, and non-normalized data mapping, leading to frequent visual misrepresentations (Kent 2020). Furthermore, computer scientists from MIT have shown that various pandemic data visualizations have contributed to fuel a vast infodemic of viral disinformation and unorthodox science relying on sophisticated data techniques (Lee et al. 2021).

In opposition to these forms of top-down mapping, data activists appropriate data to generate their own datasets, maps and visualizations to enhance social justice and enact social change. Hence, they create COVID maps to represent issues and drive creative community action. The motivations behind COVID counter-data mapping are several. Activists struggle to interrupt the dominant visual narrative of often contradictory global COVID maps. They strive to reclaim and visualize missing data from invisibilized communities and aim to offer more representative and nuanced representations from the margins (Milan & Treré 2020; Milan, Treré, & Masiero 2021). Through their counter-maps, data activists also reveal how certain areas are stigmatized and invisibilized, while others are given excessive prominence in relation to the virus. Moreover, they can invite people to submit their own maps where they represent their lockdown experiences (Bliss & Martin 2020). These maps offer crucial insight into the politics of big data, as they reframe narratives of pandemic impacts on specific, overlooked and marginalized areas and populations (Kent 2020). One clear manifestation of this aspect can be found in the series of COVID maps of China presented by Field (2020) that display the same data in different ways precisely to reveal the socio-political perspectives magnified by the decisions taken during the mapping production process.

Counter-data mapping as a form of data activism reveals how maps – and related forms of data visualization – are always socially and politically constructed. It exhibits how communities, movements and activists can reframe, rethink and reconfigure them to visually amplify the voices of the disenfranchised and the marginalized. These counter-maps can catalyse the public attention on issues of race, gender, violence and oppression. They can stimulate political intervention, change, resistance and activism, and enhance different forms of social justice.

Algorithmic Politics and Activism[2]

Data systems and algorithmic systems are entangled, and they both represent battle-grounds of contesting actors, forces and practices. Data agency and algorithmic agency are also intimately connected. As data scholar Taina Bucher (2017, p. 42) perfectly puts it, 'while algorithms certainly do things to people, people also do things to algorithms'. In recent years, academic attention has started to be oriented towards the analysis of the contexts and situations in which people 'resist, subvert and transgress against the work of algorithms, and re-purpose and re-deploy them for purposes they were not originally intended' (Kubitschko 2017, p. 26). Algorithmic politics can thus be considered as a subset of data politics that is concerned with how different groups appropriate and act upon algorithms to fulfil their political purposes (Treré & Bonini 2022, forthcoming). Paraphrasing Beraldo and Milan (2019), we can outline an 'institutional politics of algorithms', which refers to the attempts to act on algorithms undertaken from 'above' – by a state, an institution, a corporation – and a 'contentious politics of algorithms', which denotes instead all those practices initiated from 'below' – by social movements and activists. The institutional politics of algorithms include, for example, the deployment of political bots in relation to the global phenomenon of 'computational propaganda', defined by Woolley and Howard (2016, p. 4886) as 'the latest, and most ubiquitous, technical strategies to be deployed by those who wish to use information technology for social control'. Within this phenomenon, in recent years, political bots acquired a growing importance. They can be described as 'the algorithms that operate over social media, written to learn from and mimic real people so as to manipulate public opinion across a diverse range of social media and device networks' (Woolley & Howard 2016, p. 4885). They are increasingly being used across the globe to manipulate public opinion, spread propaganda, manufacture consent, artificially boost popularity and destabilize forms of progressive activism (Treré 2016).

The 'contentious politics of algorithms' refers instead to how contemporary digital activism is being progressively reshaped within algorithmically-mediated environments as Facebook, Twitter, YouTube, TikTok and Instagram. With their codes, regulations and affordances, these spaces are contributing to restructure collective action and the very conditions under which social movements operate at a profound level (Dolata 2017; Milan 2015). These platforms enable and constrain practices of digital activism in various ways and have become key actors in what German sociologist Ulrich Dolata (2017, p. 22) has termed the 'sociotechnical constitution of collective action'. This means that, on the one hand, they collect and exploit the data that users leave behind and ensure the seamless monitoring of their activities. On the other hand, their technical protocols, interface designs, default settings, features, codes and general algorithm structure have several implications for the practices of activists. In this context, the repertoires of collective action of social movements are shifting. In the datafied age, it is key for social movements to understand how algorithms work and try to use them to achieve their political aims and pursue social change and justice (Treré & Bonini 2022, forthcoming). Through understanding how algorithms constrain or enable collective action, data activists can appropriate them as 'algorithmic tacticians' (Kant 2020, p. 215), revealing the fissures of algorithmic structures that appear not as impenetrable monoliths, but rather as opportunities that can be manoeuvred to pursue social justice objectives and deploy alternative forms of resistance (Velkova & Kaun 2021).

The 'contentious politics of algorithms' is also a contested territory, with both progressive and oppressive forces struggling to leverage the opportunities offered by algorithmically-mediated landscapes. Digital media scholar Ico Maly from Tilburg University (2019a & 2019b) has used the concept of 'algorithmic activism' to tackle the rise of 'Schild & Vrienden', a recent Flemish far-right activist movement. Maly carefully analyses how 'algorithmic activists' from this movement strategically exploit the affordances of social media to reach their goals, 'boost their popularity rankings' and make their content go viral (Maly 2019b, p. 1). The manipulation or hijacking of the algorithms of social media platforms like Twitter is one of the most striking features in the practices of alt-right supporters around the world. Computer scientists Nikita Jain and colleagues (Jain, Agarwal, & Pruthi 2015) have defined 'hashtag hijacking' as a practice where hashtags are used to spread unrelated content, spam or negative sentiments to tarnish the intended motive. This became apparent during the 2016 US elections (Marwick & Lewis 2017) when alt-right groups worked collectively to get hashtags to trend through the establishment of large numbers of fake accounts. Other practices included the 'hijacking' of existing hashtags from progressive movements, such as #BlackLivesMatter. By posting messages critical of Black Lives Matter, alt-right activists diminished the ability of BLM supporters to use the hashtag to effectively connect their narratives.

A key aspect of data justice is to nurture alternative imaginaries by shedding light not only on the challenges, but also on the opportunities of such transformations. By integrating algorithms into their contentious repertoires, social movements across the world have also proven that algorithmic power can be repurposed to enhance social justice and political transformation. For example, contemporary activists can game, hijack and reappropriate these algorithms to introduce and spread alternative narratives within the media ecology. In their book #Hashtag Activism, critical communication scholars Jackson, Bailey and Welles (2020) have explored how marginalized groups use Twitter to advance counter-narratives, pre-empt political spin and build powerful networks of dissent. These scholars investigate the use and spread of hashtags such as #MeToo, #GirlsLikeUs and #BlackLivesMatter. They illustrate their power to challenge dominant understandings of gender and race, forging alliances and building strategies through storytelling. In a similar vein, in their comparative study of digital protest in Greece and Sweden, media scholars Galis and Neumayer (2016) have introduced the notion of 'cyber-material détournement'. With this notion, the two scholars refer to 'alliances and conglomerations of activists and cyber-material actors that not only perform radical politics but also reconstitute the ontologies of political participation and organisation' (Galis & Neumayer 2016, p. 4). Other authors have used the terms 'algorithmic resistance' and 'algorithmic appropriation' to address social movements' engagement with algorithms to pursue social transformation and political change through a new breed of 'hybrid media activism' (Treré 2015, 2019).

Movements can thus build alliances with algorithms to pursue their social justice objectives, demonstrating that activists are effectively integrating data and algorithms into their protest repertoire. The Mexican scenario of the last 10 years offers a relevant case in point to study these forms of activism. Since the Zapatista uprising in the 1990s, Mexico has represented an innovative laboratory of both institutional and contentious forms of digital politics. In the last decade, the country has witnessed a steep rise in forms of institutional algorithmic politics linked to propaganda and repression. Since 2010, activists and civil society organizations have frequently denounced various forms of problematic institutional algorithmic politics, including algorithmic attacks on social media linked to the criminalization of protest and segregation of dissident voices. More specifically, political strategies that rely on the appropriation of algorithms to undermine dissent through political bots have seen a great rise in the years since the 2012 national elections, up to the point where they have become one of the most crucial components of the government's political repertoire. In this scenario, forms of algorithmic activism in Mexico have often emerged to expose government's algorithmic strategies of repression, propaganda and manipulation. Mexican tech collectives, social movements and data activists are developing tactics of algorithmic activism in order to expose and try to neutralize the institutional strategies of parties and the government.

For instance, Mexican bloggers and data-mining experts, such as Alberto Escorcia, constitute a new generation of 'algorithmic activists' who have been observing and documenting the rise of bots, trolls and fake profiles in Mexico during the last decade. Escorcia publishes his analyses on his digital platform 'LoQueSigue' ('WhatFollows') (Escorcia & O'Carroll 2017). Here, he carefully dissects the institutional adoption of bots to disrupt protests, by preventing information from spreading, and to send death threats to protesters, journalists and intellectuals during several political campaigns. Relying on social network visualization tools such as Flocker and Gephi, Escorcia found ways to detect bot accounts by examining the number of connections a Twitter account has with other users. In his videos, he explains to the public the political impact of bots in Mexico, thus dispelling the opaqueness surrounding these algorithmic attacks. The activist broadcasts his analyses of hashtags, trends and data, and shares information about effective social media tactics for activists to counteract strategies of algorithmic hijacking. These tactics include the need to always post fresh content on Twitter, because the platform rewards novelty. Further, he stressed that activists must erect strong connections within their networks to show to the algorithm that these are real connections and not a set of bots. Escorcia also recommends building iterative versions of some protest-related hashtags (e.g. using numbers, such as in the case of the famous Mexican activist hashtag 'YaMeCanse' that later became 'YaMeCanse1' and 'YaMeCanse2'). This tactic is meant to avoid institutional 'bot armies' that try to drown out real conversations on Twitter using 'noise' (i.e. flooding protest hashtags with a lot of non-relevant information, usually related to pornographic or violent content that is then flagged as spam and blocked by the platform). By building iterative versions of protest-related hashtags, activists can move the conversation somewhere else and avoid the disruptions caused by institutional algorithmic strategies that try to silence, confuse and undermine data activist practices. Based in Guadalajara and affiliated with the ITESO University, since 2017 the Signa Lab has been researching and experimenting with digital methods, tools and visualization techniques to understand (and improve) the role of data and algorithms in the democratic life of contemporary Mexico. Researchers and activists at the Lab monitor and analyse digital flows of information on the Mexican platform ecosystem during key disputes and political campaigns to understand how the public discourse has been impacted by algorithmic logics that can hurt democracy. Part of the mission of the Lab is generating easy-to-read visualizations to communicate its insights to the public and expose the dangerous material implications of algorithmic politics.

The Spanish movement 15M is another interesting case in point. This movement has represented a laboratory for innovation in practices of political communication and dynamics of civic participation that contributed to reconfigure democracy itself (Flesher Fominaya 2020), radically transforming communication activism in Spain (Barbas & Postill 2017) and leading to profound socio-cultural changes (Feenstra et al. 2017). Through the tactical adoption of social media and the 'hacking/hijaking' ('hackear' in the Spanish original) of their algorithms, the movement was able to spread information, organize protests, build powerful narratives and shape both national and international journalistic coverage (Candón Mena 2013). One of the most illustrative tactics of algorithmic activism developed by Spanish activists consisted of the prearranged creation of trending topics on Twitter (Treré 2019). This tactic comprised the blended adoption of internal communication technologies and corporate social media. Tools of internal communication, such as Titanpad, were used to collectively discuss and select a list of possibly successful hashtags to build the narrative of the movement. Once a hashtag was chosen, a range of potential tweets was created accordingly and shared with other activists through a combination of various technological resources, including direct messages on Twitter, instant messaging services (WhatsApp, Telegram, Signal) and mailing lists. Various social media platforms were used to massively spread the information and reach the desired result. This tactic presupposes a deep awareness and reflective knowledge of how algorithms work. This awareness was obtained through several sequences of trial and error by activists who engaged in a constant struggle to understand how different social media algorithms operate in order to game them for their own needs. In relation to Twitter, activists formulated similar recommendations to the ones that Escorcia developed: newness and attractiveness of the hashtags; need to tweet simultaneously and avoid bots by building 'real' activist networks.

These experiences suggest that protest movements engage in tactics of algorithmic activism by leveraging the opportunities offered by social media's algorithms to various ends. First, they denounce, expose and challenge the injustices of institutional algorithmic power, reclaiming space for their own voices and narratives. Second, they do it to attract the attention of mainstream media and increase their visibility and presence in the public sphere (Maly 2019a & 2019b). Then, they do it to exercise and strengthen their 'narrative agency' (Yang 2016), that is the capacity to tell their stories and frame events and experiences in their own terms, as it is testified by global movements as diverse as #OccupyWallStreet, #BlackLivesMatter and #YoSoy132. As social movement scholar Tufekci (2017) has underlined, the strongest movements are the ones that are able to develop a 'narrative capacity', understood as the power to attract public attention and situate new issues or frames into the political debate. In the era of big data and algorithms, algorithmic activism constitutes a key tactic for the development of this capacity. Recent examples point to the flourishing of this type of data activism: the massive cheating ticket sign-ups for a Trump rally event (Lorenz, Browning, & Frenkel 2020); instances of Power-Point activism that exploit the affordances of Instagram (Nguyen 2020); the flooding by K-Pop fans of right-wing hashtags such as #whitelivesmatter and #bluelivesmatter with fan content silencing racist and aggressive voices. This new wave of algorithmic activism shows that protesters are integrating new platforms and practices into their multifaceted repertoires. Political activists are working alongside global fandoms such as K-Pop forging new activist alliances in their social justice struggles. While algorithmic activism integrates practices of hashtag activism on Twitter (Jackson et al. 2020), it comprises a wider ecosystem of platforms and tactics that go beyond the reliance on hashtags. For instance, MIT professors Kellogg, Valentine and Christin (2020) have used the term 'algoactivism' to address the individual and collective tactics of workers resisting algorithmic control. As algorithms increasingly pervade our lives, this kind of activism is becoming more mundane and has started to define the practices not only of social movements, but also of a growing number of citizens in a broader variety of social domains (Treré & Bonini 2022, forthcoming).

Finally, it should be emphasized that the integration of algorithms into the repertoires of contention of contemporary movement is not a seamless exercise, but a practice traversed by problems and frictions. For example, Danish researcher Julie Uldam (2018) has outlined how risks of state and corporate surveillance pervade these platforms and can have a negative impact on the lives of activists. Similarly, digital media scholars Etter and Albu (2021) have demonstrated that social media algorithms can have harmful consequences for protesters as they expose them – often without their knowledge – to information overload, opacity and disinformation.

Conclusion: Understanding Data Activism as a Key Component of Data Justice

This chapter has represented a journey through social movements' engagements with data and algorithms. We have investigated the mutual shaping between social movements and data, foregrounding the forms of agency and social change that are being imagined and practised in the datafied society. We have shown that studying social movements' practices is pivotal for the understanding of the foundations, challenges and the directions of data justice. Movements throughout history have influenced major societal, cultural and political shifts, and their role is especially important in the face of rising inequality, injustice and in the context of the brutal environmental crisis that we are confronting. They are also central to our understanding of technological experimentation and innovation, being at the forefront of the creation of independent media infrastructure. Protest movements represent environments where different ways of thinking about democracy, equality and justice emerge, and radical ways of using data and algorithms are envisioned and enacted. Data activism can be understood as a key part of data justice, as it draws attention to the persistent role of social movements in shaping the world we live in, even as that world is becoming more and more datafied. That is, it provides an avenue through which we can nurture alternative imaginaries and open up a discussion on current injustices and ways to overcome them, by drawing on the histories of social movements, their activist repertoires and their long trajectory of technological engagements and experimentations.

Through the evaluation of several examples of two key genres of data activism – counter-data mapping and algorithmic activism – we have reflected on the dynamics, challenges and opportunities of data engagements from below. We have disentangled the double articulation of this phenomenon (Beraldo & Milan 2019). On the one side, data activism is about reorienting datafication and using data and algorithms *as repertoire*. Hence, data activism challenges existing power relations and activates data to enhance social justice and seeks to transform our society. Contemporary social movements and activist formations resist, subvert, repurpose and reappropriate data and algorithms. They do it to envision alternative social imaginaries, foster different objectives around data, spread their narratives and amplify their voices in their quest to build a more just society. But the fact that data and algorithms are mobilized for social justice constitutes only one aspect of the ongoing struggle around the datafication of society. The engagement with data to enhance social justice often does little to challenge the premise of datafication (Hintz, Dencik, & Wahl-Jorgensen 2019). Therefore, on the other side, social movements and civil society organizations mobilize data as *stakes*, fighting against the deployment of data systems in the first place. They thus contribute not only to reorient the course of datafication to fulfil social justice needs, but also to challenge the inevitability of its application at a more structural level.

The contemporary fight around data is carried out simultaneously across these two axes: on the one side, with activists appropriating data and algorithms as part of their repertoires of contention, while on the other side denouncing the inequalities, biases, harms and violations of data systems and questioning their adoption and usefulness at a more profound level. As Dencik, Hintz and Cable (2016, p. 9) have pointed out, 'concerns with the collection, use and analysis of data need to be integrated into activists' agendas, not just to protect themselves, but also to achieve the social change they want to make'. While we have assessed plenty of examples of civil society actors that are able to effectively navigate and connect these two axes, it is key for activists and organizations across the whole spectrum of civil society – and not just the 'already converted' tech collectives and data activists – to embrace data justice as a necessary condition for their social change(s) to be achieved in an era of increasing datafication and ubiquitous algorithmic systems.

Notes

1   The research on which the 'Counter-data action' section is based has been supported by a Lakehead University SRC SSHRC Research Development Fund grant, Romeo File #1468486 (Canada), PI Sandra Jeppesen (Lakehead University) and Co-I Emiliano Treré (Cardiff University).
2   The reflections developed in the 'Algorithmic politics and activism' subsection are partly based on the AlgoRes Project, co-led by Emiliano Treré at Cardiff University (UK) and Tiziano Bonini at the University of Siena (Italy).

8
DATA AND SOCIAL JUSTICE

By Lina Dencik

As we have seen throughout this book, the increasing turn to data-driven technologies across areas of social life is part of reconfiguring not only how we might access resources and services to meet our basic needs, but perhaps more fundamentally how we come to understand the social world, how we relate to it and what matters in it. Data infrastructures not only extend and shift power dynamics in capitalism, governance and civil society, but also assert realities and visions of social order. In this sense, an engagement with data justice is as much an engagement with what Nancy Fraser (2008) refers to as the 'grammar of justice', a struggle over the what, who and how of justice, as it is an engagement with advancing just outcomes in a datafied world. A concern with data justice needs to consider not only how social justice can be advanced in relation to datafication, but also how data processes come to construct and define the very terms of social justice. That is, the ways in which we come to understand the parameters for the pursuit of rights, equality, well-being and human flourishing in a datafied society.

Although it is clear that how we make sense of the social world is central for how we also make claims about it, systems of communication, media and information infrastructures have tended to be neglected in prevalent theories of justice, often in favour of a focus on political institutions and moral ethics (Bruhn Jensen 2021). While such a focus continues to be important for ideas of justice, the nature of institutions and the parameters for moral ethics are increasingly bound up with information and communication systems. As we have seen throughout this book, the digitalization and datafication of not only communication, but social life more broadly, is increasingly key for understanding the distribution of goods, social stratifications, treatment and life-chances. The use of data for capital, control, capture and contestation requires a decidedly political engagement with datafication that takes heed of both the conditions that enable it and the power it yields. To speak of data justice is thus to recognize not only how data, its collection and use increasingly impacts on society, but also that the current constellation of datafication advances a normative vision of how social issues should be understood and resolved. That is, data is both a matter *in* and *of* justice; it embodies not only processes and outcomes of (in)justice, but also its own justifications.

In this final chapter, therefore, we take stock of the range of developments and issues we have outlined in this book and consider what they mean for social justice. Importantly, we come to this question not as philosophers, but draw on longer-standing traditions that have sought to situate and mobilize around media, information and communication technologies in social justice debates. In doing so, we engage with justice not as a stable and universalist concept, but rather, as has been a key theme of this book, one that needs to be grounded in the actual practices and lived experiences of datafication. This approach, we argue, allows us to centre data justice debates around the concerns of those most impacted, often with the least means to be heard, and privileges the historical and social context within which datafication has emerged and plays out. We therefore start the chapter by briefly tracing some of the existing debates on the intersection of justice with information, communication and media that serve as a foundation for more recent discussions on data justice. Building on these, we go on to make the case for thinking about justice beyond what political theorist Iris Marion Young (2011) refers to as the 'distribution paradigm' and instead see datafication through the lens of 'abnormal justice' (Fraser 2008) that focuses on the very conditions that underpin how justice is understood, debated and advanced. Using this approach, we can then consider the crucial question as to what data justice means in terms of political and social mobilization. Data justice is not only an engagement with what is at stake with datafication, but also the struggle over what might be appropriate responses. In particular, we consider data justice to garner meaning alongside and as part of theories and movements of social justice that attend to underlying power dynamics and conditions for social change. It is in this vein that we see debates on data justice as valuable for understanding and advancing social justice today.

Information, Communication and Media Justice

Justice concerns have often been embedded in many analyses of information infrastructures and processes of communication. Yet while information and communication has been largely overlooked in much political philosophy on justice, communication scholar Bruhn Jensen (2021) contends that the field of contemporary communication studies has also tended to shy away from normative assertions of what is good or just. Where such considerations have been foregrounded have been in the exploration of the institutional conditions of communication that have examined mass media's potential for supporting public deliberation and debate, alongside research into the contextual practices of communication that has had an orientation towards intergroup and intercultural relations. What has been less prominent has been the engagement with communication as constitutive of and substantiated through justice, as a condition for enacting different visions of how society is and should be organized. Yet as societies have become increasingly informationalized (Castells 1996), there has been a growing focus on conceptualizing the place of information and communication technologies in both procedural and substantive ideals of justice.

A prominent approach to understanding the role of information and communication technologies (ICTs) in justice comes from information studies, which has sought to consider information as a resource or a good that needs to be subject to procedures that determine its fair distribution in society (Hoffmann 2017). Such an understanding particularly aligns with John Rawls' conception of 'justice as fairness' (1971), which extends ideas of the social contract to a more generalized and abstracted level as a theory of justice. For Rawls, principles of justice do not rest on any particular conception of virtue, but rather on each person's freedom to choose his or her own conception of the good life (Sandel 2010). His concern is with the task of creating a just institutional framework within which individuals may live as they please (Cohen 2008). As information studies scholar Anna Lauren Hoffmann (2017, p. 1602) outlines, within the basic structure of contemporary liberal democratic societies, Rawls intends his principles of justice as applying to the 'basic institutions', including a constitution and the system of government it defines, systems of property for regulating the use of goods, and economic markets for distributing productive resources.

Hoffmann (2017) provides an overview that demonstrates a range of different uses of Rawls' work as it applies to information studies. A particularly important aspect is the application of Rawls to accounts of information justice that seeks to develop a systematic account of the just distribution of informational goods (Britz 2008; Drahos 1996; Hoffmann 2017, pp. 1607–1608; van den Hoven & Rooksby 2008). On this reading, 'information should count as a primary good because it is integral to rational life planning and for furthering human interests in an informational – or post-industrial – society' (Hoffmann 2017, p. 1611). This finds expression in the articulation of rights of access to information that sit alongside other basic liberties. At the same time, information holds economic value that makes it subject to specific property rights arrangements that, following Rawls, should favour the most disadvantaged. We see this, for example, in disputes over intellectual property claims and efforts towards more democratic information markets. As we have outlined in Chapter 6, this understanding continues to constitute an important part of policy debate, also in relation to data.

The emphasis on the distribution of goods and assertion of rights has extended across information, communication and media studies. Beyond justice implications in terms of individual rights to information and to freedom of thought, expression and association, understanding media and communication systems as social goods has positioned them as something that requires regulation beyond the market and that needs protection from private interests. Rawls' framework of fairness has been less prominent in these debates despite his references to publicity, deliberation and reasoning that indicate an implicit, if not explicit, concern with communicative processes and their role in procedural and substantive justice. Instead, as Bruhn Jensen (2021) argues, it has been interventions made by Jürgen Habermas, including directly in relation to Rawls' theory of justice, that have dominated normative debates on the nature of media and communication systems. In particular, Habermas' concern with transformations in the public sphere and his concepts of communicative reason and action have provided much impetus for assertions on the role of communication in processes and outcomes of justice and how media should be organized. By attaching media institutions to an ideal of the public sphere, Habermas' work has helped pave a path for media scholars to situate studies of media systems in relation to normative concerns with democracy and freedom. Moreover, in privileging communication in terms of reason and action, Habermas has advanced an understanding of ethics centred on conditions of communication as central to justice. Not only do structures of communication enact ethics, but processes of communication also serve as the basis for achieving consensus on just outcomes (Fenton & Downey 2003).

Of course, both Rawls' and Habermas' ideas have been the subject of much critique, not least in their engagement with principles and ideals that do little to account for actual, existing conditions of injustice and that can explain the terms by which such principles and ideals might be realized. Indeed, in more recent debates on justice, also in relation to information, communication and media technologies, there has been a decided shift in focus away from abstract ideals of justice. This has, not least, come to the fore in contemporary debates on universalist applications of justice as discussed in Chapter 3. Instead, drawing especially on the work of economist and philosopher Armatya Sen, discussions have emphasized actual conditions of injustice and their structural dynamics. For Sen (2009), a theory of justice that can serve as the basis of 'practical reasoning' must include ways of judging how to reduce injustice and advance justice, rather than aiming only at the characterization of perfectly just societies. Here, the focus on actual lives in the assessment of justice informs the nature and reach of the idea of justice.

In the field of media and communication studies, this has found notable expression in the use of Sen's 'capability' approach, which understands justice in terms of human lives and the freedoms that the persons can respectively exercise. This approach contends that preferences are not naturally occurring but are themselves socially formed; people start out from different bodily and other resources and so have different needs, and may need different resources to actually achieve their preferences or may just choose different functionings (Moss 2017). With regards to communication research, media scholar Nick Couldry (2019) argues that Sen's insistence on the diversity of value, understood as pluralist rather than relativist, is particularly attractive as it rejects the kind of false universalism referred to above. Moreover, a capabilities approach as advanced by Sen, Couldry argues, invites reflections on what functionings might be valued in media and communications (such as not being misrepresented, having opportunities of voice, or attributions of recognition), and the complexity of such functionings with the accelerated development of new information infrastructures.

A central contribution from Sen, therefore, has been to shift the focus away from the 'distribution paradigm' in ideas of justice and to consider more the structural dynamics of social (in)justice in shaping what choices people can and want to make about their lives (Young 2011). Feminist and critical theorist Nancy Fraser (2005), similarly, has sought to broaden the lens through which we might understand justice beyond the distribution of primary goods, most notably by situating economic dynamics of (mis) distribution alongside cultural dynamics of (mis)recognition and political dynamics of (mis)representation. In doing so, Fraser privileges an engagement with justice that shifts the axes through which 'participatory parity' might be pursued. This approach has been particularly prominent in discussions on media justice that have emphasized a need to go beyond the focus on individual rights in policy debates to engage more explicitly with media as power, a theme we have highlighted throughout this book. That is, an engagement with media that houses a reframing of 'the relationship of disenfranchised communities to political power' (Malkia Cyril at the 2007 Southeast Media Justice Conference in Knoxville Tennessee quoted in Gregg 2011, p. 92). This vision of media justice has entailed the bringing together of media reform advocates and social justice activists as a way to situate media in relation to racial, economic and gender justice to create a framework for fundamental media and social change. In this sense, media needs to be seen as an essential component of social justice, not as an end in itself but as part of the conditions within which justice can be pursued and achieved. In the words of social justice activist Malkia Cyril: 'Media is not the issue. Justice is the issue. Media is the infrastructure for how we communicate about the issue of justice' (quoted in Gregg 2011, p. 92).

Datafication and Abnormal Justice

The longer-standing traditions that have engaged with information, communication and media justice are important for understanding more recent debates on data justice. In several respects, as we have outlined through our engagement with different aspects of datafication in this book, a concern with data justice extends these discussions and builds on them as information infrastructures have become digitized and datafied. Much focus, for example, as we've discussed in earlier chapters, has been on data as a resource or a good of economic value that should be subject to property rights arrangements and market regulation. In addition, as we have seen, the growing reliance on data infrastructures for decision-making has raised pressing concerns about the possibility for deliberation, public reasoning and preference-formation. Moreover, it has extended critical questions about how we come to understand the social world and the possibilities available to us within it. That is, as activities and behaviours are turned into data-points used to assess, evaluate and process outcomes, the terms upon which we not only access basic needs, but come to reason about value, attribute and receive recognition, and participate in processes that govern our lives are put into question. To speak of data justice, therefore, is to take account of the continuities of the social justice implications of our information infrastructures, but also their increased complexity and power dynamics.

To make sense of this complexity and how datafication disrupts assumptions about justice, we can draw on Nancy Fraser's (2008) pertinent concept of 'abnormal justice' (cf. Dencik, Jansen, & Metcalfe 2018). With 'abnormal justice', Fraser advances a theory of justice that shifts our attention away from the discussion on how goods should be distributed in a just society, and instead towards the very conditions that underpin how justice is understood, debated and advanced. Reflecting on the advent of a globalizing world, Fraser (2008, p. 395) contends that 'not only substantive questions, but also the grammar of justice itself, are up for grabs'. She goes on to outline this in terms of three different 'nodes' of abnormality: (1) the 'what' of justice (the ontology); (2) the 'who' of justice (the scope); and (3) the 'how' of justice (the procedure). Using this framework, we can consider how datafication intersects these different nodes of abnormality. How datafication, in other words, disrupts the very grammar of justice (noting, as does Fraser, that abnormality has tended to be the rule rather than the exception in wordly state of affairs).

Disruption is meant in a dual sense here: how general justice claims are destabilized by datafication and how the particularities of justice about data are up for grabs. For example, as datafication asserts what counts as social knowledge, questions about the ontology of justice are unearthed. Couldry (2019) has argued that in a context of datafication the very terms upon which we come to reason about values are transforming as choice is automated and regulated by what legal scholar Karen Yeung (2017) describes as the 'hypernudge'. That is, the datafied environments we inhabit increasingly shape our understanding of what 'counts' as social knowledge, and how issues and solutions should be understood and approached. At the same time, as we have seen in previous chapters, the ontology of justice claims about data itself are not clearly defined as a question of goods, resources or property, and struggle to account for the nature of data flows and the inherent social nature of how data is generated and attributed meaning. As we have discussed in this book, data has meaning in relational terms, and circulates within a complex web of possible insights that limits the possibilities to concretize its value. We might have to ask, then, about the meaning of the 'what' of data justice.

Similarly, in thinking about the 'who' of justice, Fraser outlines a dislocation between the loci of decision-making and the subject of justice in a given matter. Assumptions about a bounded polity as the appropriate scope of justice have been significantly undermined, not least with globalization as activities and decisions in one part of the world significantly impact on those in another. As we have seen in previous chapters, this dislocation has only become more entrenched with the advent of datafication as the asymmetry between data classes creates new forms of dislocation between the data subject and processes of governance. Chapters 2 and 5 highlighted how both forms of governance and citizenship are mediated through the processing of data, often with little regard to how this may or may not correspond with lived experiences in what can be considered a significant transformation of state–corporate–citizen relations. In this sense, datafication actively generates forms of subjectification on alien terms in relation to existing conditions, particularly among marginalized groups. As Fraser (2008) argues, such dislocations risk diminishing subjects' ability to make justice claims. Furthermore, as we have seen in our discussion of data and policy frameworks in Chapter 6, including the EU's General Data Protection Regulation, the anchoring of rights around an individual data subject or a constituency of several data subjects struggles to account for how data about an individual is bound up with population-level effects (Viljoen 2020). That is, how we are to understand the relationship between the individual and the collective and the scope of data justice claims.

Finally, building on Fraser's third node of abnormality, the 'how' of justice, datafication can be seen to disrupt any shared notion of the criteria or procedure by which disputes about the 'what' and 'who' should be resolved. At one level, we see this in the shifting boundaries of sovereignty we discussed in earlier chapters on capital, governance and citizenship, where we move from territorial sovereignty to what legal scholar Pasquale (2017) has described as 'functional sovereignty', in which technology companies increasingly take on governance functions previously associated with the state. Along with that, procedures for resolving disputes become obscured or displaced. How, for example, might we address discriminatory outcomes of data-driven systems? Or more generally, what become the avenues through which justice claims about infringements on rights and freedoms might be upheld as data systems increasingly shape life-chances? We see this uncertainty about the 'how' of justice play out in disputes about the role of engineers, for example, or the assertion of computational criteria for determining and ensuring 'fairness'. Others have questioned the relevance of traditional institutional avenues, such as governments or courts, to adequately uphold justice claims in a context where processes of data-driven decision-making are obscured, or unknown, even to those who design or use such technologies. At the same time, as we saw in the previous chapters, social movements and activists continue to play a key role in advancing justice in the datafied society, either in terms of subverting dominant modes of datafication or by challenging and acting on data harms, but are also faced with significant limitations in doing so. As such, insofar as social issues are posited to have either techno-legal or social solutions, the 'how' of data justice remains up for grabs.

Responding to datafication

Allowing for the ideal and practice of data justice to itself be a source of uncertainty is part of recognizing the plurality of values that stride against dataism as a universalist discourse and the drive to reduce knowledge and experience to singular outputs. As political geographer Amoore (2019) argues, although technologies such as machine learning algorithms contain within them a multiplicity of doubts, the algorithm nonetheless condenses this multiplicity to a single output with a numeric value. In this context, reasserting doubt, or rendering doubt visible, may itself be a way to confront the epistemic injustice inherent in computational reason that we have also alluded to in previous chapters. Moreover, by situating the different facets of datafication that we have outlined in this book within the framework of abnormal justice, we can think about data justice not as simply a discussion about how to manage and govern data and data infrastructures, but rather as a concern with how datafication conditions the way justice today is pursued and achieved. As media activist Malkia Cyril said, 'the issue is justice'. In this sense, data justice has to contend with the fact that asserting what is actually at stake with datafication has not yet been settled. There is, in other words, a continued *politics* of data justice.

In understanding data justice in these terms, we are also asked to consider appropriate responses to the advancement and impact of datafication that may not necessarily take technology as its starting-point in the mobilization for social justice. This would mean a different or complementary approach to many of the dominant ways in which data-driven technologies have been approached in debates on how we might respond to the challenges of datafication. As we have outlined previously, initial concerns over the mass generation and analysis of data collection, for example, tended to highlight issues of surveillance and privacy in public debates, particularly in the immediate aftermath of the Snowden leaks first published in 2013 (Hintz, Dencik, & Wahl-Jorgensen 2019). This saw the flourishing of a range of technology and policy initiatives aimed at restricting data gathering, such as the development of privacy-enhancing tools, mainstreaming the use of encryption and lobbying around anti-surveillance issues (Dencik, Hintz, & Cable 2016). In previous chapters, we have shown how these initiatives have advanced important repertoires for resistance that directly challenge the power relations of data-driven surveillance and have provided avenues for individuals to manage aspects of their digital engagement.

However, as we have also discussed, the advancement of technological self-defence as a governance frame is limited by the onus on the individual user to protect their own privacy. As Ruppert, Isin and Bigo (2017, n.p.) describe it, many accounts of data politics are premised on an ontology of 'hyper-individualism' that nurtures a suggestion that 'ultimately it is up to you to change your behaviour to protect yourself from the dark forces of the internet'. Yet in translating some of the concerns of anti-surveillance resistance into regulation, the protection of personal data has become a particularly noteworthy frame for governance, such as the EU's General Data Protection Regulation (GDPR). The premise is that individuals should be able to claim some rights with regards to information collected about their person, and that collecting such information requires some form of consent. In this sense, it privileges the individual data subject and understands the protection of personal data as distinct from, but complementary to, individual privacy. As outlined in Chapter 6, the GDPR has paved the way for engaging with data-centric technology in a broader sense, but questions remain about both its scope and enforceability.

Perhaps in part as a response, much attention and resources have been dedicated to advancing 'data ethics' and 'AI ethics' in recent years as alternative and complimentary frameworks for response. This field has engaged a range of different streams of thought and practice, some of which continue a long-standing tradition of computer ethics while changing the level of abstraction of ethical inquiries from an information-centric to a data-centric one (Floridi & Taddeo 2016). That is, the focus shifts from a concern with how to treat information as an input and output of computing to a focus on how people access, analyse and manage data in particular, not necessarily engaging any specific technology but what digital technology manipulates (Taylor & Dencik 2020). Often this has privileged concerns with the responsible handling of data that considers risks to privacy, forms of discrimination and abuse, ensuring transparency and accountability.

In translating this into practice, we have seen the proliferation of various initiatives across industry, government and civil society, framed under 'ethics', which set out different guidelines and procedures that attend to the development, handling and deployment of data-centric technologies, particularly artificial intelligence. Government initiatives such as the UK's Centre for Data Ethics and Innovation and the establishment of high-level expert groups on ethics within the EU have advanced some avenues for outlining ethical concerns in relation to technology, whereas civil society actors have turned to data ethics as a way to advance data developments 'for good' across a range of contexts. Of particular note has been the active engagement by the technology sector itself in this response, swiftly setting up associations and creating guidelines and codes for the responsible handling of technological innovation. An early offering came in the form of the Partnership on Artificial Intelligence to Benefit People and Society, which was set up by Amazon, Google, Facebook, IBM and Microsoft in 2016 as a non-profit organization to advance 'best practices and public understanding'. Most of these companies have also subsequently attempted to set up their own ethics boards, sometimes in partnership with academics, with varying degrees of success (Naughton 2019).

While a focus on data and AI ethics has foregrounded some prominent concerns about data collection and use in a way that shifts the onus of responsibility onto developers and the data controller, it is not clear that these initiatives have resulted in any real intervention. Government entities have predominantly been set up as nominal oversight bodies without any real teeth to interfere, leaving civil society actors having to levy at the abstract level of principles and rely on the goodwill of the industry to uphold them. Corporate data ethics initiatives, meanwhile, have focused on 'micro-ethics', an orientation around the individual practitioner, and an emphasis on compliance that avoids any fundamental engagement with the bottom line or premise (Taylor & Dencik 2020). In some instances, this has led to accusations of 'ethics-washing' (Wagner 2018), allowing technology companies to engage with public concerns about their activities while continuing to avoid regulation or any major challenge to the business models that sustain them. Moreover, by actively capturing the ethics space, the very players who are creating, developing and directly profiting from these technologies have also been the ones dictating the terms upon which we are to understand both the nature of problems and what might be suitable responses. Unsurprisingly, therefore, the application of ethical frameworks within the technology sector has tended to concern itself with the actual datasets or algorithms themselves, positing that the causes of harms that emerge from data systems can be traced to 'errors' or 'bias' in the design and application, causes that essentially have technological solutions, preferably through further data collection and algorithmic sophistication.

However, the growing debate surrounding ethical challenges and the bias of algorithmic processes has helped spur on an engagement with data-driven technologies as sociotechnical systems that have an impact on people's lives. As we saw in earlier chapters, some of this is evident in emerging forms of regulation on AI, for example the emphasis on 'Trustworthy AI' and a risk-based approach to minimizing harms in AI systems at the EU level (Niklas & Dencik 2020). Yet there remain concerns about the extent to which such frameworks can actually comprehensively engage with the societal implications of datafication and how they correspond to an engagement with justice. In particular, there have been calls to centre rights, and particularly human rights, more firmly within these discussions. Drawing on human rights legislation in data governance debates goes beyond issues of privacy and the protection of personal data, while providing a sturdier point of reference than abstract principles of ethics and fairness. Using international human rights as a frame in relation to data details the specificity of potential harms and opportunities by linking them to particular rights, such as the right to freedom of association or the right to a fair trial, that can apply to different parts of social life (Human Rights, Big Data and Technology Project 2020). These assertions of rights can help inform impact assessments, for example when new AI systems are being developed or deployed (Jansen 2020; Jørgensen, Bloch Veiberg, & ten Oever 2019). By relying on universal terms of reference, a human rights framework is also effective for advocacy as an internationally recognized agreement, however much this may not play out in practice. A recent court case brought forward by NGOs in the Netherlands, for example, to challenge the use of data-centric technology in the welfare sector won in part on the basis that it was considered an infringement on human rights and supported ongoing efforts by the human rights community to demand assessments of automated systems beyond the required initial data protection impact assessment (Toh 2020).

Approaching data from a human rights perspective can therefore provide an avenue for a more holistic engagement with data-driven systems that considers a broad range of rights that pertain to people's lives. However, the notion of international human rights has historically struggled to translate into successful concrete action, and is often seen to be at the whims of geopolitical concerns and international relations. Moreover, as a framework, it has traditionally centred on the individual and civil and political rights in a way that has struggled to account for collective rights and that has tended to neglect social and economic rights (Alston 2005). Moreover, in relation to a concern with justice, both ethics and human rights narrow the scope of responses by containing them within moral and individual rights-based realms. As we have argued throughout this book, there is a need for contending with the systemic features and power relations inherent in the advancement of datafication, as a cultural, political, and economic regime and vision of social order.

Mobilizing for Social Justice in an Age of Datafication

In thinking about the mobilization for social justice in an age of datafication, we draw on those earlier traditions of media justice mentioned above that explicitly sought to situate media as a social justice issue. The aim has not necessarily been to focus on media reform *per se*, but to bring together media scholars and activists and social justice scholars and activists as a way to identify synergies between the two fields and advance a better understanding of the role of media and communication in struggles for social justice (Jansen 2011). In particular, the media justice frame has sought to privilege the insights and experiences of historically marginalized communities and the long tradition of social justice activism around the world to inform media reform debates. As such, a key contribution of the media justice approach is to draw attention to what voices are heard and which concerns are foregrounded in efforts towards media and social change. It highlights how the nature of media systems is intricately linked to social justice struggles, calling for different media representations and alternative ownership and governance structures in addressing injustices. Moreover, it calls for different movements and groups, across communication rights and socio-economic rights, to unite and find common ground amongst diverse experiences.

Similarly, mobilization under a data justice frame starts with a recognition that the burdens of datafication overwhelmingly fall on resource-poor and marginalized groups in society. This is important, as it cuts through the all-too-comfortable narrative that emerged out of the emphasis on *mass* data collection, which was particularly prominent in the aftermath of the Snowden leaks, that suggests we are all equally implicated in the datafied society. Instead, as we have outlined in this book, data justice debates have to contend with the way the development, advancement and impact of datafication is contingent upon deep historical social and economic inequalities, both domestically and globally. As a starting-point, this shifts the focus of what voices need to be centred in any understanding of what is at stake and challenges the current constitution of the decision-making table on how datafication should be negotiated. As an approach, it explicitly undermines the assertion that the technology industry should be able to dictate the scope of problems and solutions, let alone that a decision on what constitutes 'fairness' should be confined to what can be computationally determined. Perhaps more contentiously, it also asserts the need to move mobilization on data beyond the domain of communication and digital rights groups.

Instead, in line with Gangadharan and Niklas's (2019) argument about the need to 'decentre' technology in data justice debates, mobilization around data justice needs to situate technology within systemic forms of oppression in which the harms that emerge from data-driven systems are articulated by those who are predominantly impacted and those who have a history of struggle against such oppression. That is, the concern with data needs to be part of an integrated social justice agenda, one in which definitions of problems and solutions may not actually be about data. As Hoffmann (2019) has argued, we cannot afford to continue to fail to address the logics that produce advantaged and disadvantaged subjects and the underlying structural conditions against which we come to understand data harms and injustice.

In taking such an approach, we are invited to turn our attention to focus on what function datafication – as infrastructure, discourse and practice – serves in different contexts, the social and political organization that enables it, and who benefits. This opens up the parameters for response. For example, rather than seeking to locate injustices relating to discrimination in predictive policing practices within the datasets upon which machine learning systems are trained or how algorithms are designed, the challenge lies instead in engaging with the actual conditions of such practices. Making 'better' working technology will do little to address the historical and structural manifestations of the unequal and discriminatory operations of law enforcement (Jansen, Sanchez-Monedero, & Dencik 2021). Similarly, making AI 'responsible' in its deployment in workplaces to manage workers will do little to address the growing encroachment on the structures and institutions through which workers have traditionally been able to exercise voice and empower themselves in the workplace (Whittaker 2021). Or, as we argued in Chapter 2, improving data quality or algorithmic design in government uses of automated systems for administering welfare will not address the way social welfare often extends surveillance and stigmatization of the 'undeserving' poor.

Rather, we see hints of a different kind of mobilization emerging, which, to return Olin Wright's (2019) notion of 'strategic logics' that we introduced in Chapter 1, seeks to dismantle the systems that underpin the power of datafication through different repertoires of action. We saw examples of this in the previous chapter that outlined the different ways in which datafication and activism intersect. Particularly noteworthy is the framing of data justice in terms of abolitionism, as articulated by groups such as the StopLAPDSpying Coalition and the Data for Black Lives initiative. Here, the call is not for more efficient technology – or an algorithmic fix to so-called bias – but rather to recognize how technology has meaning and impact in relation to the inequalities manifest in capitalist exploitation and a history of state violence. The call is to divest resources into oppressive data systems, ban surveillance technologies such as facial recognition systems, and to 'abolish big data' that is used to measure and profile people, and instead reinvest in communities to advance education, employment opportunities and better housing (Benjamin 2019; Crooks 2019).

Alongside this, growing efforts have sought to highlight the relationship between oppressive technology systems and the labour relations that sustain them. The Tech Workers Coalition, for example, has prioritized a focus on labour organizing as a way of nurturing solidarity between technologists and social justice movements. While actual unionization remains a challenge in many parts of the digital economy, such efforts have included walk-outs and workplace protests over exploitative practices and unjust technology. For instance, in 2018, Google employees successfully pushed back on the company's involvement with the military on Project Maven, an initiative to use AI to improve the surveillance capabilities of drones. The wider #TechWontBuildIt campaign has sought to mobilize further similar actions elsewhere, while groups such as NoTech-forTyrants have started to focus collective action on the technology pipeline, challenging processes of recruitment into Big Tech and the evermore entangled relationship between academia and the technology industry.

These different actions and struggles unite around a need to tackle the actual conditions that lead to experiences of injustice as they exist on the ground rather than necessarily pouring efforts into appealing to ideal formations of data and technology in contemporary society. Moreover, mobilization in this sense is nurtured through solidarity in which the aim is not simply the creation of just institutions that enact justice 'from above', but the manifestation of justice within and through social relations as they currently exist (Cohen 2008). Holding on to the possibility of solidarity in determining how society should be organized and the role of technology within it has never been more important (Fenton et al. 2020). As Gandy (2020) has argued, such political mobilization is precisely what is needed, but also what is directly under threat with the advancement of datafication. As behaviours and activities are abstracted and reduced for the purposes of optimization, people's shared experiences, and with that their political capability, are undermined as algorithmically-defined groups come to dictate the basis of social positioning. That is, the reliance on data-driven systems advances forms of domination in the vision and creation of data subjects. A call for data justice is therefore also a call for social relations through which people can identify with each other, enact agency and mobilize on their own terms.

In this sense, the condition of 'abnormal justice' that permeates data justice debates is an important starting-point for thinking about mobilization as it destabilizes entrenched assumptions about what the issues with datafication are, who they impact, and how they can be resolved. Instead, it opens up data justice as subject to continuous struggle rather than a fixed ideal that therefore requires us to think about how justice claims, as they pertain to data, are asserted, by whom and through which avenues. Moreover, it requires us to consider data issues in historical and social context that can build on how social justice has traditionally been understood and advanced, and what conditions need to be in place for such mobilization to happen. In appealing to the importance of data justice, we see the focus on this context and such conditions to be pivotal for advancing both conceptualization and practice around data justice.

Conclusion: What is Data Justice?

In this book, we have sought to explore the growing focus on data justice from a range of different perspectives that explore not only areas of key transformation as the collection and use of data becomes more widespread, but also the implications of such transformations for society and what might be possible responses. As such, we started by situating data in the context of capitalism, highlighting the need to consider data justice in relation to the systemic features of datafication and its manifestation as a political-economic regime. This focus continued with our exploration of how governments at local, national and international levels are turning to data-driven systems as a way to operationalize contemporary forms of governance, with significant implications for how we think about citizenship. Indeed, as we have argued, a concern with data justice needs to engage not only with the way the advancement of datafication extends aspects of bureaucratization and neoliberalism that have historically permeated public administration and broader regimes of governance, but also what it means for how people come to be constituted as citizens, and their ability to influence decisions that govern their lives.

Importantly, we have argued that data justice debates need to take heed of such questions in a way that overcomes the anchoring of datafication as a universalist development. Instead, data justice has to contend with both nuance and differing contexts, as well as the epistemic injustice that has shaped much of our understanding of data developments and their implications. In this sense, we reject the assertion of data justice as a universalist ideal and instead understand it as rooted in the experiences and practices of (in)justice as it is lived, and what functionings of data may or may not be valued. We have sought to further engage with such an orientation by detailing prominent understandings of data harms as a way to explore functionings of data in relation to central justice concerns, such as redistribution, representation and recognition. We see this as a key task for attributing meaning to data justice, not least as it exposes some of the fallacies of current policy frameworks that have sought to address such harms.

Indeed, the role of policy and regulation remains at the forefront in public and scholarly understandings of how justice claims pertaining to data might be upheld, perhaps particularly in the UK and Europe. This has only intensified as digital strategies and AI policy frameworks are being rapidly devised across national, regional and global governance contexts. However, as we have argued, the dominant approach to such policy responses remains rooted in individualist frameworks that are often focused on procedural safeguards that do little to address the nature of harms that a focus on data justice foregrounds. This requires an engagement with more participatory and collectivist forms of data governance that provide avenues for communities to reason about and assert values in relation to population-level effects of datafication. As we have gone on to outline, some of this engagement has emerged from social movements and activists that have sought to create arenas for contestation around data, either through subversive ways of collecting and using data or by directly confronting datafication from community perspectives. Data justice, in this context, has been expressed as an extension of long-standing traditions of media and digital activism that have paved the way for a critical engagement with what changing information infrastructures mean for advancing social justice.

It is this question that, in essence, concerns data justice debates. It is an important one as theories of justice have tended to neglect the role of information and communication technologies despite their pertinence for how we come to understand the social world and what we want it to look like. Addressing such neglect has only become more pressing as social life is increasingly intertwined with computational infrastructures that centre on the collection and processing of data. We see our focus on data justice as a way to take heed of this challenge, but doing so through our ongoing engagement with the practices and lived experiences that surround datafication as a way to inform justice claims as they pertain to data in different contexts. As such, data justice, as we approach it in this book, cannot be formulated as a list of universal principles about the collection and use of data, but should rather be grounded in the way transformations manifest in relation to ongoing historical struggles for social justice. This requires us to decentre technology in our engagement with data justice, shift the make-up of the decision-making table, and focus on the conditions within which injustices as they pertain to data and beyond are experienced and, ultimately, how they may be changed.

REFERENCES

Ada Lovelace Institute. (2021). *Exploring Legal Mechanisms for Data Stewardship*. London: Ada Lovelace Institute. Retrieved from www.adalovelaceinstitute.org/wp-content/uploads/2021/03/Legal-mechanisms-for-data-stewardship_report_Ada_AI-Council-2.pdf

Ajana, B. (2015). Augmented borders: Big data and the ethics of immigration control. *Journal of Information, Communication and Ethics in Society*, 13(1): 58–78.

Akbari, A. (2020). Follow the thing: Data: Contestations over data from the Global South. *Antipode*, 52(2): 408–429.

Albornoz, D., Reilly, K., & Flores, M. (2019). *Community-based Data Justice: A Model for Data Collection in Informal Urban Settlements*. Development Informatics Working Paper, 82.

Ali, S. M. (2016). A brief introduction to decolonial computing. *XRDS: Crossroads, The ACM Magazine for Students*, 22(4): 16–21.

Ali, S. M. (2017). Decolonizing Information Narratives: Entangled Apocalyptics, Algorithmic Racism and the Myths of History. In *Proceedings*, 1(3): article no. 50.

Alston, P. (2005). Assessing the strengths and weaknesses of the European Social Charter's Supervisory System. In G. Búrca, B. Witte & L. Ogertschnig (Eds.), *Social Rights in Europe*. Oxford: Oxford University Press.

Alston, P. (2019). *Report of the Special Rapporteur on Extreme Poverty and Human Rights. UN General Assembly, 11 October 2019*. Retrieved from https://undocs.org/A/74/493

American Civil Liberties Union. (2013, May). *Prove Yourself to Work: The 10 Big Problems with E-Verify*. New York: American Civil Liberties Union (ACLU). Retrieved from www.aclu.org/files/assets/everify_white_paper.pdf

Amnesty International UK. (2018). *Trapped in the Matrix: Secrecy, Stigma and Bias in the Met's Gangs Database*. London: Amnesty International UK.

Amoore, L. (2019). Doubt and the algorithm: On the partial accounts of machine learning. *Theory, Culture & Society*, 36(6): 147–169.

Amoore, L. (2020). *Cloud Ethics: Algorithms and Attributes of Ourselves and Others*. Durham, NC: Duke University Press.

Amrute, S. (2016). *Encoding Race, Encoding Class*. Durham, NC: Duke University Press.

Amrute, S. (2019, November 9–12). *Tech Colonialism Today* [Keynote presentation]. EPIC 2019 Conference, Providence, RI, United States. Retrieved from https://points.datasociety.net/tech-colonialism-today-9633a9cb00ad

Anderson, B. (2016). *Imagined Communities: Reflections on the Origin and Spread of Nationalism*. London: Verso.

Anderson, D. Q. C. (2015). *A Question of Trust: Report of the Investigatory Powers Review*. London: Independent Reviewer of Terrorism Legislation. Retrieved from https://terrorismlegislationreviewer.independent.gov.uk/a-question-of-trust-report-of-the-investigatory-powers-review/

Andrejevic, M. (2020). Data civics: A response to the 'ethical turn'. *Television and New Media*, 21(6): 562–567.

Aneesh, A. (2009). Global labor: Algocratic modes of organization. *Sociological Theory*, 27(4): 347–370. doi:10.1111/j.1467-9558.2009.01352.x

Angwin, J. (2014). *Dragnet Nation: A Quest for Privacy, Security, and Freedom in a World of Relentless Surveillance*. New York: Times Books.

Angwin, J., Larson, J., Kirchner, L., & Mattu, S. (2017, April 5). Minority neighborhood pay higher car insurance premiums than white areas with the same risk. *ProPublica*. Retrieved from www.propublica.org/article/minority-neighborhoods-higher-car-insurance-premiums-white-areas-same-risk

Angwin, J., Larson, J., Mattu, S., & Kirchner, L. (2016, May 23). Machine bias. *ProPublica*. Retrieved from www.propublica.org/article/machine-bias-risk-assessments-incriminal-sentencing.

Angwin, J., Mattu, S., & Larson, J. (2015, September 1). The Tiger Mom Tax: Asians are nearly twice as likely to get a higher price from Princeton Review. *ProPublica*. Retrieved from www.propublica.org/article/asians-nearly-twice-as-likely-to-get-higher-price-from-princeton-review

Aouragh, M., Gürses, S., & Rocha, J. (2015). Let's first get things done! On division of labour and techno-political practices of delegation in times of crisis. *The Fibreculture Journal*, 26: 208–235.

Arora, P. (2016). Bottom of the data pyramid: Big data and the global south. *International Journal of Communication*, 10(19): 1681–1699.

Arora, P. (2019a). *The Next Billion Users*. Cambridge, MA: Harvard University Press.

Arora, P. (2019b). Decolonizing privacy studies. *Television & New Media*, 20(4): 366–378.

Article 29 Working Party. (2016, December 13). *Guidelines on the Right to Data Portability*. Retrieved from http://ec.europa.eu/information_society/newsroom/image/document/2016-51/wp242_en_40852.pdf

Arun, C. (2019). AI and the Global South: Designing for other worlds. In D. M. Dubber, F. Pasquale & S. Das (Eds.), *The Oxford Handbook of Ethics of AI*. Oxford: Oxford University Press.

Bâ, S. M., & Higbee, W. (Eds.). (2012). *De-Westernizing Film Studies*. Abingdon: Routledge.

Baack, S. (2015). Datafication and empowerment: How the open data movement re-articulates notions of democracy, participation, and journalism. *Big Data & Society*, 2(2), 2053951715594634.

Baptiste, N. (2014, October 13). Staggering loss of black wealth due to subprime scandal continues unabated. *The American Prospect*. Retrieved from https://prospect.org/justice/staggering-loss-black-wealth-due-subprime-scandal-continues-unabated/

Barassi, V. (2015). *Activism on the Web: Everyday Struggles against Digital Capitalism*. Abingdon: Routledge.

Barassi, V. (2020a). *Child Data Citizen: How Tech Companies are Profiling Us from before Birth*. Cambridge, MA: MIT Press.

Barassi, V. (2020b). Datafied citizens in the age of coerced digital participation. *Sociological Research Online*, 24(3): 414–429.

Barbas, A., & Postill, J. (2017). Communication activism as a school of politics: Lessons from Spain's indignados movement. *Journal of Communication*, 67(5): 646–664.

Barocas, S., & Selbst, A. D. (2016). Big data's disparate impact. *Calif. L. Rev.*, *104*, 671.

Barranquero, A., & Treré, E. (2021). Comunicación alternativa y comunitaria: La conformación del campo en Europa y el diálogo con América Latina. *Chasqui. Revista Latinoamericana de Comunicación*, 1(146): 159–182.

Barwise, T. P., & Watkins, L. (2018). The evolution of digital dominance: How and why we got to GAFA. In M. Moore & D. Tambini (Eds.), *Digital Dominance: The Power of Google, Amazon, Facebook, and Apple* (pp. 21–49). New York: Oxford University Press.

Bauböck, R. (1994). *Transnational Citizenship*. London: Edward Elgar.

Beer, D. (2014). Governing through biometrics: The biopolitics of identity. *Information, Communication & Society*, 17(8): 1051–1054. doi: 10.1080/1369118X.2014.900103

Beer, D. (2019). *The Data Gaze*. London: Sage.

Bellamy, R. (2008). *Citizenship: A Very Short Introduction*. Oxford: Oxford University Press.

Benjamin, R. (2019). *Race after Technology: Abolitionist Tools for the New Jim Code*. Cambridge: Polity Press.

Bennett, L., & Segerberg, A. (2014). *The Logic of Connective Action: Digital Media and the Personalization of Contentious Politics*. Cambridge: Cambridge University Press.

Beraldo, D., & Milan, S. (2019). From data politics to the contentious politics of data. *Big Data & Society*, 6(2).

Berry, D. (2011). The computational turn: Thinking about the digital humanities. *Culture Machine*, 12: 1–22.

Berry, M. (2019). *The Media, the Public, and the Great Financial Crisis*. Cham, Switzerland: Palgrave Macmillan.

Bhambra, G. K., Medien, K., & Tilley, L. (2020). Theory for a global age: From nativism to neoliberalism and beyond, *Current Sociology*, 68(2): 137–148.

Bhargava, R., Deahl, E., Letouzé, E., Noonan, A., Sangokoya, D., & Shoup, N. (2015). *Beyond Data Literacy* [White paper]. Data-Pop Alliance White Paper Series. Harvard Humanitarian Initiative, MIT Lad and Overseas Development Institute. Retrieved from https://dam-prod.media.mit.edu/x/2016/10/20/Beyond%20Data%20 Literacy%202015.pdf

Bhatia, R. (2018). How India's welfare revolution is starving citizens. *The New Yorker*, 16 May. Retrieved from https://www.newyorker.com/news/dispatch/how-indias-welfare-revolution-is-starving-citizens

Birhane, A. (2020). Algorithmic colonization of Africa. *SCRIPTed*, 17: 389.

Bliss, L., & Martin, J. L. (2020, June 18). Coronavirus maps show how the pandemic reshaped our world and homes. *Bloomberg*. Retrieved from www.bloomberg.com/ features/2020-coronavirus-lockdown-neighborhood-maps/

Bloch-Wehba, H. (2021, June 17). Transparency's AI problem. *Knight First Amendment Institute*. Retrieved from https://knightcolumbia.org/content/transparencys-ai-problem

Bourne, C. (2019). AI cheerleaders: Public relations, neoliberalism and artificial intelligence. *Public Relations Inquiry*, 8(2): 109–125. doi:10.1177/2046147X19835250

boyd, d. (2007). Why youth (heart) social network sites: The role of networked publics in teenage social life. In D. Buckingham (Ed.), *Youth, Identity, and Digital Media* (pp. 119–142). MacArthur Foundation Series on Digital Learning. Cambridge, MA: MIT Press.

boyd, d., & Crawford, K. (2012). Critical questions for big data. *Information, Communication & Society*, 15(5): 662–679.

Britz, J. J. (2008). Making the global information society good: A social justice perspective on the ethical dimensions of the global information society. *Journal of the American Society for Information Science and Technology*, 59: 1171–1183.

Browman, C. (2017, January 6). Data localization laws: an emerging global trend. *Jurist: Legal News and Commentary*. Retrieved from www.jurist.org/commentary/2017/01/ Courtney-Bowman-data-localization/

Bruhn Jensen, K. (2021). *A Theory of Communication and Justice*. Abingdon: Routledge.

Bruno, I., & Didier, E. (2013). *Benchmarking: l'Etat sous pression statistique*, Paris, La Découverte, coll. Zones.

Bruno, I., Didier, E., & Vitale, T. (2014). Statactivism: Forms of action between disclosure and affirmation. *Partecipazione e conflitto: The Open Journal of Sociopolitical Studies*, 7(2): 198–220.

Brunton, F., & Nissenbaum, H. (2011). Vernacular resistance to data collection and analysis: A political theory of obfuscation. *First Monday*, 16(5). Retrieved from https:// firstmonday.org/article/view/3493/2955

Bucher, T. (2017). The algorithmic imaginary: Exploring the ordinary affects of Facebook algorithms. *Information, Communication & Society*, 20(1): 30–44.

Buolamwini, J., & Gebru, T. (2018). Gender shades: Intersectional accuracy disparities in commercial gender classification. *Proceedings of Machine Learning Research*, 81(1): 1–15.

Calo, R. (2017). *Artificial Intelligence Policy: A Primer and Roadmap*. Available at SSRN: https://ssrn.com/abstract=3015350

Calzati, S. (2020). Decolonising 'data colonialism' propositions for investigating the realpolitik of today's networked ecology. *Television & New Media*, 22(8): 914–929.

Candón Mena, J. (2013). *Toma la calle, toma las redes: el movimiento# 15M en Internet*. Sevilla: Atrapasueños.

Cardullo, P., & Kitchin, R. (2019). Smart urbanism and smart citizenship: The neoliberal logic of 'citizen-focused' smart cities in Europe. *Environment and Planning C: Politics and Space*, 37(5): 813–830.

Carmi, E., Yates, S. J., Lockley, E., & Pawluczuk, A. (2020). Data citizenship: Rethinking data literacy in the age of disinformation, misinformation, and malinformation. *Internet Policy Review*, 9(2). Retrieved from https://policyreview.info/articles/analysis/data-citizenship-rethinking-data-literacy-age-disinformation-misinformation-and

Castells, M. (1996). *The Rise of the Network Society*. Malden, MA: Blackwell.

Cave, S., & Dihal, K. (2021). Race and AI: The diversity dilemma. *Philosophy & Technology*, 1–5.

Celis Bueno, C. (2017). The Attention Economy: Labour, *Time and Power in Cognitive Capitalism*. London and New York: Rowman & Littlefield.

Chacón, H. (Ed.). (2019). *Online Activism in Latin America*. Abingdon: Routledge.

Chakravartty, P., Kuo, R., Grubbs, V., & McIlwain, C. (2018). # CommunicationSoWhite. *Journal of Communication*, 68(2): 254–266.

Cheney-Lippold, J. (2016). Jus Algoritmi: How the national security agency remade citizenship. *International Journal of Communication*, 10: 1721–1742. Retrieved from http://ijoc.org/index.php/ijoc/article/view/4480

Cheney-Lippold, J. (2017). *We Are Data*. New York: New York University Press.

Chin, J., & Wong, G. (2016, November 28). China's new tool for social control: A credit rating for everything. *Wall Street Journal*. Retrieved from www.wsj.com/articles/chinas-new-tool-for-social-control-a-credit-rating-for-everything-1480351590

Christl, W. (2017, June). *Corporate Surveillance in Everyday Life* [Report for Cracked Labs]. Retrieved from http://crackedlabs.org/en/corporate-surveillance

Christophers, B. (2020). *Rentier Capitalism: Who Owns the Economy, and Who Pays for It?* London: Verso Books.

Citron, D. J., & Pasquale, F. A. (2014). The scored society: Due process for automated predictions. *Washington Law Review*, 89: 1–33. Retrieved from https://papers.ssrn.com/sol3/papers.cfm?abstract_id=2376209

Clarke, J., Coll, K. M., Dagnino, E., & Neveu, C. (2014). *Disputing Citizenship*. Bristol: Policy Press.

Clarke, J., Newman, J., Smith, N., Vidler, E., & Westmoreland, L. (2007). *Creating Citizen-Consumers: Changing Publics and Changing Public Services*. London: Sage.

Clayton, V., Sanders, M., Schoenwald, E., Surkis, L., & Gibbons, D. (2020, September). *Machine Learning in Children's Services: Summary Report*. What Works for Children's Social Care. Retrieved from https://whatworks-csc.org.uk/wp-content/uploads/WWCSC_machine_learning_in_childrens_services_does_it_work_Sep_2020_Accessible.pdf

Cohen, G. (2008). *Rescuing Justice and Equality*. Cambridge, MA: Harvard University Press.

Cohen, J. (2020). *Between Truth and Power: The Legal Constructions of Informational Capitalism*. Oxford: Oxford University Press.

Collins, H. (2021). The science of artificial intelligence and its critics. *Interdisciplinary Science Reviews* 46(1–2): 53–70, DOI: 10.1080/03080188.2020.1840821

Collins, P. H. (1990). *Black Feminist Thought: Knowledge, Consciousness, and the Politics of Empowerment*. London: Routledge.

Collins, P. H. (1997). Comment on Hekman's 'Truth and Method: Feminist Standpoint Theory Revisited': Where's the power? *Journal of Women in Culture and Society*, 22(2): 375–381.

Comaroff, J., & Comaroff, J. L. (2012). Theory from the South: Or, *How Euro-America is Evolving toward Africa*. Abingdon: Routledge.

Competition and Markets Authority (CMA) & Information Commissioner's Office (ICO). (2021). *Competition and Data Protection in Digital Markets: A Joint Statement between the CMA and ICO*. Retrieved from https://ico.org.uk/media/about-the-ico/documents/2619797/cma-ico-public-statement-20210518.pdf

Connell, R. (2014). Using Southern Theory: Decolonizing social thought in theory, research and application. *Planning Theory*, 13(2): 210–223.

Conroy, A., & Scassa, T. (2015). Promoting transparency while protecting in Open Government in Canada. *AlbertaLaw Review*, 53(175). Retrieved from https://albertalawreview.com/index.php/ALR/article/view/284

Cooiman, F. (2021). Veni vidi VC – the backend of the digital economy and its political making. *Review of International Political Economy*. doi: 10.1080/09692290.2021.1972433

Costanza-Chock, S. (2018). *Data and Discrimination* [Plenary presentation]. Data justice conference: Exploring social justice in an age of datafication. Cardiff, UK.

Costanza-Chock, S. (2020). *Design Justice: Community-Led Practices to Build the Worlds We Need*. Cambridge, MA: MIT Press.

Couldry, N. (2014). Inaugural: A necessary disenchantment: Myth, agency and injustice in a digital world. *The Sociological Review*, 62(4): 880–897.

Couldry, N. (2019). Capabilities for what? Developing Sen's Moral Theory for Communications Research. *Journal of Information Policy*, 9: 43–55.

Couldry, N., & Hepp, A. (2017). *The Mediated Construction of Reality*. Cambridge: Polity Press.

Couldry, N., & Mejias, U. A. (2018). Data colonialism: Rethinking big data's relation to the contemporary subject. *Television and New Media*, 20(4): 338.

Couldry, N., & Mejias, U. A. (2019). *The Costs of Connection*. Stanford, CA: Stanford University Press.

Couldry, N., & Mejias, U. A. (2021). The decolonial turn in data and technology research: What is at stake and where is it heading? *Information, Communication and Society*, 1–17.

Couldry, N., & Powell, A. (2014). Big data from the bottom up. *Big Data & Society*, 1(2).

Couldry, N., Stephanson, H., Fotopoulou, A., MacDonald, R., Clark, W., & Dickens, L. (2014). Digital citizenship? Narrative exchange and the changing terms of civic culture. *Citizenship Studies*, 18(6–7): 615–629.

Council of Europe. (1950). *European Convention of Human Rights*. Brussels: Council of Europe. Retrieved from www.echr.coe.int/Documents/Convention_ENG.pdf

Crenshaw, K. (1989). Demarginalizing the intersection of race and sex: A Black feminist critique of antidiscrimination doctrine feminist theory and antiracist politics. *University of Chicago Legal Forum*, 1(8): 139–167.

Crooks, R. (2019, March 22). What we mean when we say #AbolishBigData2019. *Medium*. Retrieved from https://medium.com/@rncrooks/what-we-mean-when-we-say-abolishbigdata2019-d030799ab22e

Cukier, K., & Mayer-Schönberger, V. (2013). The rise of big data: How it's changing the way we think about the world. *Foreign Affairs*, 92(3): 28–40.

Cukier, K., & Mayer-Schönberger, V. (2013). Big Data: The Essential Guide to Work, Life and Learning in the Age of Insight. Place, New York: Houghton, Mifflin Harcourt Publishing

Culpepper, P. D., & Thelen, K. (2020). Are we all Amazon Primed? Consumers and the politics of platform power. *Comparative Political Studies*, 53(2): 288–318.

Curran, J. (2012). Rethinking internet history. In J. Curran, N. Fenton & D. Freedman (Eds.), *Misunderstanding the Internet*. Abingdon: Routledge.

Currie, M., Knox, J., & McGregor, C. (2022). *Data Justice and the Right to the City*. Edinburgh: Edinburgh University Press.

Currie, M., Paris, B. S., Pasquetto, I., & Pierre, J. (2016). The conundrum of police officer-involved homicides: Counter-data in Los Angeles County. *Big Data & Society*, 3(2).

Dalton, C., & Thatcher, J. (2014, May 12). What does a critical data studies look like, and why do we care? Seven points for a critical approach to big data. *Space and Society Open Site*. Retrieved from http://societyandspace.org/2015/05/12/what-does-a-critical-data-studies-look-like-and-why-do-we-care-craig-dalton-and-jim-thatcher/

Danaher, J. (2016). The threat of algocracy: Reality, resistance and accommodation. *Philosophy & Technology*, 29: 245–268. https://doi.org/10.1007/s13347-015-0211-1

Davis, G. F. (2009). The rise and fall of finance and the end of the society of organizations. *Academy of Management Perspectives*, 23(3). doi: 10.5465/amp.2009.43479262

Dean, J. (2001). Cybersalons and civil society: Rethinking the public sphere in transnational technoculture. *Public Culture*, 13(2): 243–266.

De La Garza, A. (2020, May 28). States' automated systems are trapping citizens in bureaucratic nightmares with their lives on the line. *Time*. Retrieved from https://time.com/5840609/algorithm-unemployment/

De Liban, K. (2018) Interview. Conducted by Joanna Redden. March 12.

Demeter, M. (2019). So far, yet so close: International career paths of communication scholars from the global south. *International Journal of Communication*, 13(25).

Dencik, L. (2022). The datafied welfare state: A perspective from the UK. In A. Hepp, J. Jarke & L. Kramp (Eds.), *The Ambivalences of Data Power: New Perspectives in Critical Data Studies*. Basingstoke: Palgrave.

Dencik, L., Hintz, A., & Cable, J. (2016). Towards data justice? The ambiguity of anti-surveillance resistance in political activism. *Big Data & Society*, 3(2): 1–12. doi: 10.1177/2053951716679678

Dencik, L., Hintz, A., Redden, J., & Treré, E. (2019). Exploring data justice: Conceptions, applications and directions. *Information, Communication and Society*, 22(7): 873–881.

Dencik, L., Hintz, A., Redden, J., & Warne, H. (2018). *Data Scores as Governance*. Cardiff: Data Justice Lab. Retrieved from https://datajusticelab.org/wp-content/uploads/2018/12/data-scores-as-governance-project-report2.pdf

Dencik, L., Jansen, F., & Metcalfe, P. (2018). *A Conceptual Framework for Approaching Social Justice in an Age of Datafication* [Working Paper]. DATAJUSTICE project. Retrieved from https://datajusticeproject.net/2018/08/30/a-conceptual-framework-for-approaching-social-justice-in-an-age-of-datafication/

Dencik, L., Redden, J., Hintz, A., & Warne, H. (2019). The 'golden view': Data-driven governance in the scoring society. *Internet Policy Review*, 8(2).

Dencik, L., & Wilkin, P. (2015). *Worker Resistance and Media: Challenging Global Corporate Power in the 21st Century*. London & New York: Peter Lang.

Desrosières, A. (2015). Retroaction: How indicators feed back onto quantified actors. In R. Rottenburg, S. Merry, S. J. Park & J. Mugler (Eds.), *The World of Indicators* (pp. 329–353). Cambridge: Cambridge University Press.

D'Ignazio, C., & Klein, L. F. (2020). *Data Feminism*. Cambridge, MA: MIT Press.

Dixon, P. (2017). A failure to "Do No Harm" – India's Aadhaar biometric ID program and its inability to protect privacy in relation to measures in Europe and the U.S. *Health and Technology*, 7(4): pp. 539–567.

Dixon, P. (2013). Congressional testimony: What information do data brokers have on consumers? World Privacy Forum. Retrieved from https://www.worldprivacyforum.org/2013/12/testimony-what-information-do-data-brokers-have-on-consumers/

Dixon, P., & Gellman, R. (2014). *The Scoring of America: How Secret Consumer Scores Threaten Your Privacy and Your Future* [Report]. Lake Oswego: World Privacy Forum. Available at www.worldprivacyforum.org/wp-content/uploads/2014/04/WPF_Scoring_of_America_April2014_fs.pdf

Dodd, V. (2021, Feb. 3). A thousand young black men removed from Met gang violence prediction database, *The Guardian*. Retrieved from https://www.theguardian.com/uk-news/2021/feb/03/a-thousand-young-black-men-removed-from-met-gang-violence-prediction-database

Dodd, V. (2018, May 9). UK accused of flouting human rights in 'racialised' war on gangs. *The Guardian*. Retrieved from www.theguardian.com/uk-news/2018/may/09/uk-accused-flouting-human-rights-racialised-war-gangs

Dolata, U. (2017). *Social Movements and the Internet: The Sociotechnical Constitution of Collective Action*. SOI Discussion Paper, No. 2017-02, Universität Stuttgart, Institut für Sozialwissenschaften, Abteilung für Organisations- und Innovationssoziologie, Stuttgart.

Drahos, P. (1996). *A Philosophy of Intellectual Property*. Aldershot, UK: Dartmouth.

Dranoff, S. (2014, December 15). Identity theft: A low-income issue. *American Bar Association*. Retrieved from www.americanbar.org/groups/legal_services/publications/dialogue/volume/17/winter-2014/identity-theft–a-lowincome-issue/

Draper, N., & Turow, J. (2019). The corporate cultivation of digital resignation. *New Media and Society*, 21(8): 1824–1839.

Duffield, M. (2018). *Post-Humanitarianism: Governing Precarity in the Digital World*. Cambridge: Polity Press.

Duque Franco, I., Ortiz, C., Samper, J., & Millan, G. (2020). Mapping repertoires of collective action facing the COVID-19 pandemic in informal settlements in Latin American cities. *Environment and Urbanization*, 32(2): 523–546.

Dyer-Witheford, N., Kjøsen, A. K., & Steinhoff, J. (2020). *Inhuman Power: Artificial Intelligence and the Future of Capitalism*. London: Pluto Press.

Edwards, L., & Veale, M. (2017). Slave to the algorithm? Why a 'right to an explanation' is probably not the remedy you are looking for. *Duke Law and Technology Review*, 16(1): 18–84.

Elmer, G., Langlois, G., & Redden, J. (Eds.). (2015). *Compromised Data: From Social Media to Big Data*. New York: Bloomsbury.

Emergencia Indigena. (2020). (https://emergenciaindigena.apiboficial.org/en/).

Engstrom, D., & Ho, D. E. (2021). Artificially intelligent government: A review and an agenda. In R. Vogl (Ed.), *Research Handbook on Big Data Law* (pp. 57–86). Cheltenham, UK: Edward Elgar Publishing.

Escobar, A. (2018). *Designs for the Pluriverse: Radical Interdependence, Autonomy, and the Making of Worlds*. Durham, NC: Duke University Press.

Escobar, O., & Elstub, S. (2017, May 8). *Forms of Mini-publics*. Newcastle: newDemocracy. www.academia.edu/34630797/Forms_of_mini-publics_An_introduction_to_deliberative_innovations_in_democratic_practice

Escorcia, A., & O'Carroll, T. (2017, January 24). Mexico's misinformation wars: How organized troll networks attack and harass journalists and activists in Mexico. *OpenDemocracy*. www.opendemocracy.net/en/mexicos-misinformation-wars/

Etter, M., & Albu, O. B. (2021). Activists in the dark: Social media algorithms and collective action in two social movement organizations. *Organization*, 28(1): 68–91.

Eubanks, V. (2011). *Digital Dead End: Fighting for Social Justice in the Information Age*. Cambridge, MA: MIT Press.

Eubanks, V. (2018). *Automating Inequality*. New York: Macmillan.

Eubanks, V. (2015). Want to cut welfare? There's an app for that. *The Nation*, 27 May. Retrieved from https://www.thenation.com/article/archive/want-cut-welfare-theres-app/

Evangelista, R., & Firmino, R. (2020). Brazil. Modes of pandemic existence: territory, inequality, and technology. In L. Taylor, G. Sharma, A. Martin & S. Jameson (Eds.), *Data Justice and COVID-19: Global Perspectives (pp. 100–107)*. London: Meatspace Press.

Fanon, F. (1963). *The Wretched of the Earth* (Trans. from the French by Constance Farrington). New York: Grove Press.

Feenstra, R. A., Tormey, S., Casero-Ripollés, A., & Keane, J. (2017). *Refiguring Democracy: The Spanish Political Laboratory*. Abingdon: Routledge.

Fenton, N., Freedman, D., Schlosberg, J., & Dencik, L. (2020). *The Media Manifesto*. Cambridge: Polity Press.

Fenton, N., & Downey, J. (2003). Counter public spheres and global modernity. *Javnost – The Public*, 10(1): 15–32.

Ferdinand, S., Villaescusa-Illán, I., & Peeren, E. (Eds.). (2019). Introduction. In *Other Globes Past and Peripheral Imaginations of Globalization* (pp. 1–39). Cham, Switzerland: Palgrave Macmillan.

Field, K. "Mapping Coronavirus, Responsibly." ArGIS Blog (blog), February 25, 2020. https://www.esri.com/arcgis-blog/products/product/mapping/mapping-coronavirus-responsibly/

Fisher, M. (2009). *Capitalist Realism: Is There No Alternative?*. Winchester, UK: Zero Books

Flensburg, S., & Lomborg, S. (2021). Datafication research: mapping the field for a future agenda. *New Media & Society*, https://doi.org/10.1177/14614448211046616

Flesher Fominaya, C. (2020). *Democracy Reloaded: Inside Spain's Political Laboratory from 15-M to Podemos*. Oxford: Oxford University Press.

Floridi, L., & Taddeo, M. (2016). What is data ethics? *Philosophical Transactions of the Royal Society*, 374(2083). Retrieved from http://rsta.royalsocietypublishing.org/content/374/2083/20160360

Fotopoulou, A. (2020). Conceptualising critical data literacies for civil society organisations: Agency, care, and social responsibility. *Information, Communication & Society*, 24(11): 1640–1657. Retrieved from www.tandfonline.com/doi/full/10.1080/1369118X.2020.1716041?scroll=top&needAccess=true

Fourcade, M., & Gordon, J. (2020). Learning like a state: Statecraft in the Digital Age. *Journal of Law and Political Economy*, 1(1): 78–108.

Fourcade, M., & Healy, K. (2017). Seeing like a market. *Socio-Economic Review*, 15(1): 9–29.

Fraser, N. (1997). Justice Interruptus: Critical Reflections on the Postsocialist Condition. New York: Routledge.

Fraser, N. (2005). Mapping the feminist imagination: From redistribution to recognition to representation. *Constellations*, 12(3): 295–307.

Fraser, N. (2008). Abnormal justice. *Critical Inquiry*, 34(3): 393–422.

Freedman, D. (2008). *The Politics of Media Policy*. London: Polity Press.

Freedman, D. (2016). The internet of capital: Concentration and commodification in a world of abundance. In J. Curran, N. Fenton & D. Freedman, *Misunderstanding the Internet* (2nd ed.) London: Routledge.

Friedman, G. D., & McCarthy, T. (2020, October 1). Employment law red flags in the use of artificial intelligence in hiring. *American Bar Association.* www.americanbar.org/groups/business_law/publications/blt/2020/10/ai-in-hiring/

Fruchterman, J., & Mellea, J. (2018). Expanding employment success for people with disabilities. *Benetech.* Retrieved from https://benetech.org/wp-content/uploads/2018/11/Tech-and-Disability-Employment-Report-November-2018.pdf

Fuchs, C. (2014). *Social Media: A Critical Introduction.* London: Sage.

Fullerton, J. (2018, March 24). China's 'social credit' system bans millions from travelling. *The Telegraph.* Retrieved from www.telegraph.co.uk/news/2018/03/24/chinas-social-credit-system-bans-millions-travelling/

Gabrys, J. (2011). *Digital Rubbish: A Natural History of Electronics.* Ann Arbor, MI: University of Michigan Press.

Galis, V., & Neumayer, C. (2016). Laying claim to social media by activists: a cyber-material détournement. *Social Media & Society*, 2(3). doi: 10.1177/2056305116664360

Gandy, O. (1993). *The Panoptic Sort: A Political Economy of Personal Information.* New York: Harper Collins.

Gandy, O. (2005). Data mining, surveillance, and discrimination in the post-9/11 environment. In K. D. Haggerty & R. V. Ericson (Eds.), *The New Politics of Surveillance and Visibility* (pp. 363–384). Toronto: University of Toronto Press.

Gandy, O. (2020). *A Panoptic Sort: A Political Economy of Personal Information* (2nd ed.). Oxford: Oxford University Press.

Gangadharan, S. P., Eubanks, V., & Barocas, S. (2014). *Data And Discrimination: Collected Essays.* Open Technology Institute and New America. Retrieved from www.ftc.gov/system/files/documents/public_comments/2014/10/00078-92938.pdf (accessed September 9, 2015).

Gangadharan, S. P., & Niklas, J. (2019). Decentering technology in discourse on discrimination. *Information, Communication and Society*, 22(7): 882–899.

Ganter, S. A., & Ortega, F. (2019). The invisibility of Latin American scholarship in European media and communication studies: Challenges and opportunities of de-westernization and academic cosmopolitanism. *International Journal of Communication*, 13(24).

Garrido, S. A., Allard, M. C., Béland, J., Caccamo, E., Reigeluth, T., Agaisse, J. P. (2018, February). *IoT in the Smart City: Ethical Issues and Social Acceptability.* Montreal: Centre international de reference sur le cycle de vie des produits procédés et services. Retrieved from http://ville.montreal.qc.ca/pls/portal/docs/page/prt_vdm_fr/media/documents/ido_vi_revue_litt_final_en.pdf (accessed September 2, 2018).

Garvey, S. C. (2021). Unsavory medicine for technological civilization: Introducing 'Artificial Intelligence & its Discontents'. *Interdisciplinary Science Reviews*, 46(1–2): 1–18. doi: 10.1080/03080188.2020.1840820

Gerbaudo, P. (2017). From cyber-autonomism to cyber-populism: An ideological history of digital activism. *TripleC: Communication, Capitalism & Critique*, 15(2): 477–489.

Gillingham, P. (2016). Predictive risk modelling to prevent child maltreatment and other adverse outcomes for service users: Inside the 'Black Box' of machine learning. *The British Journal of Social Work*, 46(1): 1044–1058.

Gillingham, P. (2019). Decision support systems, social justice and algorithmic accountability in social work: A new challenge. *Practice*, 31(4): 277–290. doi:10.1080/09503153.2019.1575954

Goodin, R. E. (2008). *Innovating Democracy: Democratic Theory and Practice after the Deliberative Turn*. Oxford: Oxford University Press.

Google. (2019, September 10). *Accelerating Social Good with Artificial Intelligence*. Retrieved from https://services.google.com/fh/files/misc/accelerating_social_good_with_artificial_intelligence_go ogle_ai_impact_challenge.pdf

Graeber, D. (2015). *The Utopia of Rules: On Technology, Stupidity, and the Secret Joys of Bureaucracy*. New York: Melville House Publishing.

Graef, I. (2018). When data evolves into market power – data concentration and data abuse under competition law. In M. Moore & D. Tambini (Eds.), *Digital Dominance: The Power of Google, Amazon, Facebook, and Apple* (pp. 71–97). Oxford: Oxford University Press.

Graham, M. (2013). Geography/internet: Ethereal alternate dimensions of cyberspace or grounded augmented realities? *The Geographical Journal*, 179(2): 177–182.

Graham, M., Kitchin, R., Mattern, S., & Shaw, J. (2019). How to run a city like Amazon. In M. Graham, R. Kitchin, S. Mattern & J. Shaw (Eds.), *How to Run a City like Amazon, and Other Fables* (pp. 1–12). London: Meatspace Press.

Gray, J. (2018). Three aspects of data worlds. *Krisis: Journal for Contemporary Philosophy*, 1: 5–17.

Gray, J., & Bounegru, L. (2019). What a difference a dataset makes? Data journalism and/as data activism. In J. Evans, S. Ruane & H. Southall (Eds.), *Data in Society: Challenging Statistics in an Age of Globalisation*. Bristol: Policy Press.

Gray, M., & Suri, S. (2019). *Ghost Work: How to Stop Silicon Valley from Building a New Underclass*. Boston, MA: Houghton Mifflin Harcourt.

Gregg, N. (2011). Media is not the issue, justice is the issue. In S. C. Jansen, J. Pooley & L. Taub-Pervizpour (Eds.), *Media and Social Justice* (pp. 83–95). Basingstoke & New York: Palgrave Macmillan.

Gunaratne, S. A. (2009). Emerging global divides in media and communication theory: European universalism versus non-Western reactions. *Asian Journal of Communication*, 19(4): 366–383.

Gunaratne, S. A. (2010). De-Westernizing communication/social science research: Opportunities and limitations. *Media, Culture & Society*, 32(3): 473–500.

Gürses, S., Dobbe, R., & Poon, M. (2020). *Introduction to the Programmable Infrastructures Event*. TU Delft. Retrieved from www.tudelft.nl/tbm/programmable-infrastructures

Gürses, S., & Van Hoboken, J. (2017). Privacy after the agile turn. In J. Polonetsky, O. Tene & E. Selinger (Eds.), *Cambridge Handbook of Consumer Privacy*. Cambridge: Cambridge University Press. Retrieved from https://osf.io/preprints/socarxiv/9gy73/

Gutiérrez, M. (2018). *Data Activism and Social Change*. New York: Springer.

Hacking, I. (2007). Kinds of people: Moving targets. *Proceedings of the British Academy*, 151: 285–318.

Hanafi, S. (2020). Global sociology revisited: Toward new directions. *Current Sociology*, 68(1): 3–21.

Hannigan, R. (2014, November 3). The Web is a terrorist's command-and-control network of choice. *Financial Times*. Retrieved from www.ft.com/cms/s/2/c89b6c58-6342-11e4-8a63-00144feabdc0.html#axzz3TywRsOQ2

Hargittai, E. (2020). Potential biases in big data: Omitted voices on social media. *Social Science Computer Review*, 38(1): 10–24.

Harris, L. M., & Hazen, H. D. (2006). Power of maps: (Counter) mapping for conservation. *ACME: An International Journal for Critical Geographies*, 4(1): 99–130.

Harvey, D. (1992). *The Condition of Postmodernity*. Oxford: Wiley-Blackwell.

Harvey, D. (2007a). *A Brief History of Neoliberalism*. Oxford: Oxford University Press.

Harvey, D. (2007b). Neoliberalism as creative destruction. *The Annals of the American Academy of Political and Social Science*, 610(1): 21–44.

Harwell, D. (2019, April 10). Is your pregnancy app sharing your intimate data with boss? *The Washington Post*. Retrieved from www.washingtonpost.com/technology/2019/04/10/tracking-your-pregnancy-an-app-may-be-more-public-than-you-think/?arc404=true

Hearn, A. (2022). The collateralized personality: creatability and resistance in the age of automated credit-scoring and lending. *Cultural Studies*, DOI: 10.1080/09502386.2022.2042576

Heeks, R. (2017). A Structural Model and Manifesto for Data Justice for International Development. *Development Informatics Working Paper Series*, No. 69.

Helmond, A. (2015). The platformization of the Web: Making web data platform ready. *Social Media + Society*, 1(2). doi: 10.1177/2056305115603080

Henman, P. (2018). Of algorithms, Apps and advice: digital social policy and service delivery. *Journal of Asian Public Policy*, 12(2): 1–19.

Hintz, A., & Brand, J. (2019). *Data Policies: Regulatory Approaches for Data-driven Platforms in the UK and EU [Research Report]*. Cardiff University.

Hintz, A., & Brown, I. (2017). Enabling digital citizenship? The reshaping of surveillance policy after Snowden. *International Journal of Communication*, 11: 782–801.

Hintz, A., Dencik, L., & Wahl-Jorgensen, K. (2019). *Digital Citizenship in a Datafied Society*. Cambridge: Polity Press.

Hill, K. (2020, December 29). Another arrest, and jail time, due to a bad facial recognition match. *The New York Times*. Retrieved from https://www.nytimes.com/2020/12/29/technology/facial-recognition-misidentify-jail.html

Hoffmann, A. L. (2017). Beyond distributions and primary goods: Assessing applications of rawls in information science and technology literature since 1990. *Journal for Information Science and Technology*, 68(7): 1601–1618.

Hoffmann, A. L. (2018). Data violence and how bad engineering choices can damage society. *Medium*, 30 April. Retrieved from https://medium.com/s/story/data-violence-and-how-bad-engineering-choices-can-damage-society-39e44150e1d4

Hoffmann, A. L. (2019). Where fairness fails: Data, algorithms, and the limits of antidiscrimination discourse. *Information, Communication & Society*, 22(7): 900–915.

Hoffmann, A. L. (2020). Terms of inclusion: Data, discourse, violence. *New Media & Society*, 23(12): 3539–3556.

Hu, M. (2015). Big data blacklisting. *Florida Law Review*, 67: 1735–1809.

Hudson, M. (2014). *The Bubble and Beyond* (2nd ed.). Glashütte: ISLET.

Human Rights, Big Data and Technology Project. (2020). (Available at www.hrbdt.ac.uk/)

Hurley, M., & Adebayo, J. (2016). Credit scoring in the era of big data. *Yale Journal of Law and Technology*, 18(1): 1–69.

Hvistendahl, M. (2017, December 12). Inside China's vast new experiment in social ranking. *Wired*. Available at www.wired.com/story/age-of-social-credit/

Isin, E. (2012). *Citizens without Frontiers*. London: Bloomsbury.

Isin, E., & Ruppert, E. (2015). *Becoming Digital Citizens*. Lanham, MD: Rowman & Littlefield.

Isin, E., & Ruppert, E. (2019). Data's empire: Postcolonial data politics. In D. Bigo, E. Isin & E. Ruppert (Eds.), *Data Politics: Worlds, Subjects, Rights* (pp. 207–227). Abingdon: Routledge.

Jackson, S. J., Bailey, M., & Welles, B. F. (2020). *# HashtagActivism: Networks of Race and Gender Justice*. Cambridge, MA: MIT Press.

Jain, N., Agarwal, P., & Pruthi, J. (2015). HashJacker-detection and analysis of hashtag hijacking on Twitter. *International Journal of Computer Applications*, 114(19): 17–20.

Jansen, F. (2020). *Consultation on the White Paper on AI – a European Approach. Submission. DATAJUSTICE project*. Retrieved from https://datajusticeproject.net/wp-content/uploads/sites/30/2020/06/Submission-to-AI-WP-Fieke-Jansen.pdf

Jansen, F., Sanchez-Monedero, J., & Dencik, L. (2021, forthcoming). Biometric identity systems in law enforcement and the politics of (voice)recognition: The case of SiiP. *Big Data and Society*.

Jansen, S. C. (2011). Introduction: Media, democracy, human rights, and social justice. In S. C. Jansen, J. Pooley & L. Taub-Pervizpour (Eds.), *Media and Social Justice* (pp. 1–23). Basingstoke & New York: Palgrave Macmillan.

Jefferson, E. (2018, April 24). No, China isn't Black Mirror – social credit scores are more complex and sinister than that. *New Statesman*. Retrieved from www.newstatesman.com/world/asia/2018/04/no-china-isn-t-black-mirror-social-credit-scores-are-more-complex-and-sinister

Johns, F. (2021). Governance by Data. *Annual Review of Law and Social Science*, 17(1): 53–71.

Johnson, J. (2018). *Toward Information Justice: Technology, Politics, and Policy for Data in Higher Education*. Springer.

Jordan, T. (2020). *The Digital Economy*. Cambridge: Polity Press.

Jørgensen, R. F., Bloch Veiberg, C., & ten Oever, N. (2019). Exploring the role of HRIA in the information and communication technologies sector. In N. Götzmann (Ed.), *Handbook on Human Rights Impact Assessment*. Cheltenham: Edward Elgar Publishing.

Joshi, D. (2020). Unpacking algorithmic harms in India. The AI Observatory. Retrieved from https://ai-observatory.in/

Kaltheuner, F., & Bietti, E. (2017). Data is power: Towards additional guidance on profiling and automated decision-making in the GDPR. *Journal of Information Rights, Policy and Practice*, 2(2): 1–17. Retrieved from https://jirpp.winchesteruniversitypress.org/articles/abstract/10.21039/irpandp.v2i2.45/

Kant, T. (2020). *Making it Personal: Algorithmic Personalization, Identity, and Everyday Life*. Oxford: Oxford University Press.

Kaplan, E. (2015). The spy who fired me: The human costs of workplace monitoring, *Harper's Magazine*. Retrieved from https://harpers.org/archive/2015/03/the-spy-who-fired-me/3/

Kaye, D. (2015). *Report of the Special Rapporteur on the Promotion and Protection of the Right to Freedom of Opinion and Expression*. New York: United Nations. Retrieved from www.ohchr.org/EN/Issues/FreedomOpinion/Pages/OpinionIndex.aspx

Keddell, E. (2015). The ethics of predictive risk modelling in the Aotearoa/New Zealand child welfare context: Child abuse prevention or neo-liberal tool? *Critical Social Policy*, 35(1): 69–88. doi:10.1177/0261018314543224

Kellogg, K. C., Valentine, M. A., & Christin, A. (2020). Algorithms at work: The new contested terrain of control. *Academy of Management Annals*, 14(1): 366–410.

Kelly, K. (2016). The Inevitable: Understanding the 12 Technological Forces that Will Shape Our Future. Harmondsworth: Penguin.

Kennedy, H. (2018). Living with data: Aligning data studies and data activism through a focus on everyday experiences of datafication. *Krisis: Journal for Contemporary Philosophy*, 1: 18–30.

Kennedy, H., Poell, T., & Van Dijck, J. (2015). Data and agency. *Big Data & Society*, 2(2).

Kent, A. J. (2020). Mapping and counter-mapping COVID-19: From crisis to cartocracy. *The Cartographic Journal*, 57(3): 187–195.

Khiabany, G. (2003). De-Westernizing media theory, or reverse Orientalism: Islamic communication as theorized by Hamid Mowlana. *Media, Culture & Society*, 25(3): 415–422.

Kidd, D. (2019). Extra-activism: Counter-mapping and data justice. *Information, Communication & Society*, 22(7): 954–970.

Kitchin, R. (2015). Continuous geosurveillance in the 'Smart City'. *Dystopia*. Retrieved from http://dismagazine.com/dystopia/73066/rob-kitchin-spatial-big-data-and-geosurveillance/

Kitchin, R., & Lauriault, T. P. (2014). *Towards Critical Data Studies: Charting and Unpacking Data Assemblages and Their Work* [The Programmable City Working Paper]. Maynooth University. Retrieved from http://ssrn.com/abstract=2474112

Kitchin, K. (2014). *The Data Revolution: Big Data, Open Data, Data Infrastructures and Their Consequences*. London: Sage.

Klein, N. (2014). *This Changes Everything: Capitalism vs. the Climate*. London: Allan Lane.

Kubitschko, S. (2017). Acting on media technologies and infrastructures: Expanding the media as practice approach. *Media, Culture & Society*, 40(4): 629–635.

Kukutai, T., & Taylor, J. (Eds.). (2016). *Indigenous Data Sovereignty: Toward an Agenda*. Canberra: ANU Press.

Kwet, M. (2019). Digital colonialism: US empire and the new imperialism in the Global South. *Race & Class*, 60(4): 3–26.

Lanier, J. (2013). *Who Owns the Future?* Harmondsworth: Penguin.

Larkin, B. (2013). The politics and poetics of infrastructure. *Annual Review of Anthropology*, 42: 327–343.

Layton, V., Sanders, M., Schoenwald, E., Surkis, L., & Gibbons, D. (2020). *Machine learning in children's services: Summary report. What Works for Children's Social Care*. Retrieved https://whatworks-csc.org.uk/wp-content/uploads/WWCSC_machine_learning_in_childrens_services_does_it_work_Sep_2020_Accessible-4.pdf

Lecher, C. (2018, March 21). What happens when an algorithm cuts your health care? *The Verge*. Retrieved from www.theverge.com/2018/3/21/17144260/healthcare-medicaid-algorithm-arkansas-cerebral-palsy

Lee, C., Yang, T., Inchoco, G., Jones, G. M., & Satyanarayan, A. (2021). Viral visualizations: How coronavirus skeptics use orthodox data practices to promote unorthodox science online. *Proceedings of the 2021 CHI Conference on Human Factors in Computing Systems*, Yokohama, Japan. Association for Computing Machinery.

Lehtiniemi, T., & Ruckenstein, M. (2019). The social imaginaries of data activism. *Big Data & Society*, 6(1).

Lewis, J. E. (2021, May 28). From Impoverished Intelligence to Abundant Intelligence. *Medium*, Retrieved from https://jasonedwardlewis.medium.com/from-impoverished-intelligence-to-abundant-intelligences-90559f718e7f

Lewis, J. E. (Ed.). (2020). *Indigenous Protocol and Artificial Intelligence* [Position Paper]. Honolulu, Hawaii: The Initiative for Indigenous Futures and the Canadian Institute for Advanced Research (CIFAR).

Linklater, A. (2002). Cosmopolitan citizenship. In E. Isin & B. S. Turner (Eds.), *Handbook of Citizenship Studies* (pp. 317–332). London: Sage.

Lister, R. (1997). *Citizenship: Feminist Perspectives*. Basingstoke: Macmillan.

Liu, W. (2019). *Abolish Silicon Valley*. London: Repeater Books.

Livingstone, S. (2019). Audiences in an age of datafication: Critical questions for media research. *Television & New Media*, 20(2): 170–183.

Lorenz, T., Browning, K., & Frenkel, S. (2020, June 21). TikTok teens and K-pop stans say they sank Trump's Tulsa rally. *The New York Times*.

Lum, K., & Isaac, W. (2016). To predict and serve. *Significance*, 13(5): 14–19. Retrieved from https://rss.onlinelibrary.wiley.com/doi/full/10.1111/j.1740-9713.2016.00960.x

Lv, A., & Luo, T. (2018). Asymmetrical power between internet giants and users in China. *International Journal of Communication*, 12: 3877–3895. Retrieved from https://ijoc.org/index.php/ijoc/article/view/8543

Lyon, D. (2002). *Surveillance as Social Sorting: Privacy, Risk and Automated Discrimination.* New York: Routledge.

Lyon, D. (2015). *Surveillance after Snowden.* Cambridge: Polity Press.

Ma, W. (2022). The Future of Social Media in the Scoring Society: An Empirical Investigation of the Implications of the 2014–2020 Social Credit System for Social Media in China. [Doctoral thesis]. Cardiff University.

Madden, M., Gilman, M., Levy, K., & Marwick, A. (2017). Privacy, poverty, and big data: A matrix of vulnerabilities for poor Americans. *Washington University Law Review*, 95(1): pp. 52–125.

Madianou, M. (2019). Technocolonialism: Digital innovation and data practices in the humanitarian response to refugee crises. *Social Media & Society*, 5(3): 1–13. doi: 10.1177/205630511986314

Maeckelbergh, M. (2016). From Digital Tools to Political Infrastructure. London: Sage.

Magalhães, J. C., & Couldry, N. (2020). Giving by taking away: Big Tech, data colonialism and the reconfiguration of social good. *International Journal of Communication*, 15: 343–362.

Maly, I. (2019a, November 26). Algorithmic populism and algorithmic activism. *Diggit Magazine*.

Maly, I. (2019b). New right metapolitics and the algorithmic activism of Schild & Vrienden. *Social Media & Society*, 5(2).

Manovich, L. (2012). Trending: The promises and the challenges of big social data. In M. K. Gold (Ed.), *Debates in the Digital Humanities* (pp. 460–475). Minneapolis, MN: University of Minnesota Press.

Marazzi, C. (2008). Capital and Language: From the New Economy to the War Economy. Los Angeles, CA: Semiotext(e).

Marshall, T. H. (1950). *Citizenship and Social Class, and Other Essays.* Cambridge: Cambridge University Press.

Marwick, A., & Lewis, R. (2017). *Media Manipulation and Disinformation Online.* New York: Data & Society Research Institute.

Masiero, S., Milan, S., & Treré, E. (2021). COVID-19 from the margins: Crafting a (cosmopolitan) theory. *Global Media Journal-German Edition*, 11(1).

Masiero, S., & Shakthi, S. (2020). Grappling with Aadhaar: Biometrics, social identity and the Indian state. *South Asia Multidisciplinary Academic Journal*, 23.

Mateescu, A., & Nguyen, A. (2019). *Workplace Monitoring & Surveillance: Data & Society.* Retrieved from https://datasociety.net/wp-content/uploads/2019/02/DS_Workplace_Monitoring_Surveillance_Explainer.pdf

McCann, D., Hall, M., & Warin, R. (2018). *Controlled by Calculations? Power and Accountability in the Digital Economy* [Report]. London: New Economics Foundation. Available at https://neweconomics.org/2018/06/controlled-by-calculations

McCandless, D., & Evans, T. (2021). World's biggest data breaches & hacks. *Information is Beautiful*. October. Retrieved from https://www.informationisbeautiful.net/visualizations/worlds-biggest-data-breaches-hacks/

McGeveran, W. (2019). The duty of data security. *Minnesota Law Review*, 103: 1135–1208.

McNevin, A. (2011). *Contesting Citizenship: Irregular Migrants and New Frontiers of the Political*. New York: Columbia University Press.

McQuillan, D. (2019, June 7). *AI Realism and Structural Alternatives*. Talk presented at the Data Justice Lab, Cardiff. Retrieved from http://danmcquillan.io/ai_realism.html

Medina, E. (2014). Cybernetic Revolutionaries: Technology and Politics in Allende's Chile. Cambridge, MA: MIT Press.

Mellado, C. (2011). Examining professional and academic culture in Chilean journalism and mass communication education. *Journalism Studies*, 12(3): 375–391.

Meng, A., & DiSalvo, C. (2018). Grassroots resource mobilization through counter-data action. *Big Data & Society*, 5(2).

Metcalfe, P., & Dencik, L. (2019). The politics of big borders: Data (in)justice and the governance of refugees. *First Monday*, 24(4). https://doi.org/10.5210/fm.v24i4.9934

Metz, R. (2018, August 17). This company embeds microchips in its employees, and they love it. *MIT Technology Review*. Retrieved from www.technologyreview.com/2018/08/17/140994/this-company-embeds-microchips-in-its-employees-and-they-love-it/

Mignolo, W. (2003). *The Darker Side of the Renaissance: Literacy, Territoriality, and Colonization*. Ann Arbor, MI: University of Michigan Press.

Mignolo, W. D., & Walsh, C. E. (2018). On decoloniality. Durham: Duke University Press.

Milan, S. (2013). Social Movements and Their Technologies: Wiring Social Change. Basingstoke: Palgrave Macmillan.

Milan, S. (2015). When algorithms shape collective action: Social media and the dynamics of cloud protesting. *Social Media & Society*, 1(2).

Milan, S. (2017). Data activism as the new frontier of media activism. In G. Yang & V. Pickard (Eds.), *Media Activism in the Digital Age* (pp. 151–163). London & New York: Routledge.

Milan, S. (2018). Political agency, digital traces, and bottom-up data practices. *International Journal of Communication*, 12: 507–525.

Milan, S., & Treré, E. (2019). Big data from the South (s): Beyond data universalism. *Television & New Media*, 20(4): 319–335.

Milan, S., & Treré, E. (2020). The rise of the data poor: The COVID-19 pandemic seen from the margins. *Social Media & Society*, 6(3).

Milan, S., & Treré, E. (2021). Latin American visions for a Digital New Deal: Learning from critical ecology, liberation pedagogy and autonomous design. In S. Sarkar & A. Korjan (Eds.), *A Digital New Deal: Visions of Justice in a Post-Covid World* (pp. 101–111). Bangalore, India: IT for Change. Retrieved from https://itforchange.net/digital-new-deal/

Milan, S., Treré, E., & Masiero, S. (2021). COVID-19 from the Margins: Pandemic Invisibilities, Policies and Resistance in the Datafied Society. Amsterdam: Institute of Network Cultures.

Milner, Y., & Traub, A. (2021). *Data Capitalism + Algorithmic Racism*. Data for Black Lives and Demos. Retrieved from www.demos.org/sites/default/files/2021-05/Demos_%20 D4BL_Data_Capitalism_Algorithmic_Racism.pdf

Mohamed, S., Png, M., & Isaac, W. (2020). Decolonial AI: Decolonial theory as sociotechnical foresight in artificial intelligence. *Philosophy & Technology*, 33(4): 659–684.

Molla, R. (2020, October 30). As Covid-19 surges, the world's biggest tech companies report staggering profits. *Vox*. Retrieved from www.vox.com/recode/2020/10/30/ 21541699/big-tech-google-facebook-amazon-apple-coronavirus-profits

Molnar, P., & Gill, L. (2018). *Bots at the Gate: A Human Rights Analysis of Automated Decision-Making in Canada's Immigration and Refugee System*. Toronto: The Citizen Lab and University of Toronto. Retrieved from https://citizenlab.ca/wp-content/ uploads/2018/09/IHRP-Automated-Systems-Report-Web-V2.pdf

Moosavi, L. (2020). The decolonial bandwagon and the dangers of intellectual decolonisation. *International Review of Sociology*, 30(2): 332–354.

Morozov, E. (2014). To Save Everything, *Click Here: The Folly of Technological Solutionism*. New York: Public Affairs.

Morozov, E. (2015, June 23). Digital technologies and the future of data capitalism. *Social Europe*. Retrieved from https://socialeurope.eu/digital-technologies-and-the-future- of-data-capitalism

Mosco, V. (2014). *To the Cloud: Big Data in a Turbulent World*. New York: Routledge.

Mosco, V. (2017). *Becoming Digital: Toward a Post-Internet Society*. Bingley, UK: Emerald.

Moss, G. (2017). Media, capabilities and justification. *Media Culture & Society*, 40(1): 94–109.

Mossberger, K., Tolbert, C., & McNeal, R. S. (2007). *Digital Citizenship: The Internet, Society, and Participation*. Cambridge, MA: MIT Press.

Mouffe, C. (2000). *The Democratic Paradox*. London: Verso Books.

Moulier Boutang, Y. (2011). *Cognitive Capitalism*. Cambridge & Malden, MA: Polity Press.

Mulgan, G., & Straub, V. (2019). *The New Ecosystem of Trust: How Data Trusts, Collaboratives and Coops Can Help Govern Data for the Maximum Public Benefit* [Report]. Nesta. Retrieved from www.nesta.org.uk/blog/new-ecosystem-trust/

Mumford, D. (2021). Data colonialism: Compelling and useful, but whither epistemes? *Information, Communication & Society*, 1–6.

Mutsvairo, B. (Ed.). (2018). *The Palgrave Handbook of Media and Communication Research in Africa*. Basingstoke: Palgrave Macmillan.

Naughton, J. (2019, April 7). Are big tech's efforts to show it cares about data ethics another diversion? *The Guardian*. Retrieved from www.theguardian.com/ commentisfree/2019/apr/07/big-tech-data-ethics-diversion-google-advisory-council

Nelson, A., Hawn, L., & Zanti, S. (2020). A framework for centering racial equity throughout the administrative data life cycle. *International Journal of Population Data Science*, 5(3): 1–10.

Newman, N. (2014). How big data enables economic harm to consumers, especially to low-income and other vulnerable sectors of the population. *Journal of Internet Law*, 18(6): 11–23.

Nguyen, T. (2020, August 12). How social justice slideshows took over Instagram. PowerPoint activism is everywhere on Instagram. Why do these posts look so familiar? *Vox*. www.vox.com/the-goods/21359098/social-justice-slideshows-instagram-activism

Niklas, J., & Dencik, L. (2020). *European Artificial Intelligence Policy: Mapping the Institutional Landscape*. Working Paper. Retrieved from https://datajusticeproject.net/wp-content/uploads/sites/30/2020/07/WP_AI-Policy-in-Europe.pdf

Niklas, J., & Dencik, L. (2021). What rights matter? Examining the place of social rights in the EU's artificial intelligence policy debate. *Internet Policy Review*, 10(3). https://doi.org/10.14763/2021.3.1579

Noble, S. U. (2018). *Algorithms of Oppression*. New York: New York University Press.

OECD (2020). *Innovative Citizen Participation and New Democratic Institutions: Catching the Deliberative Wave*, Paris: OECD Publishing. https://doi.org/10.1787/339306da-en.

O'Connor, K. L. P. (2003). Eliminating the rape-kit backlog: Bringing necessary changes to the criminal justice system. *UMKC Law Review*, 72: 193–214.

Office of Oversight and Investigations Majority Staff (2013). A review of the data broker industry: Collection, use, and sale of consumer data for marketing purposes, staff report for chairman rockefeller, Dec. 18. Retrieved from https://www.commerce.senate.gov/public/_cache/files/0d2b3642-6221-4888-a631-08f2f255b577/AE5D72CBE7F44F5BFC846BECE22C875B.12.18.13-senate-commerce-committee-report-on-data-broker-industry.pdf

O'Hara, K. (2019). *Data Trusts: Ethics, Architecture and Governance for Trustworthy Data Stewardship* [White paper]. Web Science Institute. Retrieved from https://eprints.soton.ac.uk/428276/

Olin Wright, E. (2019). *How to be an Anti-Capitalist in the 21st Century*. London: Verso.

O'Neil, C. (2016a, September 1). How algorithms rule our working lives. *The Guardian*. Retrieved from www.theguardian.com/science/2016/sep/01/how-algorithms-rule-our-working-lives

O'Neil, C. (2016b). *Weapons of Math Destruction: How Big Data Increases Inequality and Threatens Democracy*. New York: Crown Publishing.

Onuoha, M. (2018). *On Algorithmic Violence: Attempts at Fleshing Out the Concept of Algorithmic Violence*. Retrieved from https://github.com/MimiOnuoha/On-Algorithmic-Violence

Pangrazio, L. (2016). Reconceptualising critical digital literacy. *Discourse: Studies in the Cultural Politics of Education*, 37(2): 163–174.

Pangrazio, L., & Sefton-Green, J. (2020). The social utility of 'data literacy'. *Learning, Media and Technology*, 45(2): 208–220.

Papacharissi, Z. (2010). *A Private Sphere: Democracy in a Digital Age*. Cambridge: Polity Press.

Pappas, G. F. (2017). The limitations and dangers of decolonial philosophies: Lessons from Zapatista Luis Villoro. *Radical Philosophy Review*, 20(2): 265–295.

Pasquale, F. (2015). *The Black Box Society: The Secret Algorithms That Control Money and Information*. Boston, MA: Harvard University Press.

Pasquale, F. (2017). From territorial to functional sovereignty: The case of Amazon. *Law and Political Economy*. Retrieved from https://lpeblog.org/2017/12/06/from-territorial-to-functional-sovereignty-the-case-of-amazon/

Patriquin, L. (2020). *Permanent Citizens' Assemblies: A New Model for Public Deliberation*. London & New York: Rowman & Littlefield International.

Poon, M. (2016). Corporate capitalism and the growing power of big data: Review essay. *Science, Technology & Human Values*, 41(6): 1088–1108.

Potts, M. (2012, November 21). The collapse of black wealth. *The American Prospect*. Retrieved from https://prospect.org/civil-rights/collapse-black-wealth/

Qui, J., Gregg, M. & Crawford, K. (2014). Circuits of labour: A labour theory of the iPhone era. *tripleC*, 12(2): 564–581.

Radcliffe, S. A. (2022). *Decolonizing geography: An introduction*. Cambridge: Polity Press.

Rahman, K. S., & Thelen, K. (2019). The rise of the platform business model and the transformation of twenty-first century capitalism. *Politics & Society*, 47(2): 177–204.

Rainie, L., & Wellman, B. (2012). *Networked: The New Social Operating System*. Cambridge, MA: MIT Press.

Rainie, S. C., Kukutai, T., Walter, M., Figueroa-Rodríguez, O. L., Walker, J., & Axelsson, P. (2019). Indigenous data sovereignty. In T. Davies, S. B. Walker, M. Rubinstein & F. Perini (Eds.), *The State of Open Data: Histories and Horizons* (pp. 300–319). Cape Town and Ottawa: African Minds and the International Development Research Centre (IDRC).

Rao, U., & Nair, V. (2019). Aadhaar: Governing with biometrics. *South Asia: Journal of South Asian Studies*, 42(3): 469–481.

Ratcliffe, R. (2019). How a glitch in India's biometric welfare system can be lethal. *The Guardian*, 16 October. Retrieved from https://www.theguardian.com/technology/2019/oct/16/glitch-india-biometric-welfare-system-starvation

Ratto, M., & Boler, M. (Eds.). (2014). *DIY Citizenship: Critical Making and Social Media*. Cambridge, MA: MIT Press.

Rawls, J. (1971). *A Theory of Justice*. Oxford: Oxford University Press.

Redden, J. (2015). Big data as system of knowledge: Investigating Canadian governance. In G. Langlois, J. Redden & G. Elmer (Eds.), *Compromised Data: From Social Media to Big Data* (pp. 17–39). New York: Bloomsbury.

Redden, J. (2018a). Democratic governance in an age of datafication: Lessons from mapping government discourses and practices. *Big Data & Society*, July. https://doi.org/10.1177/2053951718809145

Redden, J. (2018b). The harm that data do. *Scientific American*, 319(5). Retrieved from https://datajusticelab.org/data-harm-record/ www.scientificamerican.com/article/the-harm-that-data-do/

Redden, J., Brand, J., & Terzieva, V. (2020). Data Harm Record. *Data Justice Lab*. Retrieved from https://datajusticelab.org/data-harm-record/

Redden, J., Dencik, L., & Warne H. (2020). Datafied child welfare services: Politics, economics and power. *Policy Studies*, 41(5): 507–526. doi: 10.1080/01442872.2020.1724928

Reilly, K. (2020, April). The challenge of decolonizing big data through citizen data audits. *Big Data Sur*. Retrieved from https://data-activism.net/2020/04/bigdatasur-the-challenge-of-decolonizing-big-data-through-citizen-data-audits-1-3/

Rheingold, H. (2002). *Smart mobs: The next social revolution*. Basic Books.

Ricaurte, P. (2019). Data epistemologies, the coloniality of power, and resistance. *Television & New Media*, 20(4): 350–365.

Richardson, R., Schultz, J. M., & Southerland, V. (2019). Litigating Algorithms 2019 US Report: New Challenges to Government Use of Algorithmic Decision Systems. AI Now. September. Retrieved from https://ainowinstitute.org/litigatingalgorithms-2019-us.pdf

Richardson, R. (2021). Racial segregation and the data-driven society: How our failure to reckon with root causes perpetuates separate and unequal realities. *Berkeley Technology Law Journal*, 36(3): 101–139. Retrieved from https://ssrn.com/abstract=3850317

Ringer, F. (1992). *Fields of Knowledge: French Academic Culture in Comparative Perspective, 1890–1920*. Cambridge: Cambridge University Press.

Roberts, D. (2019). Digitizing the Carceral State. *Harvard Law Review*, 132: 1695–1728.

Robertson, K., Khoo, C., & Song, Y. (2020). *To Surveil and Predict: A Human Rights Analysis of Algorithmic Policing in Canada*. Toronto: The Citizen Lab and University of Toronto. https://citizenlab.ca/wp-content/uploads/2020/09/To-Surveil-and-Predict.pdf

Roberts, D. E. (2019). Book Review: *Digitizing the Carceral State*. *Harvard Law Review*, 132: 1695–1728.

Rodríguez, C. (2001). *Fissures in the Mediascape: An International Study of Citizens' Media*. Mahwah, NJ: Hampton Press.

Rodríguez, C. (2017). Studying media at the margins: Learning from the field. In V. Pickard & G. Yang (Eds.), *Media Activism in the Digital Age* (pp. 49–60). London & New York: Routledge.

Rosenblat, A., Wikelius, K., boyd, d., Gangadharan, S. P., & Yu, C. (2014). Data & civil rights: Employment primer. *Data & Society*, Retrieved from http://www.datacivilrights.org/pubs/2014-1030/Employment.pdf

Ruppert, E., Harvey, P., Lury, C., Mackenzie, A., McNally, R., Baker, S. A., Kallianos, Y., & Lewis, C. (2015). *Background: A Social Framework for Big Data*. Project Report. CRESC, University of Manchester and Open University. Available at http://research.gold.ac.uk/13484/1/SFBD%20Background.pdf

Ruppert, E., Isin, E., & Bigo, D. (2017). Data politics. *Big Data & Society*, July–December: 1–7. Retrieved from http://journals.sagepub.com/doi/abs/10.1177/2053951717717749

Sadowski, J. (2019). When data is capital: Datafication, accumulation, and extraction. *Big Data & Society*, January–June: 1–12.

Sadowski, J. (2020a). The internet of landlords: Digital platforms and new mechanisms of rentier capitalism. *Antipode*, 52(2): 562–580.

Sadowski, J. (2020b). Too Smart: How Digital Capitalism is Extracting Data, *Controlling Our Lives, and Taking Over the World*. Cambridge, MA: MIT Press.

Salganik, M. J., Lundberg, I., Kindel, A. T., Ahearn, C. E., Al-Ghoneim, K., Almaatouq, A., Altschul, D. M., Brand, J. E., Carnegie, N. B., Compton, R. J., & Datta. D. (2020). Measuring the predictability of life outcomes with a scientific mass collaboration. *Proceedings of the National Academy of Science*, 117: 8398–8403. doi: 10.1073/pnas.1915006117

Sánchez-Monedero, J., & Dencik, L. (2018). *How to (Partially) Evaluate Automated Decision Systems*. [Working Paper]. Datajusticeproject.net. Retrieved from https://datajusticeproject.net/wp-content/uploads/sites/30/2018/12/WP-How-to-evaluate-automated-decision-systems.pdf

Sánchez-Monedero, J., & Dencik, L. (2020, August 3). The politics of deceptive borders: 'Biomarkers of deceit' and the case of iBorderCtrl. *Information, Communication & Society*. doi: 10.1080/1369118X.2020.1792530

Sánchez-Monedero, J., Dencik, L., & Edwards, L. (2020). What does it mean to 'solve' the problem of discrimination in hiring? Social, technical and legal perspectives from the UK on automated hiring systems. *FAT* '20: ACM Proceedings of the 2020 Conference on Fairness, Accountability and Transparency*, pp. 458–468. https://doi.org/10.1145/3351095.3372849

Sandel, M. (2010). *Justice: What's the Right Thing To Do*? London: Penguin Books.

Sander, I. (2020). What is critical big data literacy and how can it be implemented? *Internet Policy Review*, 9(2): 1–22. Retrieved from https://policyreview.info/articles/analysis/what-critical-big-data-literacy-and-how-can-it-be-implemented

Sanders, M. (2020, September). Machine learning: Now is a time to stop and think. *What Works for Children's Social Care*. Retrieved from https://whatworks-csc.org.uk/blog/machine-learning-now-is-a-time-to-stop-and-think

San Francisco Chronicle (1993, January 1). Clinton offers a high-tech plan: $17 billion initiative unveiled in Silicon Valley. *San Francisco Chronicle*.

Santos, B. (2014). *Epistemologies of the South: Justice against Epistemicide*. London: Routledge.

Sastre Domínguez, P., & Gordo López, Á. J. (2019). Data activism versus algorithmic control: New governance models, old asymmetries. *Revista Científica de Información y Comunicación*, (16): 183–208.

Scholz, T. (Ed.). (2013). *Digital Labor: The Internet as Playground and Factory*. New York & London: Routledge.

Schrock, A. R. (2016). Civic hacking as data activism and advocacy: A history from publicity to open government data. *New Media & Society*, 18(4): 581–599.

Scott, J. (1999). *Seeing Like a State: How Certain Schemes to Improve the Human Condition Have Failed*. New Haven, CT: Yale University Press.

Segura, M. S., & Waisbord, S. (2019). Between data capitalism and data citizenship. *Television & New Media*, 20(4): 412–419.

Sell, Susan K. (2013). The revenge of the 'nerds': Collective action against intellectual property maximalism in the Global Information Age. *International Studies Review*, 15(1): 67–85.

Sen, A. (2009). *The Idea of Justice*. Cambridge, MA: Harvard University Press.

Singh, R., & Guzmán, L. R. (2021). *Parables of AI in/from the Global South*. http://ranjitsingh.me/parables-of-ai-in-from-the-global-south/

Smith, G. (2009). *Democratic Innovations: Designing Institutions for Citizen Participation*. Cambridge: Cambridge University Press.

Smith, L. T. (2012). *Decolonizing Methodologies: Research and Indigenous Peoples*. London: Zed Books.

Snow, J. (2018, July 26). Amazon's face recognition falsely matched 28 Members of Congress with mugshots. *American Civil Liberties Union (ACLU)*. Retrieved from www.aclunc.org/blog/amazon-s-face-recognition-falsely-matched-28-members-congress-mugshots

Solon, O. (2017). Big brother isn't just watching: Workplace surviellance can track your every move. *The Guardian*, 6 November. Retrieved from https://www.theguardian.com/world/2017/nov/06/workplace-surveillance-big-brother-technology

Solove, D. J., & Citron, D. (2016). Risk and anxiety: A theory of data breach harms. *Texas Law Review*, 96(737). Retrieved from https://ssrn.com/abstract=2885638

Soysal, Y. N. (1994). *Limits of Citizenship: Migrants and Postnational Membership in Europe*. Chicago, IL: The University of Chicago Press.

Spade, D. (2011). *Normal Life: Administrative Violence, Critical Trans Politics and the Limits of the Law*. Boston, MA: South End Press.

Srnicek, N. (2017). *Platform Capitalism*. Cambridge: Polity Press.

Srnicek, N. (2020). Data, compute, labour. *Ada Lovelace Institute*. Available at www.adalovelaceinstitute.org/data-compute-labour/

Standing, G. (2012). *The Precariat: The New Dangerous Class*. London: Bloomsbury.

Stark, L., Greene, D., & Hoffmann, A. L. (2021). Critical perspectives on governance mechanisms for AI/ML systems. In J. Roberge & M. Castelle (Eds.), *The Cultural Life of Machine Learning*. Cham, Switzerland: Palgrave Macmillan. https://doi.org/10.1007/978-3-030-56286-1_9

Sutherland, C., Mazeka, B., Buthelezi, S., Khumalo, D., & Martel, P. (2019). Making informal settlements 'visible' through datafication: A case study of Quarry Road West Informal Settlement, Durban, South Africa. *Development Informatics Working Paper*, 83.

Suzina, A. (2020). English as *lingua franca*: Or the sterilisation of scientific work. *Media, Culture & Society*, 43(1): 171–179.

Taylor, J. (2019, August 14). Major breach found in biometrics system used by banks, UK police and defence firms. *The Guardian*, 14 August. Retrieved from https://www.theguardian.com/technology/2019/aug/14/major-breach-found-in-biometrics-system-used-by-banks-uk-police-and-defence-firms#:~:text=The%20fingerprints%20of%20over%201,police%2C%20defence%20contractors%20and%20banks.

Taylor, L., & Dencik, L. (2020). Constructing Commercial Data Ethics. *Technology and Regulation*, 2020, 1–10. https://doi.org/10.26116/techreg.2020.001

Taylor, L., & Dencik, L. (2020, October 4). Constructing commercial data ethics. *Regulation & Technology*.

Taylor, L., Sharma, G., Martin, A., & Jameson, S. (Eds.). (2020). *Data Justice and COVID-19: Global Perspectives*. London: Meatspace Press.

Terranova, T. (2000). Free labour: Producing culture for the digital economy. *Social Text*, 63, 18(2).

Thatcher, J., O'Sullivan, D., & Mahmoudi, D. (2016). Data colonialism through accumulation by dispossession: New metaphors for daily data. *Environment and Planning D: Society and Space*, 34(6): 990–1006.

The Economist. (2016, December 17). China invents the digital totalitarian state. *The Economist*. Retrieved from www.economist.com/briefing/2016/12/17/china-invents-the-digital-totalitarian-state

The Royal Society. (2017). *Data Management and Use: Governance in the 21st Century*. A joint report by the British Academy and the Royal Society. Available at https://royalsociety.org/-/media/policy/projects/data-governance/data-management-governance.pdf

Thompson, P., & Briken, K. (2017). Actually existing capitalism: Some digital delusions. In K. Briken, S. Chillas, M. Krzywdzinski & A. Marks (Eds.), *The New Digital Workplace: How New Technologies Revolutionise Work* (pp. 241–263) (Critical Perspectives on Work and Employment). Basingstoke: Macmillan.

Tilly, C. (1997). A primer on citizenship. *Theory and Society*, 26(4): 599–602.

Tilly, C. (2008). *Contentious Performances*. Cambridge: Cambridge University Press.

Tilly, C., & Tarrow, S. G. (2015). *Contentious Politics*. Oxford: Oxford University Press.

Toh, A. (2020). Dutch ruling a victory for rights of the poor. *Human Rights Watch*. Retrieved from www.hrw.org/news/2020/02/06/dutch-ruling-victory-rights-poor

Toupin, S. (2016). Gesturing towards anti-colonial hacking and its infrastructure. *Journal of Peer Production*, 9.

Treré, E. (2012). Social movements as information ecologies: Exploring the coevolution of multiple Internet technologies for activism. *International Journal of Communication*, 6, 19.

Treré, E. (2015). Reclaiming, proclaiming, and maintaining collective identity in the# YoSoy132 movement in Mexico: An examination of digital frontstage and backstage activism through social media and instant messaging platforms. *Information, Communication & Society*, 18(8): 901–915.

Treré, E. (2016). The dark side of digital politics: Understanding the algorithmic manufacturing of consent and the hindering of online dissidence. *IDS Bulletin*, 47(1).

Treré, E. (2019). *Hybrid Media Activism: Ecologies, Imaginaries, Algorithms*. Abingdon: Routledge.

Treré, E., & Bonini, T. (2022, forthcoming). Amplification, evasion, hijacking: algorithms as repertoire for social movements and the struggle for visibility. *Social Movement Studies*.

Tronti, M. (1962). Factory and society. *Operaismo in English*. Available at https://operaismoinenglish.files.wordpress.com/2013/06/factory-and-society.pdf

Trottier, D. (2015). Open source intelligence, social media and law enforcement: Visions, constraints and critiques. *European Journal of Cultural Studies*, 18(4–5): 530–547.

Tuck, E., & Yang, K. W. (2012). Decolonization is not a metaphor. *Decolonization: Indigeneity, Education & Society*, 1(1): 1–40.

Tufekci, Z. (2017). *Twitter and Tear Gas: The Power and Fragility of Networked Protest*. New Haven, CT: Yale University Press.

Turner, B. S. (2009). T.H. Marshall, social rights and English national identity. *Citizenship Studies*, 13(1): 65–73.

Turner, B. S. (2017). Contemporary citizenship: Four types. *Journal of Citizenship and Globalisation Studies*, 1(1): 10–23.

Uldam, J. (2018). Social media visibility: Challenges to activism. *Media, Culture & Society*, 40(1): 41–58.

van den Hoven, J., & Rooksby, E. (2008). Distributive justice and the value of information: A (broadly) Rawlsian approach. In J. van denHoven & J. Weckert (Eds.), *Information Technology and Moral Philosophy* (pp. 376–396). Cambridge: Cambridge University Press.

Van Dijck, J. (2014). Datafication, dataism and dataveillance: Big Data between scientific paradigm and ideology. *Surveillance & Society*, 12(2): 197–208.

Van Doorn, N., & Badger, A. (2020). *Where Data and Finance Meet: Dual Value Production in the Gig Economy*. Working Paper. *Platform Labor*. Retrieved from https://platformlabor. net/output/dual-value-production-gig-economy

Veale, M., & Brass, I. (2019). Administration by Algorithm? Public Management Meets Public Sector Machine Learning. In K. Yeung and M. Lodge (Eds.), *Algorithmic Regulation*. Oxford: Oxford University Press.

Velkova, J., & Kaun, A. (2021). Algorithmic resistance: Media practices and the politics of repair. *Information, Communication & Society*, 24(4): 523–540.

Vera, L. A., Walker, D., Murphy, M., Mansfield, B., Siad, L. M., Ogden, J., & EDGI (2019). When data justice and environmental justice meet: Formulating a response to extractive logic through environmental data justice. *Information, Communication & Society*, 22(7): 1012–1028.

Vercellone, C. (2005, November 4–5). *The hypothesis of cognitive capitalism. [Conference presentation]. Historical Materialism Annual Conference, Birkbeck College and SOAS*. Retrieved from https://halshs.archives-ouvertes.fr/file/index/docid/273641/filename/The_hypothesis_of_Cognitive_Capitalismhall.pdf

Viljoen, S. (2020). A relational theory of data governance. *Yale Law Journal*, 131(2): 573–654. Available at SSRN: https://ssrn.com/abstract=3727562

Vivienne, S., McCosker, A., & Johns, A. (2016). Digital citizenship as fluid interface: Between control, contest and culture. In A. McCosker, S. Vivienne & A. Johns (Eds.), *Negotiating Digital Citizenship: Control, Contest and Culture* (pp. 1–18). London: Rowman & Littlefield.

Wachter, S., Mittelstadt, B., & Floridi, L. (2017). Why a right to explanation of automated decision-making does not exist in the General Data Protection Regulation. *International Data Privacy Law*, 7(2): 76–99.

Wagner, B. (2018). Ethics as an escape from regulation: From 'ethics-washing' to ethics-shopping? In E. Bayamlioglu, I. Baraliuc, L. Janssens & M. Hildebrandt (Eds.), *Being Profiled*. Amsterdam: Amsterdam University Press.

Wahl-Jorgensen, K., Bennett, L., & Taylor, G. (2017). The normalization of surveillance and the invisibility of digital citizenship: Media debates after the Snowden revelations. *International Journal of Communication*, 11: 740–762. Retrieved from https://ijoc.org/index.php/ijoc/article/view/5523

Waisbord, S., & Mellado, C. (2014). De-westernizing communication studies: A reassessment. *Communication Theory*, 24(4): 361–372.

Wallerstein, I. (2004). *World-Systems Analysis*. Durham, NC: Duke University Press.

Walter, M. (2020). Indigenous sovereignty and the Australian state: Relations in a globalising era. In A. Moreton-Robinson (Ed.), *Sovereign Subjects* (pp. 155–167). Abingdon: Routledge.

Walzer, M. (1970). *Obligations: Essays on Disobedience, War, and Citizenship*. Cambridge, MA: Harvard University Press.

Wark, M. (2019). *Capital is Dead: Is this Something Worse?* London: Verso.

Whittaker, M. (2021, February 5). *Ethics of AI in the Workplace [Conference presentation]*. *International Conference on AI in Work, Innovation, Productivity, and Skills*. Paris: OECD.

Whittaker, M., Alper, M., Bennett, C. L., Henren, S., Kaziunas, L., Mills, M., Morris, M. R., Rankin, J., Rogers, E., Salas, M., & Myers West, S. (2019, November). *Disability, Bias, and AI*. New York: AI Now Institute. Retrieved from https://ainowinstitute.org/disabilitybiasai-2019.pdf

Whitaker, M., Crawford, K., Dobbe, R., Fried, G., Kaziunas, E., Mathur, V., Myers West, S., Richardson, R., Schultz, J., & Schwartz, O. (2018). *AI Now Report 2018*, Retrieved https://ainowinstitute.org/AI_Now_2018_Report.pdf

Willow, A. J. (2013). Doing sovereignty in Native North America: Anishinaabe counter-mapping and the struggle for land-based self-determination. *Human Ecology*, 41(6): 871–884.

Winickoff, D. E., & Winickoff, R. N. (2003). The Charitable Trust as a model for genomic biobanks. *New England Journal of Medicine*, 349(12): 1180–1184.

Wizner, B. (2017). What changed after Snowden? A US perspective. *International Journal of Communication*, 11: 897–901.

Wolf, A. (2021). Robodebt was an algorithmic weapon of calculated political cruelty. *The Canberra Times*, 14 April. Retrieved from https://www.canberratimes.com.au/story/6775350/robodebt-was-an-algorithmic-weapon-of-calculated-political-cruelty/

Wood, A. J. (2020). *Despotism on Demand: How Power Operates in the Flexible Workplace*. Ithaca, NY: Cornell University Press.

Wood, A. J., & Lehdonvirta, V. (2021). Antagonism beyond employment: How the 'subordinated agency' of labour platforms generates conflict in the remote gig economy. *Socio-Economic Review*, 19(4): 1369–1396.

Woolley, S. C., & Howard, P. N. (2016). Automation, algorithms, and politics| political communication, computational propaganda, and autonomous agents — Introduction. *International Journal of Communication*, 10(9).

Yang, G. (2016). Narrative agency in hashtag activism: The case of #BlackLivesMatter. *Media and Communication*, 4(4): 13.

Yeung, K. (2017). 'Hypernudge': Big Data as a mode of regulation by design. *Information, Communication & Society*, 20(1): 118–136.

Yeung, K. (2018). Algorithmic regulation: A critical interrogation. *Regulation and Governance*, 12(4): 505–523.

Yeung, K., & Lodge, M. (eds.) (2019). *Algorithmic Regulation*. Oxford: Oxford University Press.

Young, I. M. (2011). *Justice and the Politics of Difference*. Princeton, NJ & Oxford: Princeton University Press.

Zivi, K. (2012). *Making Rights Claims: A Practice of Democratic Citizenship*. Oxford: Oxford University Press.

Žižek, S. (n.d.). Appendix: Multiculturalism, the Reality of an Illusion. Retrieved from www.lacan.com/essays/?page_id=454

Zuboff, S. (2015). Big Other: Surveillance capitalism and the prospect of an information civilization. *Journal of Information Technology*, 30(1): 75–89.

Zuboff, S. (2019). *The Age of Surveillance Capitalism: The Fight for a Human Future at the New Frontier of Power*. New York: Profile Books.

Zysman, M., & Kenney, M. (2018). The next phase in the digital revolution. *Communications of the ACM*, 81(2).

INDEX